The Dogs I've Known in Two Wars

Book One: IRAQ

By

Dennis R. Blocker & Dennis R. Blocker II

"I'm William van de Water. Passionate hobby photographer and big animal/dog lover. I live in Belgium with my wife Anita and Ranco, our Malinois. It was the love for the Belgian Malinois and photo editing that brought Dennis and I together. In my heart I knew I had to accept the request to create the cover for this book. I hope you enjoy it."

williamvdwater@gmail.com

Dedication

To My Dear Wife

Deborah K. Lemke Blocker

Many of us who go off to war are often caught up with preparing the things we will need in our backpacks and storage chests. In addition we seek to prepare our minds. This took some effort and I'm certain many of us failed to stop and realize how our dear wives felt as they washed, dried, and ironed our clothes, placed them out on the bed and made certain we had all we needed for the trip into war. We never put ourselves in their shoes and wondered what they were thinking. For me I never contemplated the extremely deep hurt in her heart and soul knowing it would be a long time before she would see me again. Maybe the thought crossed her mind that she might never see me alive after this day of parting.

I'm convinced I did not take all of this into consideration as I just described. Yes! I thanked Debbie for all of the time she put into getting my things ready for me, but I never considered how she was feeling while doing it. I was too caught up in the enormity of it all, you know, everything I had to get done prior to this early 0400hrs morning "Pack Your Bags" and press off to war mentality. For this I'm truly sorry my dearest Debbie, the love of my life.

Debbie and I kissed good-bye at the San Antonio International Airport that early morning in October of 2005 knowing we may never see one another again. Of course we told one another how much we loved each other, then we parted.

For the next thirteen months she took care of things at home. The yard work, repairs of the house, the cars, then taking care of our six dogs. This was enormous!

My Debbie was in her own war!

Debbie, I dedicate this book with **ALL** of my heart to you because of your unselfish love for me, and for those things I mentioned above. Last of all for the many hours we were separated from one another as I wrote this book. Thank you for encouraging me to write my story. I suspect that if it were not for your encouragement over these past eight years this book would not have been written.

With all of my love and thankfulness to you!

Love Den!

Breeds of Dogs in the War on Terrorism

I feel it's most appropriate to mention the three breeds of dogs which were used in the war effort during my time in Baghdad. These dogs performed exceptionally well during a tortuous time in the history of Iraq. There were daily rocket and mortar attacks as well as sporadic weapons fire of unknown caliber. In addition, there was the constant threat of suicide bombers, whose presence was felt daily as explosions rocketed the city.

Add to this environment the intense heat, unbearable dust, sand and annoying hordes of biting flies well then you have yourself a day in hell on earth. Yet, these amazing dogs performed at peak performance each and every day and night.

In my book I mention only German Shepherds and Belgian Malinois because those were the breeds I worked with. However, I did see several Labs who were performing exceptional work in other areas. If you, the private citizen, own one of these breeds give them a hug and a kiss because their cousins are doing tremendous work across the globe.

You should be as proud of them as we were!

Table of Contents

Introduction

I was asked by an author, "What is driving you to write this book about the war dogs you've worked with, trained, and supervised when in Iraq and Afghanistan?"

I'd never been asked this before so I proceeded to tell her what was on my heart and mind. When I finished explaining my reasons she said, "Dennis, what you just told me needs to be written in the very front pages of your book, as your 'Introduction.' It needs to be put on paper because what I heard was your passion and burden to tell these stories." I thanked her for her advice, and since then I've given it much thought. My life experiences have taught me to take advice from successful people. So, here goes!

Now, please keep in mind while you're reading, I'm not a gifted writer, I'm just an average American guy who must tell the stories of what I experienced and witnessed while working alongside these truly amazing dogs. Being with them during their moments of bravery, fear, and yes fun times is something I'll never forget. Most of these dogs are dead by now. It's been thirteen years since I was with them in that dusty, blood-soaked city and most of them were two years of age or just a bit older at that time therefore, if they were still alive they'd be about fifteen to sixteen years old.

Conflicting thoughts troubled my mind, "I'm not a gifted writer" and for that matter "I've never written a book before." The one point that persistently haunted me was, "If I don't tell their story, well then, who will?" Obviously, the dogs would go to their graves never able to tell their own story so they would need an ambassador of sorts. In my simple way of thinking, "If I tell their stories it will bring them back to life."

Was there any other option for me? No, I couldn't let my fear of writing spoil the chance for these dogs to receive their due. Believe me, they are "due" a lot.

I knew I had to attempt to write this book because after all is said and done it's about these dogs, not me. I just happened to be lucky enough to handle them and train them. It's all about their legacy.

A friend of mine named Sherri adopted an MWD (Military Working Dog), a Belgian Malinois named Kormi. I asked her if she knew any of the dog's history. Sherri answered, "We know nothing, other than that she was a bomb dog." This fact was so sad and served as inspiration and motivation for me to get this book written.

It's been a journey of eight years and yes, it's been a long hard trek. Writing a book requires immense discipline and time. It was the management of time that was a huge challenge. I had many health issues and responsibilities so it was not easy to sit down and type away. However, one inspiration was a vision of these dogs back when they were alive, virile and serving our country in their prime. I realized that the majority of them were dead, lying in a grave, or compressed in an urn atop a fireplace. They would never again sniff out explosives or seek out insurgents. They'd never bark or wag their tails in glee at a job well done. They were gone forever and there was no one to tell their stories, to name them or to honor their faithful service.

I couldn't let that happen so I buckled down and got busy typing stories even if it was only for a few minutes at a time. I tried to type at least once a day. Every sentence was an accomplishment and a milestone. Slowly, over time it all came together and now here we are.

While Stateside I had helped train many of the bomb dogs which were deploying into Iraq. In this position I had seen them grow into professional hunters and in turn I had grown with them. It was awesome watching these dogs I had trained, who were now working with handlers, accomplishing great things as a team. My goal had always been to advance these K9 teams to new heights. I wanted them proficient but always improving their craft and learning, always learning. Just passing the acceptable standard was never enough. We needed to be better, never complacent.

In Iraq I was fortunate enough to end up with two large, beautiful and highly intelligent German Shepherds as my bomb dogs. I went into the war with one, and soon found myself caring for another additional one. It's a crazy story how that all went down but you'll find that out soon enough.

After being with these war dogs in Iraq for thirteen long and very hot months I developed a better understanding of them. I'll never forget those amazing moments of bravery, terror, levity and fear nor the selflessness exhibited by these amazing animals. I'm so thankful that I now get to tell their story.

Now, please sit back, get comfortable and enjoy "The Dogs I've Known In 2 Wars, Book One: Iraq"

Thank you from the bottom of my heart and remember,

"War Dogs Rule the Blackness of the Night!"

Dennis R. Blocker Sr.
Texas
25 September 2019

Ancient Dust

I know I am not the first foreign warrior to die in the sand just a few feet from the Tigris River. Ironically, perhaps in this very spot where I'm down on my knees, stumbling and inhaling clouds of dust, a Roman Legionnaire drew his last breath. Maybe a Mongol bowman from the hordes of Hulagu Khan used his last moments of consciousness here to think of his family thousands of miles away. My thoughts may have turned to my family and life back in America were it not for the annoying jerking, pulling on my left wrist.

My whole body was screaming at me to sleep, to just let go but the erratic yanking on my left arm kept jolting me back to consciousness, to the resoluteness of survival. Though my eyes refused to see, instincts had kicked in and I was trying to stand. It was a weird battle between flesh and soul. I would have liked to rest, it was definitely beckoning to me, but something deep within began yelling to "get up, keep moving". I vigorously shook my head trying to will myself out of this stupor, out of this veil of blackness. Then of course there was also that irritating, annoying sensation of pulling, jerking on my left wrist.

Pokie

My journey to the banks of the Tigris River didn't begin with my decision to come to Iraq, nor did it begin with my decision to become a K9 handler. The starting point was not even my decision to join the United States Air Force and become an Air Force Cop. It was most definitely not from my teenage years as a gang member hooligan protecting my turf in Milwaukee. My journey to the ancient banks of the Tigris River began when I was just a seven-year-old boy, in a tiny town in Michigan with a little big-hearted dog named Pokie.

My buddy Pokie was a light-hearted black and white Border Collie my dad brought home to the family. I loved his unique markings: half of his face was white and the other half black. We were instant friends, inseparable.

One of our many adventures would take us out to the woods around Eagle Lake, Michigan where we would hunt rabbits, birds and small mammals with my popgun. I vividly recall the wonderful fragrance of the strong beautiful trees that grew so tall they seemed to touch the sky. Firs, Birch, Jack Pines, Hemlock and Evergreens populated every few feet of space providing an excellent hunting ground and ample shade. Sometimes the tree canopy was so thick the light struggled to make its way through the mass of leaves and branches. Large moss-covered rocks served as the perfect place to rest when it was time to hunker down and listen to the sounds of the forest. Pokie never left my side. His vigilant presence steadied my nerves as there were black bears and coyotes about.

My trusty dog and I would quietly stalk through the woods listening for the chirp of birds or the faint snap of a twig. Every once in a while, I would catch a glimpse of a rabbit quietly gnawing on some greenery. Other times I would watch the playful scamper of a family of chipmunks. Slowly I would raise my gun, bring the sights to bear on the center of the unsuspecting animal and slowly begin to squeeze the trigger. It always seemed that at this moment Pokie would spot the nervous animals and immediately give chase. "Pokie!" Too late, the prey was off like lightning, with Pokie in hot pursuit. I would storm home, throw open the door and yell out to my mother that Pokie was, "Not allowed to leave the house!" Soon however, my anger would subside and Pokie, sensing my mood, was lying beside me on the floor as I played with my marbles.

My hunting trips with Pokie always ended the same way, with frustrated shouts of anger, and the cork at the end of my popgun always idle. Truth was though, I could not bear the thought of hunting without him by my side and so day after day we would go hunting and day after day my prize eluded me.

Pokie was the first dog I ever loved and he would not be the last. His devotion to me made quite an impression on my young heart. In fact, I would say his love for me opened a new chamber of my heart

I never knew existed. He endeared himself to me in the most amazing ways.

Every school day he would accompany me to the county bus stop. When the long bus came to a squeaking halt the doors would open and Pokie would accompany me right up to the steps. I would board the bus and immediately run all the way to the back window because I knew what was coming next. With my buddies gathering around and with bated breath we would watch as the bus began to pull away. Pokie would bark and begin to chase after the bus. Picking up speed we all howled with laughter as Pokie made a good effort to keep pace. Soon though Pokie would give up as we pulled further and further away. We would watch as this hilarious dog applied his own brakes and then panting would turn back toward home. He had resigned to another loss in a race with the bus but perhaps tomorrow he would win.

Day after day this was how my school day would begin. Then, when I returned home, Pokie would be there at the bus stop waiting for me, right beside our country mailbox. Together, side by side, we would walk back home ready for another adventure.

Soon it was winter and with it came the bountiful Michigan snow which accumulated quickly and made traveling on the roads treacherous. One day, during Christmas break, Pokie and I were out playing on the country road in front of our house. Snowplows had previously come through and created huge snowbanks which my four-legged companion and I climbed and burrowed into. Suddenly we both heard the deep growling sound of a large engined vehicle coming our way. It was a snowplow clearing our country road again. Pokie heard the engine noise and I suspect was reminded of our school bus. He darted from my side and began to chase the snowplow, bounding through the snow in great leaps and barking wildly, I was screaming, "Pokie! Come here! Pokie!" Suddenly the white of the snowbank was splashed with a quick spray of red. I was frantically screaming, running, crying "Pokie!" The snowplow never stopped; the driver probably oblivious to the fact that his plow had connected with my best friend's head.

Reaching Pokie I was surprised to see he was still alive. I ran for help. Surprisingly, my stalwart companion survived, but he would never be the same. Something in his inner being had been damaged. My heart was broken and even after all of these years I still feel the pain of the loss of my best friend. In a scene reminding me of Old Yeller our formerly passive and friendly Pokie would growl at us and show his teeth when we walked by or walked too close. He never trusted anyone again. One day, after returning home from school he was gone. No explanation was given, he was just gone. It was not until decades later that I would hear from my mother that he had been taken to the pound by dad.

Pokie was the first dog I ever loved and reflecting back on those days of long ago when we chased rabbits and squirrels, I can't help but feel melancholy. Fondly do I remember how we wrestled and played and how my heart leapt when I would see him waiting for me at the bus stop. My companion, my best friend.

Pokie had planted a seed in me, a love for dogs that would ensure that no matter where life took me there would always be at least one in my home. Because of Pokie all three of my children have fond memories of their own childhood canine friends: Stretch, Pupper, Cinnamon, Blind Barney, Kisie, Peanut, Kimya and Dallas. My grandchildren have likewise felt and basked in the love of their fury companions: Rosa Lee, Cal, Scarlett, Shadow, Elsie and Clifford. The legacy of Pokie lives on through the love our family has for dogs and because of Pokie's love I would one day learn to train both men and dogs to protect human life and to hunt those whose deeds and intentions are evil.

Dennis Blocker Baghdad '05 and '06

Part One

Checkpoint Two

First Foot Falls

I must admit though that when I first stepped off the creaking and dented platform of the cargo plane at Baghdad International Airport, I was most definitely not thinking about Pokie. I was thinking about survival. I was keenly aware and mindful of dangers and possible threats. In fact, when teaching at the Air Force Police Academy at Lackland Air Force Base[1], I instructed on terrorist tactics, convoy strategies and the dangers of choke points. With those years of experience under my belt my head was always on a swivel and once I stepped off the cargo plane and onto Iraqi soil it was situational awareness to the max.

Those who have been in combat or who have worked law enforcement will know what I mean. I did a quick scan of my environment checking for the highest elevation in the vicinity, places I would choose if I were a sniper. I quickly surveyed the perimeter of the airport to see if there were walls or just chain link fencing. I wasn't going to assume the area was secure. Guys who assumed things got killed. Not me. I would assume nothing.

I then inspected the airport employees to see if they knew how to handle the machinery that would be used to unload our gear of if they seemed awkward and unfamiliar with their tasks. I was seeking anything, clues that made someone seem out of place. Was I over cautious? Darn right I was.

Let's get real. I had no illusions about where I was. There was no time for romanticizing this place of Babylon and the ancient kings of old. This was one of the deadliest places on the planet, especially for an American and even more so for those working with K9 bomb dogs. It would be a cold day in Hell before I allowed myself to be shot being a tourist in this place. Vigilance would serve to keep me, my men and our dogs alive.

---

[1] The Air Force Base is located in San Antonio, Texas and is also where all Air Force recruits receive their basic training.

I was a long way from training dogs and handlers back in Texas. It's one thing to train dogs and men and quite another to put the training into use in real world situations. Especially when the stakes were so high. I mean, face it, an environment where people are actively trying to kill you is as real and as intense as it gets. I had been in plenty of real-world situations in the military, most of which are still classified, but I had never been actively pursuing explosives. This was new territory for me.

I knew the mechanics were basically the same as any other dog team search. Back in Texas we trained many dogs to detect drugs coming across the border from Mexico. The same search pattern used in seeking out drugs would be used in searching for explosives but there were even variations in those details.

For starters, I knew that searching for drugs alongside a Texas highway was dangerous but my students and I never had to worry that the car would blow up in our faces. We worried about passing vehicles and perhaps a driver or passenger who had a warrant and thus didn't want to go to jail. Iraq was different in that the road could kill with IEDs, the cars could kill with VBIEDs[2] and evil men in plain sight or in hidden places would actively try to kill us with any weapon at hand. The fact that a bounty of $25,000 had been placed on K9 Explosive Detection Dogs (EDD's) seemed to insure the likelihood of our deaths.

Yes, Iraq was a new ball game for me and I would have to learn quickly to keep my odds of dying in the sand low. Fortunately I had over two decades of military experience to draw from and a military bearing that told everyone I was there for business, not to make friends. I was there to keep people alive not to just hold a leash and collect a paycheck.

---

[2] IED stood for Improvised Explosive Device and was usually buried alongside a road or under a pressure plate in the road. VBIED was Vehicle Borne Improvised Explosive Device, aka "Car Bomb"

Reading reports and declassified documents had been a huge asset but it really came down to personal connections and becoming an information sponge. I would not allow ego to keep me from asking questions. I was on a crash course to learn as much as possible.

Why? Simple. I wanted to stay alive, to get back home to my family and I darn sure wanted to keep my dogs and our teams safe. There was much to learn and I got right to it. So, as soon as my feet hit the Iraqi tarmac it was game on.

I knew the stakes and realized I could die but I had made my peace with God and had things organized back home ensuring my wife and family were cared for. First footfalls in Iraq and then game face.

The Invisible Killer

With the aircraft finally on Iraqi soil our first order of business was to load our dogs and gear aboard several trucks that had come to pick us up. Of course our first instinct was to "break"[3] our dogs and allow them a chance to stretch their legs. Unfortunately there was no time for this task because we needed to quickly clear the area because enemy mortar teams had recently taken delight in firing on stationary targets on the flight line.

With the trucks loaded we made a short drive to Camp Striker, a US Army camp specializing in logistics and life support that was located inside the protective perimeter around Baghdad International Airport. The entire area surrounding the airport had been stunningly converted into a mega US military installation called Victory Base Complex. The "Complex" consisted of ten US

---

[3] To "break" a dog does not have the same meaning as "breaking" a horse. In the dog world it refers to providing the canines an opportunity to relieve their bowels.

military bases[4] that provided various missions from logistics to assault. I must say it was impressive and sometimes ironic. For example, driving down a road I could see the unfinished shell of a palace I later learned Saddam Hussein had given the lofty and laughable title, "Victory Over America Palace."[5] Very ironic to have the palace surrounded by not one, or even two but ten United States military bases. Maybe Saddam should have given the unfinished palace the title of "Let's Provide the Americans a Nice Building for Their Headquarters."

Anyway, the area we had been assigned was surprisingly nice. For some reason I had visions of a musty old green army tent with open flaps for "air conditioning." You can imagine my surprise when we were shown several large modern tents that were huge, clean and air conditioned. First things first though, caring for our dogs, so I joined the others in doing the most important task: removing the dogs from their crates, giving them a chance to relieve their bowels and then watering them.

The last dog I had to water was a Belgian Malinois named Buffie. When I opened his crate, I noticed that his water dish was pushed all the way to the back. He had already been taken out and given a break so I only needed to refill his water. Unfortunately I had to bring Buffie out so I could get to his dish. When I attempted to put this Mal back into the crate he turned to run. I quickly spun him around and guided him back into the crate but he did a quick counter spin and attempted to make a run for it. I reached up to gently push him back in but as soon as my hand pressed against Buffie's chest he quickly turned and bit my right forearm. He had been cooped up for many hours and was in no mood to be locked back into the confined

---

[4] Victory Fuel Point, Camp Slayer, Camp Striker, Camp Cropper, Camp Liberty, Radwaniyah Palace, Camp Dublin, Sather Air Base, Logistics Base Seitz and Camp Victory

[5] This was to flaunt Iraq's supposed victory over the United States in the first Gulf War (2 August 1990 – 28 February 1991)

space. As soon as Buffie bit me I could tell he knew that he had messed up. I shoved him back into his crate.

The wound was nothing dramatic, just a few bloody puncture marks which I cleansed and then quickly forgot about as we were busy getting our dogs and gear squared away. After returning to my quarters it was time to pick a collapsible olive colored canvas bed. I selected one that looked like it would support my weight, threw my sleeping bag on top and then placed my two backpacks alongside. I was definitely getting the feel that I was in an active combat area. There were no soft comforters, no doilies beside the cot and definitely no room service. I was, "Not in Kansas anymore."

I lay on my cot and inspected my forearm which, other than the slightly oozing wounds, looked fine. I did some minor first aid covering the small puncture sites with some triple antibiotic and a dressing, that was it. I wasn't angry about getting bit for it's a given when working with these dogs. Every canine trainer and handler will have stories and scars that bear testimony to the effort and time required to transform these amazing animals into carefully crafted and honed detection dogs. Getting bit was no big deal. However, there was a big deal taking place under my skin. I did not know it then but a small strain of Staphylococcal Bacteria[6] had been deposited into my wound and would soon begin to multiply and make a good effort at killing me. For the moment though my thoughts were on the coming convoy down the most dangerous highway on the planet, Route Irish.

---

[6] If you've heard anyone say they had a "Staph infection" well this was it and it would prove to be a doozy.

Route Irish

I fully expected to make enemy contact during our journey to the Green Zone.[7] I had seen the news reports about the dangers and had even been briefed on the subject before departure for Iraq. Television reports about the influx of IEDs, VBIEDs and suicide bombers were regular fare for viewers in America and these broadcasts were gruesome, frightening and sadly, accurate.

By the time I arrived in Iraq in mid-October 2005 there had already been 13,944 civilian deaths in that year alone. Staggering when you realize that number was not **since** the war but rather for the single year of 2005. Heck, it hadn't even been a year yet as it was only October. I didn't know the numbers at the time but looking back they serve as a very real testament to the danger we were all heading into. As it would turn out 2006 would set a whole new record for bloodshed but of course we didn't know that at the time.

With these ominous thoughts racing through my mind I made sure to call my family back home and once again tell them of my love and inform them that I had arrived safely. I dared not tell my wife of the danger yet to be faced, traveling from the airport to the Green Zone, however, when speaking with my son Dennis, candor was paramount. I made sure that my son knew where my will was located and reiterated my wishes regarding the disposition of my remains should I not survive the drive to the GZ or my time in Iraq. Too soon the conversation was over and it was back to preparations for the convoy on the morrow.

The route we had to travel had been given the code name "Route Irish". Secretly I wondered if it was a touch of military dark humor implying it was "luck" that decided who made it alive down the route. As far as I knew I had no Irish ancestors so I would have to trust God. Only an idiot would have claimed to have no fear knowing the gauntlet we had to run. The very real threat was manifested in our convoy's requirement to be escorted by US Army vehicles with helicopter gunships overhead.

---

[7] Also known as the "International Zone" or "IZ"

Now some in our group may have thought we were special to receive such impressive care but I smiled at the thought knowing the real reason the Army was involved was due to our amazing canines. In our convoy we had over thirty-six of the most highly trained and disciplined dogs on the planet each representing hundreds of hours of training and thousands of dollars in expense. Each canine had the potential to save unknown numbers of lives so they were given the royal treatment. High praise if you ask me. Sure we were the handlers but these canines were awesome and everyone from the top down knew it.

So did the insurgents who were offered a bounty of $25,000 for each canine killed. This was the main reason we had such impressive security. The threat was genuine and the money offered would be life changing for any Iraqi, Syrian or Iranian insurgent bent on changing his living conditions. The danger was real and the stakes never higher. The insurgents were serious, I was sure serious and it was evident the US Army was serious so it really surprised me when later I discovered some of my men had no idea it was, well, serious. Sometimes I would just shake my head in disbelief but more on that in later stories.

Pushing our looming date with Route Irish out of my mind I set about making sure the dogs were given a chance to stretch their legs, relieve their bowels and lap up some water. Then after squaring away the dogs and realizing there was some time to kill, I went looking for a place to purchase some sunglasses. I needed to protect my eyes from the incredibly bright sun but also to keep debris from flying into my eyeballs.

At the small "PX"[8] I found they had a pitiful selection so decided to wait until safe in the Green Zone where I hoped more variety awaited. By this time my stomach was letting me know it had a hankering to eat but the line to the DFAC (Dining Facility) was just

---

[8] "PX" is the Post Exchange and is much like a miniature Wal-Mart but designated for military use, and Contractors working for the State Department.

too long so I settled on the Gatorade purchased earlier at the PX and made my way back to the tent.

That night, while lying on my rack, I reflected back on the phone conversation with Debbie, my wife. In my mind I mulled over the conversation and could not help but reminisce about our life together and the memories we shared. Typing these thoughts down now it all seems a bit overly dramatic but at the time, dying was a very real possibility and I guess I couldn't help but reminisce.

Back in October 1968[9] I was an eighteen-year-old punk who had grown up on the streets of Milwaukee, Wisconsin thumping heads and sometimes getting thumped myself. I had previously dropped out of high school in the later part of the 10th grade and never went back. To keep me out of the crosshairs of the State of Wisconsin my mother signed me up with a vocational school where I was learning to be a chef. The apprenticeship was a two-year program which, surprisingly, I really enjoyed.

After completing the course at the Milwaukee Institute of Technology the students would be moved into various restaurants throughout the State. I would say there were about ten of us in the class at the time and most were just like me: stubborn kids, down on their luck and looking for a break in life. The school, the instructors and our training gave us a glimmer of hope for the future.

In no time at all we had graduated and were assigned restaurants. I was pleasantly surprised to learn that my internship would take me to the small resort town of Rhinelander. But where the heck was Rhinelander? I pulled out a map and found it was in the northern part of the state nestled in what was called the North Woods. Hmm...North Woods. That had a nice sound to it.

In Rhinelander I was introduced to the man who was to be my boss and mentor for the next two years. As his apprentice chef I would start out making $1.78 an hour, which was good money. A nice upper apartment just a few blocks from where I'd be working

---

[9] It was almost thirty-seven years to that date in October 2005.

happened to be the right price. I had few belongings so the walls were bare and the floors devoid of furniture but it was mine. I was on my own, self-sufficient and loving it.

In the kitchen I was learning a great deal from the head Chef who, much to my relief, turned out to be a great guy. The restaurant had been in the family for thirty years so the place had a nice cozy feel to it. I liked working there a lot.

My life seemed to be on a good track and there were few worries other than the fact that the Vietnam War was hot and heavy and my draft number might have been called up. You know what though, I was really doing well. In fact, I decided to make the four-and-a-half-hour drive down to Milwaukee to visit my folks and let them see for themselves.

Just prior to departing for Milwaukee I received some hot news from a pal describing a huge Halloween party going down at a friend's house. I was looking forward to seeing my buddies and showing everyone how well I had done on my own. There was a smile on my face and money in my pocket.

After the four and a half hour drive my first stop was to my folks who I had not seen in a couple months. I entered through the kitchen door, just as always, and made my way into the living room where I was immediately struck by what felt like a bolt of lightning. There, sitting on the couch in my parents living room, was the most beautiful girl I had ever seen in my life.

My sister Doreen introduced her to me but this cutie's beauty and unexpected appearance in my folk's home caught me by surprise. I just stood there like an idiot unable to speak and incapable of forming thoughts. I was panicking. My brain finally engaged, "What did Doreen say this babe's name was?" I could see my sister's mouth moving but could not comprehend her words so I looked this beautiful chick in the eyes, "What did you say your name was?" She responded shyly, "Deborah, Deborah Lemke." I was a cocky guy and very sure of myself and could always be counted on for a good line but this babe made me speechless. After the customary hello I turned to talk to my parents and siblings. I would not find out until years later but at that moment Deborah thought to herself, "This is the man I'm going to marry."

So, as I lay on my bunk thinking of those times of long ago, I couldn't help but realize that Halloween 2005 was only two weeks away. I chuckled to myself because October 31st, 1968 was the best "trick or treat" I ever had. It was a trick because Doreen had set it all up and of course it was a treat because on that night I met the love of my life, the woman who would be my wife for fifty years[10] and counting. She would be the mother of our three children and grandmother to eight. It was the best day of my life.

As I lay on my canvas rack I was quickly returned to reality when one of the K9 handlers entered the tent and bellowed that the convoy had been postponed. Frustrating to say the least. My attitude was more like, "Let's get this over with." Kind of like doing all the prep for a colonoscopy and being told on arrival at the clinic that the technicians will have to reschedule. At that moment you just want to get it over with. Well, it's a horrible analogy but you get the point.

I was a little frustrated but there was nothing to be done for we were at the mercy of the military who, as it turned out, had determined there were not enough escort vehicles available to safely make such a journey. Having been in the military I knew they had a darn good reason for the postponement. So, we waited.

The next day we learned that our new time was set for 1500 hrs. This news was a little disturbing because our first convoy, which had been canceled, was to take place in the dark of night, zero dark thirty, when the population was asleep and our forces could utilize thermal sights to scan for threats. In the middle of the day when the entire city was on the move did not seem like a good idea. Once again though we were servants to the will of the military and their time schedule. We would obey and hopefully not die. The image of iron ducks at a carnival did seem similar to our plight but I hoped not.

---

[10] As of this writing in 2019

The hours passed quickly and it was time to load up. As we approached our transportation, I was horrified to see that we would be riding in the open beds of pickup trucks. Inwardly I laughed with resignation for this was getting better and better, but outwardly I was stoic. Oh well, nothing to do but soldier on. I kept my reservations to myself for a good leader never disseminates fear or discord. Fear is a contagion, very much like a virus, and once released it is almost impossible to reign in. So, I kept my mouth shut and exuded an air of confidence and professionalism. Just another day on the job. Just another convoy run.

In addition to our pickup trucks there were two medium sized refrigerated cargo trucks that would transport our canines. For the handlers there were the open beds of pickup trucks and our air conditioning was the wind created as we sped down the dusty highway. Several of the guys joked about our current standing in the "Most Important Assets" category. We knew we were replaceable but the dogs were harder to find. We all joked about it but we loved our dogs and knew refrigeration was the best thing for them in this heat.

As we prepared to move out, two desert sand colored US Army HUMVEEs, drove to the front of the column while two more took up positions at the rear. It was our escort. Atop each HUMVEE was a gunner peering down the barrel of a menacing black machine gun. These fellas were serious. Overhead I could hear the chop of wind and looked up to see an Apache helicopter gunship circling. As we began to move out, so did the Apache, keeping pace. We were in good hands and it made us feel a lot better seeing the veteran warriors with us. Having twenty-one years of military experience myself I had the awareness that these assets were with us because there was a very real necessity for them. This thought made me swallow hard and say a prayer as our vehicles pulled out. My safety was now in the very capable hands of the US Army and God in heaven.

The Army set the pace and it was a fast one. The drivers maintained only a few feet of distance between vehicles so no civilian could maneuver between. I glanced forward over the cab of our truck and could see broiling clouds of khaki colored dust and dirt rolling out from under the trucks in our convoy. The sensation of our caravan swaying from side to side in gentle swells is a vivid memory of that trip as the lead vehicle avoided possible IED positions or suspicious areas. From the air I am sure our convoy resembled a sleek and fast-moving snake.

Our speeding caravan had to pass under a few bridges which I knew were the perfect places to drop a hand grenade into a passing truck filled with a bunch of unarmed guys in an open bed. As we neared each bridge, I scanned its walls searching for a bobbing head but thankfully no one took a crack at us. I did have the thought that these locations were excellent places for an IED and as we passed each intersection I cringed, expecting an explosion. I glanced down and my hands were clenched shut. Waiting. Nothing. Whew.

Suddenly we came to a huge highway intersection which had previously been given the code name "Objective Moe" when the 3rd Infantry Division made its famous "Thunder Run" on April 7th, 2003. The interchange had been held by US infantry and armored units against a relentless onslaught of RPGs and machine gun fire. US commanders on scene reported dozens of burning vehicles that had attempted to ram American tanks. Other civilian vehicles served to transport gunmen to the scene and were shredded with weapons fire. US soldiers described the scene with hundreds of dead Iraqi soldiers and foreign fighters littering the ground in all directions. It all happened in this very interchange less than two years before but thankfully it was quiet now and we coasted through in a matter of seconds.

In less than thirty minutes both the Army and the Lord delivered us into the relative safety of the Green Zone, a.k.a. International Zone. I was pleasantly surprised that our journey to the IZ was uneventful. In fact, if my whole time in Iraq proved as exciting as the convoy ride down Route Irish, well, that would be just fine with me. I had already lived a life full of excitement and a nice period of boredom would be welcome.

29

On the way to Iraq I let Toris know I'm there with him on the journey.

**Toris' crate has my black computer bag placed on top.
Picture taken after safe arrival in Green Zone**

Zing!

It was a huge relief when we finally arrived safe and sound into the Green Zone. Of course I knew we were still in danger but for me the threat level had dropped considerably. Now that I was in the GZ I had to check in with our director of K9 operations, Mitch Raleigh[11], who would be giving us our assignments. I had seen him walking around the area and knew he was squared away. His bearing bore all the hallmarks of prior military and of someone comfortable in command. I looked forward to meeting him.

Soon it was time for all of the new handlers to report to the K9 administration building for our first meeting with Mr. Raleigh. There were at least twenty-five to thirty guys assembled and as we filed into the main office, we were instructed to form a line starting at Mr. Raleigh's desk. I was probably about the fifteenth guy in line so I was outside his office, against the wall facing toward his open door. Soon the line would move slightly forward and a man would emerge from Mr. Raleigh's private office and head out the main door.

One by one the men had a talk with our director and one by one the men exited his office and departed outside. Soon I was through his office door and could see his room was a mini command center. Directly across from the door was a long desk that spanned the entire width of the back wall. Over this desk were charts for each checkpoint, rosters I presumed. Above these, on the ceiling, were lights angled in such a way that they cast their light down on the rosters and assignments.

To my right there was a giant map of the Green Zone displaying all of the checkpoints. It was impressive but I could tell this space also doubled as his residence because there was a metal framed bed off to the left and a shower stall and restroom. He literally worked and lived out of his office. Impressively efficient.

---

[11] A pseudonym for security reasons.

As Mr. Raleigh finished with a handler he would walk over to a chart and write down the name of the man he had just talked with. As I drew closer and closer, I noticed that there was a folder resting in his lap. He never touched it. He would ask the next man in line for his name and then reach over and flip through the various folders on the desk but never touching the one in his lap.

Soon it was my turn and as I stepped forward, he smiled up at me and asked, "Can I have your name please?" My answer was crisp and respectful, "Dennis Blocker sir." He looked up at me and then down to the mysterious folder in his lap. It was my resume.

Flipping through my folder he began to recite some of my qualifications, certifications and levels of experience which told me he had spent considerable time studying my resume. Mr. Raleigh continued, "You've got an interesting record Blocker. Twenty-one years military, been all over the world, a cop, trained police dogs, war dogs, FBI dogs. Taught every subject known to police work and combat. You're the second oldest man here." He let that sink in for a minute. Yeah, he was a master at this sort of thing. Then he continued as I silently stood there, "Out of respect for your age and experience level I am allowing you to choose where you'd like to work."

I told him what was on my heart, "Sir, I want to work where I feel I'd be making a difference. I don't want an easy assignment. Please post me to the most dangerous checkpoint there is."

Mr. Raleigh looked up at me and said, "Ok Blocker, I was hoping you'd say something like that. I have the perfect place for you. In fact, I'd like to assign you as the 'K9 Team Leader' for Checkpoint Two. It's the most dangerous checkpoint in Baghdad. It's in the 'Red Zone' so you'll be outside the wire, so to speak. You'll be in charge of six other K9 teams, giving you a total of seven teams at your checkpoint. Just outside your area is an Iraqi Police Station, which gets a lot of attention by insurgents. Something else you should know is that Checkpoint Two is the entrance to the Iraqi Interim

Government[12]. This is where the Iraqi Prime Minister and his staff conduct the business of the newly formed Iraqi Government. So, as you can imagine, this makes the area a 'High Priority' target."

Mr. Raleigh let the words and their ramifications sink in and then continued, "So, Blocker, do you still want Checkpoint Two?" My response was immediate, "Sir, sounds perfect." He revealed a slight smile as he stood and reached out to shake my hand, "Then Blocker, it's yours." I shook his hand and thanked him.

As I turned to leave, he remembered something, "Oh! Blocker! One last thing. I'll select handlers for your checkpoint but I want you to screen them and take them under your wing. Those you feel cannot handle this type of high profile target I'll allow you to replace. I want you to have handlers you believe will be able to handle business when the…" he looked around the room in a playful way and continued, "stuff hits the fan." I smiled, nodded my head and said, "Roger that sir, will do."

I was so thrilled to know that I would be allowed to surround myself with handlers I trusted. My checkpoint was in fact going to be the most dangerous but this was fine with me. I had never been one to just stand idly around so I was doubly excited to learn that I would literally be there during the making of Iraqi history as I protected the Prime Minister of Iraq. Pretty cool.

I thought to myself, "Ok Blocker, you got what you asked for."

After leaving Mr. Raleigh's office I met up with K9 trainer Isaac Reynolds.[13] Isaac was giving me a walking tour of the facilities we would call home for the next several months. "PUFF! ZING!" A bullet at supersonic speed smacked the earth between us and

---

[12] Also referred to as "IIG"

[13] An alias to protect his identity as he is still working K9 contracts in foreign lands.

careened off into a barrier wall. I had not been in the GZ for half a day and someone had already shot at me! My sense of safety was obviously misguided so my guard went back up and would remain elevated for the rest of my time in Iraq. Lesson learned.

Isaac then led me to a truck we would use to run errands, "I want to show you around the Green Zone and then your checkpoint so hop in." As we drove Isaac pointed to various buildings describing the services provided: medical, veterinary, PX, and "WHACK!" A bullet plowed into the windshield creating a small spider web of cracked glass. Isaac immediately floored the gas pedal and we made what I would learn was record time to Checkpoint Two.

Crap! This was the second time I had been shot at in a matter of a few hours! I could just imagine a grizzled soldier looking at a buddy and saying, "You know, a guy could get killed around here." This place was dangerous and I was now more certain than ever that I would most likely not survive.

In such circumstances a person has two choices: either give in to the fear and dwell solely on it or decide that you're already a goner so you might as well do the best job you can. I thought to myself, "Who knows, maybe I can keep someone alive and make my sacrifice mean something." Time to buckle down and get to work, make the most of the time allotted to me.

Now I don't mention these events and how I dealt with them to make myself into some super warrior or amazing leader. The truth is that I was scared. Only a fool would not have been. However, like I mentioned earlier, it's what one does with that fear that separates the different types of people. Let's be real. Rational people flee the presence of danger. However, there are some whose DNA contains a little something extra that gives them a sort of purpose, a calling to protect others. This attribute is often called, "It."

You might hear a soldier say, "Man, that guy has it." The attribute is courage and is seen in a small section of society. Several jobs require the trait so are therefore by default havens for courageous people. We know such people as firefighters, policemen, EMS and

US service men and women. These types frequently put their own lives in danger to protect or rescue others. One important point about these people is that each one of them will not have known if they had what it took until their first rescue attempt, their first armed burglary call or their first battle.

For me that testing had come years earlier while in the military and I had stood fast. Was I terrified? Yes. However, I had a sort of inner voice that calmed me down, shunted the building anxiety, made me refer to my training and then insisted I apply the knowledge. This is why we harp on training so much. The heat of the moment is not the time to break out the training manual and refer to the index. Train. Train. Train!

Only the fool brags about what he or she will do in various situations. The wise person says nothing, but quietly prepares for the moment of crisis, hoping they will have what it takes. There is not a person alive who will know what category they fall into until they are in danger; until the imminent threat of peril draws near.

I have often put myself into the shoes of those who faced such jarring times. I think of the captain of the Titanic and the men who knew they were going to die yet continued to perform their jobs even to the last possible moment seeking to save as many women and children as possible. Then there are the heroic passengers of United Flight 93 on September 11th, 2001. They knew their plane was going to be used as a weapon but rather than sit and do nothing they talked it over and decided that they could not allow themselves to be used as a weapon against their own countrymen. They rushed the cockpit of their airliner, wrested control from the terrorists and the rest of the story is history.

Thankfully such dreadful experiences during a lifetime are few and far between. Most intense predicaments are not as dramatic as the few instances I mentioned. Such tests of courage come in the form of a rescue from a burning building, or during a hold-up in a bank. Perhaps it is the scrawny kid in high school who inspires those standing round to intercede for kids being bullied. Courage rests in the hearts of men, women and children of all ages, races and creeds and what's marvelous about courage is that it sometimes pops up when you least expect it.

My thoughts on survival and courage at this time in Baghdad reminded me of an incident I had survived in North Dakota back on October 26th of 1973. Israel and Egypt were at war and the Soviet Union threatened to send in troops to protect Egypt. This would have been disastrous for the world as the United States was bound to protect Israel. Could anything be worse than the Soviets and Americans in all out combat? I don't think so. Especially at that time in history.

I was a young three striper, a Buck Sergeant, and my wife and I were stationed at Grand Forks Air Force Base in North Dakota. While events in the Middle East threatened to annihilate the world, Debbie and I were enjoying a beautiful dinner over at a friend's home. It was a great time as we enjoyed a tasty meal and some amazing conversation. The air was filled with laughter.

Later that night, I would say around 0200 hrs., the phone rang and a voice on the other end informed me, "Sergeant Blocker there is a recall underway. Get here immediately." "What's going on?" I asked. The caller stated, "I can't tell you. Just get here right away." I figured it was a drill or base exercise to test our readiness. I kissed Debbie and said I would be back soon.

When I arrived at the headquarters building my stomach dropped because absolutely everyone was there. I thought, "Oh man, this isn't good." Soon we were briefed that all of the B-52 bombers on base were being armed with nuclear weapons and that B-52s in maintenance were being rush jobbed and all the in-flight refuelers, such as the KC-135s, were being fueled up and readied to accompany the bombers.

We checked out our weapons, donned our cold weather parkas and made our way to our assigned posts. Mine was an entry control gate into a Priority B Area[14], the flight line. I stamped my feet and tried to stay warm but I must say the gear I had was doing a good job. My area quickly went from Priority B to Priority A as nuclear weapons passed within feet of me on their way to dozens of B52 bombers that were parked in a large concrete paved area that was ten football fields long and over 500 feet wide. The bombers were silent, sitting, waiting for their lethal loads to be delivered into their bellies.

Other bombers had been loaded and were now slowly exiting the loading area maneuvering along the paved routes that would deliver them to the taxiway. Further to my left were bombers sitting idle, nose to tail on the final trek of paved road leading to the runway. There they sat: dark, idling, looking like a school of barracuda waiting for the opportunity to pounce. Then I noticed a single B52 sitting alone, ready, waiting for the word to go as it sat on the end of the actual runway. I instantly knew that if it did indeed take off, life as we knew it was over.

The Soviet Union had ratcheted up their readiness and threatened to send troops to the Middle East so the United States had responded in kind. As Brezhnev and Nixon[15] traded wartime rhetoric and beat their shields with swords, nuclear weapons were readied for the extinction of the human race. I vividly recall thinking of Debbie fast asleep in our warm bed. I knew that if the missiles started flying there would be no coming back from the ramifications. They would launch and then we would launch and it would all be over. No more habitable world. It was surreal.

I recall watching quarter sized snowflakes slowly drifting through the glow of the stadium sized lights around the flight line.

---

[14] Priority B Area was an area that was classified as non-nuclear. Priority A was an asset that was unique and irreplaceable, such as a nuclear warhead. Priority C would be an aircraft that was down for maintenance.

[15] The two Heads of State were Soviet Leader Leonid I. Brezhnev and US President Richard M. Nixon

The pungent and unique smell of JP4 aviation fuel assaulted my nose and was held hostage by the low-lying bank of snow filled clouds overhead. With my M16 slung over my shoulder I studied the scene and thought, "Well, this is it. All of this snow is going to melt and we are all going to be toast. I'm not going to see Debbie and bless her heart she has no idea she is about to die." I was scared. Of course I was scared. I wanted to run home, hold Debbie in my arms and then "head for the hills" with her. However, I steadied myself, remained at my post and prepared for the world's largest fireworks show.

Millions of people were about to die but I did my job and it was my first inkling that I would have what it took to stand firm during an emergency. Thankfully, Nixon and Brezhnev worked it all out and within 24 hours the emergency was over. It had been a close call. President Nixon spoke of the emergency the following day and said that it was, "The most difficult crisis we've had since the Cuban missile crisis of 1962." Well, it was definitely a crisis but we had performed our jobs expertly and we knew the country was ready, and personally, I knew I was ready.

In Baghdad I knew I would once again need to have courage. I had men and dogs depending on me and I could not let them down. Failure was not an option.

My first few hours in the Green Zone had taught me just how dangerous this place was. I knew I would be tested in the months ahead but I just hoped I would survive the experience.

The Setup

Well, my request to be assigned to the most dangerous checkpoint had been granted. It was called Checkpoint Two, or CP2 if I wanted to be cool and make it sound like a Star Wars droid. The name meant little to me then but later would serve to remind me of many moments when eternity teetered on a single decision.

Many folks wonder why I would ask for the most dangerous posting. Simple, really, I had the knowledge and experience to keep people alive and I've never been one to sit by and let others handle a heavier load. Call me old fashioned but I really wanted to do my part and represent my family, our name, my State of Texas and the United States admirably.

Asking for the most dangerous assignment also considerably reduced any fear of the unknown because "knowing" a place is dangerous automatically eliminates unnecessary contemplation. It's a sort of, "Well, now that we got that out of the way we can get to work." Hazardous environments make men and women vigilant, it's just natural. This would give me and my team an edge, making us more aware of our surroundings. A less dangerous posting might tend to lull us into a false sense of security. I needed my guys attentive, on track and eager to fulfill our mission of protecting those in our charge.

With such a dangerous posting my first order of business was to familiarize myself with Checkpoint Two.[16] It would be my post in the foreseeable future, so it was imperative I get to know the layout and the current operating procedures in place there.

First, the big shocker was that I would not be guarding Americans. Turns out the checkpoint I was assigned guarded the offices of the new Iraqi Interim Government. The US had spent considerable national treasure to help form the new government and thus had a huge stake in its success. Now I knew there were thousands who lived in Baghdad who would actively seek the fall of this new government and the probability of an attack was very likely. This of course meant that CP2 held the highest degree of danger for those working there. I was fine with that.

My job would be to hold Checkpoint Two to such a high level of security that insurgents would know access through our gate was not

---

[16] From this point forward Checkpoint Two may be referred to as CP2, CP Two, Checkpoint 2

going to happen. To insurgents the prize would be blowing up one of the IIG buildings, not a checkpoint manned by a few people. Therefore, I needed to make security so tight that any probes[17] sent by the insurgents would be found every time. The tests would come. It was a given. The contest was on, life and death hung in the balance. My chief concern would be in attaining the men and dogs who would share my work ethic and resolve. Time would tell who these men would be. Our director had already told me I could remove any men or dogs who did not measure up. It was a measure I was willing to use should the need arise.

To bring me up to speed I received several manuals and digital reports that detailed how the insurgents were manufacturing explosives and delivering them to targets. One of the documents caught my attention because it specifically referred to my checkpoint.

Eleven days before I arrived in Baghdad there was an assassination attempt on an Iraqi general as his driver attempted to turn toward Checkpoint Two. The insurgent car blocked his path and detonated his explosive packed vehicle gravely wounding the general and his guards. Thankfully the only one to die was the suicide bomber.

The explosion took place on Yaffa Street which bordered the walls that protected the Iraqi Interim Government office buildings. To drive home the threat we faced, I was informed that CP2 was the only one of dozens in the International Zone to be classified as actually in the Red Zone.

---

[17] For example, at one checkpoint a canine discovered a shoe box tied with twine mounted under an Iraqi contractor's truck. Inside the box was a baby shoe, some yarn, a couple pencils and pens and a few other items. There was explosive residue in the box and it was definitely out of the ordinary. This may have been a probe by the insurgents to see if our teams would find the box mounted there. A probe was anything the insurgents would think that if found would indicate high proficiency on our part. A probe had to be monitored which of course meant there was an insurgent in the Green Zone watching this Security and Bomb Dog Team to see if they noticed the shoe box.

So, just how would an insurgent get to our checkpoint? Looking over maps and then conducting a walkthrough of the checkpoint I learned how vehicles gained access to our area and how many we could expect. Turned out our control point would sometimes search up to a thousand vehicles in a single day, so it was quite busy.

The first contact drivers made with a security detail was out near an access road that intersected with Yaffa Street. The position was staffed with Iraqi military and police personnel who checked IDs and inquired about the reasons for entering. If anyone looked suspicious, had dubious reasons for being there or acted nervous they were directed to exit their vehicles for interrogation. Of course the soldiers and police were also looking into the vehicles to see if there were explosives lying about or materials used to make explosives. If there was anything suspicious the vehicle was then moved off to the side and further investigation undertaken and other entities called.

Drivers then maneuvered their vehicles through a corridor of tightly connected "Texas Walls" or "T-Walls." These walls stood twelve feet high, were made of steel-reinforced concrete and as they were in sections could be connected to form long perimeters.[18] It was through this T-wall corridor that drivers had to maneuver their vehicles. The design was such that there was only room for a single lane of traffic going one way and no room to turn around. The odor of vehicle exhaust and cigarette smoke combined with the oppressive heat from the sun and these vehicles closely packed made for a very uncomfortable experience for vehicle operators.

Once down this path there was a twelve-foot high wheeled heavy gauged metal gate where Peruvian and Chilean guards stood with automatic rifles in hand. It was a show of force and it was at this point that vehicles were given a visual search by these guards. Once

---

[18] The T-wall or "Texas Wall" has a smaller cousin called a "Jersey Wall" and a larger cousin called an "Alaska Wall" which stands about twenty feet high. As you can imagine Texans don't like talking about these bigger walls.

satisfied that everything was in order the guards would allow ten or twelve cars to pass through.

Passing through the rolling iron gate a driver would then have to make a sharp right turn proceed a few feet and then make another right turn followed by an immediate left turn. This path down the T-wall corridor was designed so that vehicles would not have the opportunity to build speed and thus momentum to break through our area. Cars were crawling along by the time they reached us.

After this final left turn, we would begin to see the fronts of cars as they made their way toward us. A Peruvian guard would be standing there directing the cars to move into one of two lanes ahead of them. The lanes were separated by a Jersey Wall which was also made of steel-reinforced concrete but only stood about three-foot high thus allowing the guards and K9 handlers to maintain eye contact at all times.

With a total of six vehicles in each lane our security personnel would direct the drivers to turn their engines off, pop their trunk and hood and exit the vehicles. They were warned not to have any interaction with a cell phone[19] unless they had a death wish. Guns would come up and then there was the possibility of getting shot. Signs in Arabic and English were posted everywhere warning drivers to the fact that deadly force was authorized.

Readers should remember that for months all around Baghdad explosions had rocked the city as car bombs (VBIED) and IEDs[20] had detonated killing hundreds. These former cops and hardened soldiers from Peru and Chile were not playing around as was evidenced by their solid and grim expressions.

---

[19] We all knew cell phones were a common trigger device for detonation of explosives.

[20] "Improvised Explosive Device". These were usually artillery rounds or mortar rounds that had explosives attached to them and were buried alongside a road in hopes of destroying targets driving by.

With search mirrors in hand our security detail inspected the undercarriages of vehicles while other guards performed visual checks of the interiors. The security men were instructed by me to not open or touch anything on the vehicle so that possible triggering devices would not be tripped.

Next, the security detail, satisfied that all was visually clear, would indicate to us that it was time for the K9 teams to proceed with our search. Once our search was accomplished the drivers were allowed to enter their vehicles and continue on with their business. All of these procedures and steps meant long delays for those attempting to bring their vehicles into the IIG parking lot. However, despite the rantings, the shouting, and the blaring horns there would be no change in the procedure because lives were on the line. A sentinel tower stood thirty yards forward of the parked vehicles and the machine gun poking out of the gun port served to remind the drivers that this was serious business

Security was necessarily tight but even with the Peruvian and Chilean guards standing around with automatic rifles the dog handlers carried personal protection. We were all qualified and approved to wear a sidearm and in addition we had been trained and qualified on automatic rifles. The thought was that should a fire fight break out and our security detail wounded or killed, we would then pick up these automatic rifles and defend ourselves. Of course we also had the additional benefit of our canines. My German Shepherd Toris was trained in patrol work as well as explosives detection. This meant Toris could find bombs but also take down insurgents with his sharp teeth and bone crushing jaws. It was something Toris had done on previous deployments with another handler. I must confess that Toris was a nice, "Ace up my sleeve."

For additional insurance we had a radio network that would allow us to call US troops should the need arise. On that point there was almost always a huge US Army M1 Abram tank staring down the preliminary Iraqi military checkpoint ready to blow anyone away should they feel so inclined to die for their beliefs. The specter of that tank sitting there was reassuring to us and unnerving to absolutely everyone else.

As I made notes on my inspection of Checkpoint Two, I began to form plans on how security and conditions could be improved. Walking toward my quarters for the night my mind raced with ideas, problems and solutions. Challenge accepted.

Toris quenching his thirst.

Toris and I at Checkpoint Two

Stumbling Block

Let's face it, if you are a K9 handler working in war zones or in law enforcement you are probably an alpha type personality. In our situation in Baghdad, handlers were not hired unless they had worked for at least two years in either law enforcement or the military. There is something about having the lives of others on the line that tends to either steel you or encourage you to choose another field of employment.

The benefit of working with veterans was that for the most part they were tried and true. Now, as we will see, Baghdad took things to a whole new level for these guys and several would not be able to stand under the stress. For the most part though the men chosen were capable of performing their jobs under dire circumstances.

Everyone knows there are two sides to a coin and the flip side of competent canine handlers is that many of these guys had ego's the size of Texas. In an environment with battle tested men who have no history together there is a sort of proving period that men feel they must survive to earn the respect of the others. Of course, this was all self-induced as there was no pressure from me for these guys to appear hardy or talk tough because for me actions speak louder than words.

Show me you're a good handler by demonstrating a flow between you and your dog during searches. Let me find your kennel is spotless and the water bowl always containing fresh water. Let me see the dog look at you with adoration in its eyes. "Show" me you're a good handler don't scream at me, "I've been doing this for twenty years and I'm a good handler!" In that instant you have shown me you are not a good handler and probably have some serious problems with ego.

Ah, ego, there it is, the biggest stumbling block keeping a good handler or trainer from progressing to a great one.

The guys I would be working with at checkpoint two were quite a mix. I had previously met the men during our introductory meeting when we first arrived in the Green Zone. Now I was going to see their work ethic and interactions with their canines.

Several of the men were from South Africa and I was to find that the majority of these men were outstanding. They had a tremendous work ethic and were hard chargers always ready to put in a full day's work and eager to learn from their mistakes. With anything in life, though there are always a couple guys who just seem to buck the way things are done. Fortunately I knew I had a fail-safe in this regard because our boss Mitchell Raleigh had already informed me that I had the right to remove anyone I wished off of Checkpoint Two. I was to discover that I would have to use this option within two days of taking over the checkpoint.

You see, I was looking for guys who could take instruction without getting their feelings hurt. Our checkpoint needed handlers with a tremendous work ethic and a desire to do their best every single day. CP2 required handlers who knew their craft, had a great relationship with their canine and were not puffed up with pride in themselves.

In the military I had learned a unique way to sort out the troublemakers. It was a little speech I would give to the team assembled for a "meet and greet" of sorts. Just glancing around the room I could already pick out some of the guys with huge chips on their shoulders. It made me grin.

I began the meeting, "Hello my name is Dennis Blocker and I will be the team lead for Checkpoint Two. I'm here to protect the lives of our countrymen, our Allies and assets. I am not here to make friends. I don't want to make friends because if a friend gets killed I'll have to live with that the rest of my life. This will make me feel bad and possibly not allow me to perform my job as well. So, some of you in this room will hate me and that's fine. I'm here to keep you and your dogs alive and make sure you perform your tasks efficiently and appropriately. If you don't like the way I run things you are more than welcome to transfer to another checkpoint or go home. I'm okay with that."

Some of the guys had smiles on their faces and I could see they were enjoying this. I thought, "Good, I have some guys I can work with." Others though were stone faced and were already bristling. It's the same the world over with the species of men. They meet other males and feel the need to puff out their chest and see who has the biggest muscles. I didn't have time for that crap and our work was way too serious so I needed to nip this in the bud quick.

One of the fellas who quickly became a problem was a South African. Let's call him Chip. Well this guy Chip always seemed to be in a bad mood. He was like a bull in a cage always looking for a fight. We've all seen the type. I could only describe him as a loner and in this setting that is dangerous.

Within a day word was passed to me that Chip was trying to lead an insurrection and have me removed from the checkpoint. This dude would not take instruction or critiques on his efforts with his dog. It was really quite amazing how strong willed he was in refusing even the slightest bit of instruction. I marveled at the amount of energy he wasted maintaining the anger and chip on his shoulder.

Obviously, I had to confront Chip so one day I walked up to him and asked, "Chip, what's your problem with me? Tell me man to man what's up." He just stood there in silence and blinked a few times. As he was not offering an answer I continued, "Chip, if you're going to work Checkpoint Two you need to be a team player and you need to take instruction." He just stood there like a mute robot failing to acknowledge that I was even speaking with him. Blinking. Breathing. Motionless. After a few seconds of silence he turned and walked off.

I went to our director and asked, "Sir, just to confirm, you did say I could have whoever I wanted and could trade out anyone I did not want. Is this correct?" Mr. Raleigh smiled and said, "Yes, that's correct. Tell me the name and they are gone. I don't need a reason, just a name. I know your past, your military history and your reputation." Wow, that was fast, "Yes sir."

So, on the second day I gave our director the word and Chip Hollowman was no longer at Checkpoint Two. Two of his fellow countrymen that he had worked up into a frenzy were likewise sent to another checkpoint a couple days later. There was no way I was going to allow any ill will or concealed anger to fester at my checkpoint. We needed to work together and to trust each other. There was no room or time for deception, backstabbing or injured egos. I needed men, not children.

The other handler, Bill Swanson,[21] was a South African with a lot of experience but also a keen desire to better his skills as a K9 handler. He was continuously asking for advice and looking for tips on how to perform better and get the most out of his dog. A true joy to work with, Bill possessed an amazing work ethic and was absolutely fearless. Bill was comfortable in his skin and derived his self-worth from his work and a mission accomplished. Swanson was not looking to impress but only to put in a solid day's work and keep people alive. Over time we would bond, becoming brothers.

I can tell you that some of my own countrymen, even fellow Texans were a constant thorn in my side. One guy, we will call Bert Swamp, was a real winner. Somehow, he managed to slither through the cracks and attain a contract in Baghdad. I was mystified by this because the only experience he had was training Lab Retrievers to fetch ducks.[22]

---

[21] A pseudonym (fictitious name) for security reasons. Many dog handlers still work in war torn lands and it is an easy thing to use Google to find an address. With this in mind the names of these men have been changed.

[22] Nothing against those who train dogs to fetch ducks. We are all trainers but there is a huge difference between a tranquil pond in the American Midwest and a war zone in the Middle East. This is why they required police and military experience.

Bert wanted to work with me at Checkpoint Two. Looking back I'm not sure why, unless he desired a familiar face around. He knew my work ethic and that I was serious about our directive in Baghdad. He also knew I would be the lead at CP2 so I'm not sure how he thought his antics would fly.

Anyway, I had worked with Mr. Swamp back in Texas and would marvel as he strutted around wearing a hunting vest that had dozens of pockets on the front and a huge pocket in the back to carry ducks. Poor guy was always trying to impress the fellas with how official and distinguished he looked. He constantly bragged about all of the many dogs he had trained.[23] Fact was he had never trained an explosives dog and had never worked in law enforcement or served in the military.

Bert did not take instruction very well and would often complain to others, "I'm more qualified than Dennis so I should be the Team Lead at Checkpoint Two." What an ego! It was bizarre how he ended up in Baghdad. I walked up to him and asked, "Bert, how many dogs have you trained? I hear you are more qualified than I am." Swamp stammered a bit, looked down at his feet and began tabulating the many dogs he had trained and then proudly said, "At least a dozen." I then revealed to him a figure I had not told anyone else up to that point, "Well, I've trained over one hundred explosive, drug, patrol and search dogs in the last twelve months so you might want to listen and learn."

After a short visit with Mr. Raleigh the obstinate Mr. Swamp was removed from Checkpoint Two. In a matter of days I just about had

---

[23] Bert Swamp was going to adopt one of our wash-out dogs named Boss who will appear later in the book. I warned Bert that the dog was dangerous and not to be trusted. Bert would not listen and I heard later that he did in fact adopt Boss and one day at his home back in the States Boss mauled Bert. A friend stated the guy had over 200 bite wounds. I remembered back to the day when I had warned him that Boss was dangerous and could only be handled by very few experienced and seasoned handlers.

my group of guys whittled down to a serious, hardworking and trustworthy core.

In Baghdad, with a directive to keep the Prime Minister of Iraq alive, I was not going to settle for second best. I could not afford to have men on my team who were only interested in looking cool or impressing other people. My requirement was for fellas not afraid to sweat, willing to put in long hours and committed to treating each day as the most important of their tour. In short, we had each other's back. Having picked my team and whittling it down to the men I thought possessed the best character, sharpest dogs and work ethic it was now time to see if I had chosen wisely. Baghdad would test us as a team, that was certain and the test was closer than we could have ever imagined.

Toris and I searching for explosives during the first Iraqi elections.

In the Jaws of Death

I'd just finished eating at the DFAC (Dining Facility) and made way for the kennels because it was time to check on my bomb dog Toris. I needed to get him out of his crate so he could stretch his legs and take a nice long walk which would afford him the opportunity to read the "Doggie News."[24]

When I opened Toris' crate I gave him a cheery, "Come on boy, let's go." Toris was looking up at me but he wouldn't budge. A second attempt, "Hey, come on let's play ball." Nope. Nothing. At this point, I'm becoming extremely worried. All of my alarm bells are going off but I give Toris one more opportunity to convince me he's ok. I reach into my ball bag and pull out the black Kong[25] that he loves. I toss it just short of the crate door and watch as his huge almond colored eyes follow the Kong as it bounces and comes to rest a few inches from his face. He didn't budge an inch. Ok, this is an emergency! Toris lives for the joy of chomping down on that Kong. His apathy for his favorite chew toy told me I had to get moving on this.

It's hard to describe the attachment you have to your dog, unless of course you have one of your own. In addition to being my companion he was also my battle buddy which took our connection to a whole other level. He would give his life for me and I would do the same for him and now here's my buddy lying prostrate, unmoving, barely blinking. I was terrified and my heart was

---

[24] "Doggie News" is when the dog is sniffing the ground, walls, trees, grass, etc.... checking out the messages left by other dogs and animals. Dogs take in so much information through their nose. They are a lot like graffiti artists, and vandals, who spray paint graffiti on buildings, bridges, etc....saying "We Have Been Here, We Are Leaving Our Mark." It is exactly the same in the canine world.

[25] A "Kong" is a non-toxic rubber toy with a hollow center designed to allow dogs to enjoy their natural desires to chew things. Every handler was required to have two on their person at all times.

breaking. We have so much to do, so many bad guys to catch! We've only been here a matter of a few days and now this. Time for action.

I reached into the crate and grabbed him by his soft collar which displayed two American flags on either side of an Iraqi flag. Very gently but deliberately I pulled him slowly out of the crate while at the same time saying, "It's going to be alright buddy, I'm here with you." Once out of the crate he refused to stand but finally I coaxed him into it. It took some time but slowly and wobbly he gingerly took to his paws. This was so bizarre for only a few hours prior he was running and jumping and enjoying life.

I tossed his Kong in front of him, again, no response. He just stared at it with those big beautiful almond colored eyes. I did a quick physical check of his body to make certain he did not have any type of bite wound from a spider or snake. Nope. Nothing suspicious. I then conducted a quick visual scan of his crate looking for blood, stool, urine, vomit anything that was not supposed to be there or that might give me a clue. There was nothing.

When I looked back at Toris I observed that he was attempting to vomit, but nothing would come up. Suddenly I noticed that his stomach looked distended and that in particular the right side of his abdomen seemed to be enlarged. Instantly I knew what the problem was. Bloat!

Bloat is a condition in dogs relating to the stomach. The condition is predominant in tall canines like Great Danes and German Shepherds. With bloat the stomach flips inside the abdomen and then as gas builds up in the stomach it causes the twist to become more rigid and tighter. Soon the twist is so tight that blood no longer flows to the other organs and in particular the pancreas. Soon the oxygen deprived pancreas releases toxic hormones which can suddenly cause the heart to cease beating. If the pancreas does not kill the canine then the dying layers of stomach tissue and intestines most surely will as they fester and cause the dog to become septic. Veterinarians say that bloat kills about 30% of the dogs who are diagnosed. This percentage is dependent on serious interventions such as surgery otherwise it is always fatal.

So, when I saw these symptoms in Toris I knew the clock had already started on his recovery. I hoped I had found it in time but realizing hope was not enough I quickly walked over to where my friend and Head K9 trainer was standing talking to another trainer. I interrupted their conversation "Isaac! Look at Toris. Look at his entire body from where you are at. What do you think?" He looked, noticed he was unsuccessfully trying to vomit. Isaac could see Toris' stomach was extended and that his breathing was labored. "Man Dennis," Isaac said as he glanced back to me, "I think Toris has bloat. Let's load him into my vehicle and get him to the Veterinarian's office right now. We cannot waist a second of time, Toris, is in the jaws of death."

We loaded him into the vehicle and sped off to the Veterinarian's clinic which was thankfully only a few blocks away. As we are driving it suddenly hits me that it is dark out which means business hours are long over. I blurt out my thoughts, "Oh man I bet they are closed." Isaac didn't answer but focused on the road that we were quickly devouring with our tires. When we skidded up to the large iron gate, I was horrified to see that it was chained shut with a big lock. Off in the distance I could see the buildings but there were no lights on. I thought, "Well, maybe they have blackout curtains pulled to keep light from shining out the windows." My heart was sinking.

Then I noticed an inconspicuous button off to the side that had all the appearances of being a sort of doorbell. I pressed the button and prayed someone would answer but I knew there was no way anyone would answer a buzzer after the gate had been locked for the night. A few awful seconds passed but suddenly I could hear what sounded like a door opening in the distance. I looked all around but could not make out the location of the door because the area was shrouded in darkness. A voice reached out to us, "Can I Help You?" Elated but desperate I both pleaded and beckoned, "I have my German Shepherd here! I believe he has bloat! He needs to be seen by the doctor, please hurry, he's in bad shape!" The voice yelled back, "I'll be right there! I have to get the keys for the gate!"

What a relief! Help was on the way! I ran back to the truck and checked on Toris, who was panting even harder now. I said, "It's ok Buddy, you're going to be just fine in a bit, hang in there." I jumped into the passenger seat and glanced over at Isaac who looked very tense. He was revving the engine a bit and I could see sweat streaming down the side of his face. "How's Toris?" he asked while staring straight ahead. I replied, "He's panting harder. I don't know how much time he has."

At that moment we could hear the chain on the gate being loosed from the big heavy lock. The chain fell to the ground and we were waved through. As we pulled alongside our savior he yelled, "Go to the center of the largest building and enter through the middle door. Our medical team will be assembling there." Wait. Did I just hear him say a medical team was assembling for Toris? I was overcome with joy and thankfulness but time was ticking so I swallowed the lump in my throat and we sped toward the indicated building.

We slid to a stop and both Isaac and I bailed out of our doors running to the back of the truck. We each grabbed a side of Toris' crate and took off running for the entrance. When we burst through the doors a team of people were waiting and quickly took the crate from us. Running with Toris they approached a stainless-steel surgical table. The room was bathed in bright surgical lights and the aroma of both sterility and disinfectant assaulted my nose. This was a professional surgical ward.

Around the room were various tools, machines and monitors. I could see suction canisters and green surgical towels laid out with shiny instruments neatly laid in a row. Seconds later entered a man through the door in which we had all just come through. He was wearing scrubs but I surmised that he was a military man and that he was in a position of leadership. He had that military bearing about him and that is exactly what we were looking for. Someone with confidence and experience.

He introduced himself, "Hello sir, I am Lieutenant Colonel Thompson, I'm the Chief Veterinarian." Wasting no time and no further pleasantries he glanced around the room filling with people and said, "I know many of us do not know one another, and thus have never worked together. Most of us have just arrived today but that is all behind us. Here's our very first 'Big Case' together, a case of bloat. This is a death sentence for this war dog. We have a mission, to save his life. You know your jobs so let's get to saving this boy's life."

I had noticed that no one stirred while he was talking and that a few were nodding their heads in agreement with the message he was giving. I was very moved. The respect and admiration these professionals from various States and backgrounds were showing Toris was humbling and filled me with pride in my boy and in them. I knew he was in good hands.

Colonel Thompson instructed one of the medical staff to get a very large syringe type hand pump with a large gauge needle. Dr. Thompson then turned toward me and asked that I place a muzzle on Toris' face to prevent a possible bite on one of his technicians. I had previously told the Colonel that Toris did not like men so the Doctor didn't want to take any chances. When I was moving the muzzle toward his face Toris made eye contact with me and I could see fear. This was an emotion I had never seen in his eyes and it caught me off guard for a nanosecond but I scratched his head, smiled really big and said, "It's going to be okay; they are here to make you feel better." With that his eyes seemed content and relaxed and I could see he seemed to understand what was going on. I placed the muzzle and the IV was started.

The handpump was readied and Toris was given a sedative through the IV that had been started. Soon Toris eyes began to flicker and he was finally resting. Then the needle was inserted through Toris' side and into his enlarged stomach. Success on the very first attempt! The skilled technician would pull back on the plunger sucking trapped air from the stomach. Over and over the plunger was pulled and slowly I could see the difference being made as Toris' massively extended abdomen began to return to its normal size.

Now Toris' stomach almost looked normal again after several minutes decompressing his stomach. Meanwhile other members of the team now began to shave the underside of his body, a process that literally only took seconds to complete. Once his belly was shaved technicians scrubbed Toris' soft belly with the antiseptic Hibiclens and Doctor Thompson called out to the X-Ray Techs standing beside their machine, "There will be no need for films. This is an obvious case of bloat. Thank you."

The radiology techs stepped aside and Colonel Thompson instructed the team, "Go ahead and start the IV fluids, hook him up to the monitor and let's move Toris into the surgical suite. Time is against us." His voice was so calm, so comforting yet direct and sure. I knew Toris was meant to have this doctor and this team who had only arrived this very day into Baghdad.

Doctor Thompson looked at me and asked, "Mr. Blocker, do you want to be in the room when we operate on Toris?" My answer was quick, "Yes sir, I want to be at my battle buddies' side during all of this." The Doc looked over his shoulder and instructed someone to get me some scrubs to wear, a face mask and then I was shown how to scrub my hands and arms. The doctor was taking no chances with introducing bacteria into the environment.

As I departed to accomplish these tasks the Doc looked back at me and said, "By the time you get back we should be finished setting everything up and ready to begin the surgery." I nodded and said, "Yes sir, thank you" and then followed a tech who got me appropriately attired.

In less than five minutes I was in the surgical suite with the doctor and his newly minted team who were being welcomed to Baghdad in a most memorable way by Toris. When I entered Colonel Thompson directed me to stand at the end of the surgical table near Toris' tail. The Doc asked, "Are you sure you can handle this? You're going to see blood and the insides of your dog as I pull them out to inspect them. Mr. Blocker you will be able to tell people that you know your dog 'inside and out!'" This joke was perfectly timed and one the Doc had probably said hundreds of times through the years but it was effective. I laughed and felt much more at ease.

The doc was sorting his instruments around in various positions when he asked, "Blocker, are you sure you're ok?" My response was quick, "Yes sir, I can handle this just fine." Colonel Thompson asked, "Then why are your fists clenched so tight. Your knuckles are pure white?" I looked down and sure enough my hands were two clenched fists and my knuckles were white and shaking. I had not realized I was doing this. I looked at the Doc and said, "I can handle this Sir. I'm nervous and scared for my boy Toris. What do you think Doc, is he going to make it?"

Doctor Thompson looked at me and asked, "What's your first name Blocker?" I responded in military fashion as I had lived for twenty-one years, "Dennis Sir! My first name is Dennis." He paused and then moving towels and sponges around his sterile field he looked up at me through surgical protective glasses and said, "Dennis, I'll let you know once I get into Toris' abdomen. Once I can look to see if the blood supply to various organs has not been cut off too long, and if I do not see anything that looks black or dark in color then I will know for sure. If most of these organs have gone without a blood supply for an extended period of time there will be nothing we can do. Let's wait and see what we find."

Doc turned from me and all the medical staff were standing around Toris. The lights in the room were dimmed down and huge surgical lights swung in above my boy Toris' resting body. The skilled technicians placed sterile green towels all around Toris being certain to cover every square inch of his body but being careful to leave his abdomen exposed. I glanced down at my hands and could see they were clenched into a fist again. I looked over at the doc but he was busy now with Toris and not looking my way. Colonel Thompson was all about Toris.

"Scalpel" The instrument was deliberately, almost forcefully, placed into his open gloved hand[26] and as it was the tech declared "scalpel." They were so professional and I felt privileged to watch them work together.

I swallowed hard as the scalpel was closing the distance down towards Toris' shaved belly. Funny, but I vividly recall thinking how clean his belly looked. I was amazed at the steady hand and precision of Doctor Thompson as he cut a straight line down along the entirety of my buddy's abdomen. I was surprised that blood was not spilling out everywhere after such a huge incision had been made. The OR Tech was holding a tool which appeared to prevent the incised skin from bleeding. I was amazed.

Colonel Thompson looked at me and asked, "Dennis, you ok?" "Yes Sir, I'm fine!" He then reached in and started to move and pull organs up and out of Toris' open abdominal cavity. I heard the Doc say, "Yep, Yes Sir, here's the turned stomach, Dennis look at this," I moved in next to the Doc's side and leaned in just a bit to see inside Toris' stomach. The Doc pointed out where the esophagus joins the upper part of the stomach and then he showed where the small intestine joins with the lower portion of the stomach.

Doctor Thompson then said, "Look at how the stomach had turned, causing his esophagus and small intestine to become knotted." Doc was examining with his surgical gloved hands each organ and every inch of the intestines ensuring their integrity. So far everything other than the knots looked good.

---

[26] The movement reminded me of the observation shift I did at the Level 1 Trauma Center my son worked at. My son informed me that when doctors ask for instruments, he did not hold them out for the doctor but rather you forcefully put them into their hands so they could grasp it with surety.

"Oh! Oh!" the words I did not want to hear from the doctor had escaped his lips. He then said, "The spleen looks like it was cut short on blood supply, come look at this Dennis." So I quickly came up alongside the Doc again and he said, "This is Tori's spleen I'm holding in my hands, do you see this dark purple area right here?" Sure enough, I could see the discoloration, "Yes Sir, what's that mean?" Colonel Thompson explained, "It means you got your boy Toris here just in time. This area was not getting enough blood supply and was beginning to die. I believe it will be fine now, we got in here just in time. However, if you had delayed this by another hour or two, he would have been dead by morning."

The thought made me shudder. I had been feeling tired after a full day and as I had already taken care of Toris earlier it was not necessary to check on him but the fact is that I did check on him again before hitting the sack. My hands were shaking at what a close call it had been.

Colonel Thompson continued his much-appreciated narration, "This was the first organ which was starting to die Dennis. From what I see here, Toris is going to make it through this. He will have some recovery time of course but I really believe that in about ten days he'll be fine, good enough to go back to doing what he came here for, sniffing out explosives/bombs and saving lives." I could see the glint in the doctor's eye as he said these last words to me. It made me tear up witnessing the admiration Doctor Thompson had for Toris. To this doctor canines were not just patients, they were heroes and I will never forget the honor shown to Toris by Colonel Thompson.

I watched as they washed each organ with sterile fluid and placed each gently back into the correct place. It was so impressive! What an amazing surgical team! To think this was the first case they had worked on as a team astounded me. I had been watching a dance as they moved around the table, around the room and around each other flawlessly, perfectly in step. To say I was thankful just feels so inadequate.

With all the organs in place Doctor Thompson turned to me and said, "Now that everything is cleaned and back where it's supposed to be, I'm going to do one more thing. I am going to stich Toris' stomach to the underside of his skin, this is going to significantly decrease the chances of Toris ever getting bloat again." I had a huge smile on my face.

Within a few minutes the stomach was sewn to the wall of the abdominal cavity and Toris was stapled shut, cleaned once again, then lifted to another table with clean sheets and a heated blanket. His IV lines dangled on a pole with wheels and his monitors chimed the comforting tones of equilibrium. I was relieved.

Of course, there was still a recovery to be made and there was always the chance of a blood clot but for now Toris seemed to be out of the "woods". Back in the reception room we had originally occupied I asked Colonel Thompson if I could stay with Toris, my battle buddy. The thought of him there without me nearby was too much for me to bear. I told the doc that I would take him out for walks and free up his staff to tend to other details.

I knew Toris was not the kind of dog who liked lying around and I figured he would be trying to walk as soon as possible. My presence would expedite his recovery and Doctor Thompson agreed, "Sure, it will be fine with me Dennis, you can bunk down on my office floor with him. I'll get you a blanket to lay on."

Within a few minutes Toris began to stir and I could see his eyelids twitch. His eyes opened and the first thing he felt was my fingers rubbing up under his neck to his chin. He always loved this. Toris rolled his eyes up to look at me as I was leaning down to give him a kiss between his big German Shepherd almond colored eyes. As I was backing away, he leaned up and gave me a couple of slobbery doggy kisses alongside my face.

I am sure he could see the relief and happiness in my eyes. I bent down once again but this time I whispered into his big ear, "You're going to be fine big boy, I love you." Again, he leaned up with his muzzle and gave me some doggy kisses.

Within a few minutes the doc was back with a blanket in his hands. He walked me over to his office which was nothing special, just a small room with cement floors. When I made the request to stay with Toris I had no illusions of comfort. However, there was a window unit air conditioner, which had a nice hum to it and was putting out comfortably cool air. This would do nicely.

The plan was for the team of vet techs to lift Toris from the table onto a layer of blankets insulated by the heated blanket. Toris was awake now and I knew that any males[27] coming near were going to get their jugulars ripped out. So I asked Doctor Thompson if I could put the muzzle back on Toris. The Colonel gave me a quick "Thumbs Up" sign.

With the muzzle secured over Toris snout it was now safe to move this war veteran. The techs gathered around Toris whose eyes were darting back and forth examining the threats gathering round. They gingerly and expertly lifted Toris in his layers of blankets and softly laid him on the floor of Doctor Thompson's office. The techs insured the IV lines were not tangled and that the monitor leads were clear of his mouth and the power cord plugged into the wall.

Once Toris was in place and looked comfortable, I removed the muzzle. Slowly he lifted himself up with one paw and gave me another big sloppy wet kiss on my face. He was happy and so was I!

A minute later Colonel Thompson entered with a pan of water for Toris, "It will be good for him to drink a little but be sure he does not have too much. He has been through a lot tonight and we want to slowly reboot his system." Doctor Thompson looked at both of us on the floor of his office, smiled and said, "Good night" and then as he stepped toward the door remembered to tell me something, "I will be shutting down the lights of the facility once we have everything

---

[27] Toris seemed to tolerate females. The male species of humans he had little affinity for.

squared away but there will be enough light that you can make your way around, you know, in case Toris wants to get up to relieve his bowels." Once again, I thanked the doc for everything and wished him a good night.

On the floor I slept with my arm resting on the base of Toris' mobile IV pole. In this way I would know if he was stirring and wanted to go potty. Twice during the night he wanted to go outside. The first time he stood he made a little whimpering sound but toughed it out. I helped him stand but he took over once erect and walked out into the cool and refreshing air. With not the least bit difficulty he urinated and deposited a nice firm stool which was a relief to see. It was about 0200 hrs. and all was quiet in Baghdad for a change. Oh, wait, there it is, the far-off sound of gunfire. Yeah, I guess some things never change and some guys never seem to sleep.

The second time Toris woke up, he stood on his own. What woke me was my arm falling off the wheelbase of the IV stand because Toris was up and walking. I said, "Ok buddy, good job, you got up on your own. You sure are one tough seasoned war dog. Good boy Toris." He slowly and gingerly walked down the corridor to the door that led outside. He marked a good spot with pee and turned to go back to his warm blanket. He looked great and I was relieved to see that his systems seemed to be working fine.

I woke in the morning to find the yellow rays of sunshine piercing the windows and illuminating the room. I looked over at my boy Toris who was already looking straight into my eyes. I'll never forget his expression, a look of love and thankfulness, it blessed my heart. As long as I live, I'll never forget that moment, it truly was special for both of us.

I knew that the doc would be by soon with the start of a new day of work so I wanted to get Toris up and have him pee before then. Toris picked a new spot, sniffed around a bit and lifted his leg. As I looked out over the buildings and the surroundings Boom! Boom! Two loud explosions a few blocks away sent a huge shock wave that slammed through our courtyard. The insurgents were bidding us a Baghdad wake up call. Toris looked back at me, we locked eyes and the look Toris gave I will never forget. Unfazed, unflinching and with a resolute expression Toris seemed to indicate, "I've already escaped the jaws of death. We got this! Let's get to work!" What an incredible dog![28]

General Patton and the "Dude!"

On June 5th, 1944 just one day before the Allied invasion of Normandy, France, General Patton stood before his beloved men whom he would lead through Europe. The general knew hard days of fighting were ahead of them and he had something to say. As a combat veteran himself, Patton had no interest in hiding the realities of warfare from his men for it would dishonor their service. On this day before the largest invasion of all time the famous general talked with them about the days ahead, days of death, toil, struggle, loss, cold, bloodshed and fear. Yes, fear.

General Patton is famously known for slapping soldiers who shirked their duty to fight. In fact, the general suffered many demotions and setbacks in his career because of these demonstrations of anger. What few know is that in this speech to his men, just days before they were to be unleashed upon the Germans, Patton addressed the issue of fear in combat. It was inspiring and would serve to bolster his men in the hard and bloody months ahead.

Impeccably dressed and with boots and a helmet that shined General Patton said, "Yes, every man is scared in his first battle. If he says he's not, he's a liar. Some men are cowards but they fight the same as the brave men or they get the hell slammed out of them watching men fight who are just as scared as they are. The real hero

---

[28] For the next ten days Toris laid on thick blankets next to my bed. He recovered very well, getting stronger and stronger with each new day. On the 11th day after his surgery, we were back at CP2 "Rocking and Rolling" once again, searching for car/truck bombs and other explosives, yes, we were in the War. Salute to Dr. Thompson and his amazing medical Staff.

is the man who fights even though he is scared. Some men get over their fright in a minute under fire. For some, it takes an hour. For some, it takes days. But a real man will never let his fear of death overpower his honor, his sense of duty to his country, and his innate manhood."

In that moment, General Patton had set hundreds of minds at ease for his men now knew they were not cowards for feeling fear. It was natural. The general let the men know that even he had felt fear. Such a statement was liberating for these warriors. It settled them and allowed them to focus on their jobs which was, "killing Nazis."

Having served in the military for over twenty-one years I was in many circumstances where I felt fear. I never let fear cloud and overpower my mind because my sense of duty was always stronger. Now, I am not tooting my own horn here I am just revealing how I personally react and think in these situations. General Patton was right in that every man and woman will feel fear in these situations but what they do with that fear is the determining factor on how they will feel when looking in the mirror. Some cannot bare up to the strain of combat and that is okay, it is not for everyone. However, when you sign up and other's lives are on the line a warrior has a responsibility to hold the line until ordered to stand down.

For we canine handlers in Iraq it was different in that we were not clearing homes or advancing through cities street by street. There were K9 teams in the armed forces who did this and they were incredibly brave. Danger was just as present to us though because we were working the only checkpoint classified as still in the Red Zone. This classification of course meant that it was the most dangerous, vulnerable and most likely checkpoint to be attacked. Once this fact began to set in with some of the guys on our teams, well, it consumed them and clouded their minds to the point they could not function or perform their tasks properly.

A frightened and terrified handler will rush through his vehicle searches and thus potentially permit an insurgent access to the Iraqi Interim Government, and concurrently multiple high value targets. We were specifically tasked with ensuring this did not happen. Such a directive naturally has inherent dangers. I knew this and I assumed that the handlers signing up for the job new this. Of course I will admit that there is a difference between "knowing" and "knowing." The specter of death has a way of making one evaluate what they "know" about the dangers in their job.

All of the handlers had the "information" that we were going to work various checkpoints and that some of these areas were more dangerous than others. It was not until the first mortar or rocket exploded nearby that previous bits of instruction became realities of existence. These explosions served to educate everyone to the new world that we found ourselves immersed in. The thought that months of such deadly experiences lay ahead was too much for some men.

Fear consumes and worst of all it spreads. In any battle in any war there are numerous accounts of victorious soldiers fleeing because of the infectious fear displayed by a single screaming soldier breaking rank. This was something I could not allow to happen in our environment. I needed to weed out those who could not focus on their job. Lives depended on our attention to detail and I did not have to wait long for one such fearmonger to identify himself.

We had only been on the job a couple weeks and were receiving daily mortar attacks. Occasionally a bullet would zing by or ricochet off the ground in a cloud of dust reminding us all that we were in a war zone. One day a new kind of threat made its debut to us and it had a dramatic impact on some of our dog handlers.

RPG's, rocket propelled grenades, came screeching into our airspace from locations across the Tigris River. These rockets travel at 940 feet a second, which means these death dealing explosives are crossing three football fields every second. As we were quite close to the bad guys, we had very little time to take cover from RPGs. Usually, no time.

These weapons were designed to punch holes in tanks and buildings so their destructive force was respected by us all. When the rocket came in, we all hit the dirt and tried to get as much of our bodies under our helmets as we could. Wham! The explosion was tremendous but not close enough to endanger our men and dogs. I waited another second or two and began to stand, dusting off my shirt and pants. Then I heard a shrill voice, "I didn't sign up for this! That's it! I'm out of here! Get me out of here now!"

I couldn't process what I was hearing. It finally registered that this guy was quitting. I tried to quiet him down and reason with him but he was not having it, "Dude! I didn't sign up for this, real rockets and mortars flying over my head and exploding! I'm out of here, going back home!" With surprise I asked, "Are you for real? You just got here. What did you think this war was fought with, cotton balls and rubber bullets?" He just stared at me wild eyed, so consumed with fear that nothing I said was registering.

I took him off to the side because I didn't want him to feel embarrassed and I didn't want his display of fear spreading to the other handlers. I calmly told him, "You're right, it's best that you go home, because you will get yourself, your dog, and maybe others killed because of your fear." I tried to do what General Patton had done with his men many years before, I tried to set him at ease by acknowledging the elephant in the room, "Look man, we all have fear, but you're in a panic and people die with that sort of fear because they become blind with hysteria. Panicking and fearful people are not able to make rational decisions. Then there are others who fear, but they are able to process the situation around them and make rational decisions." He just stared at me with wild, terrified eyes. Nothing was registering with him so I continued, "It's best you go home my friend, you've made the right decision."

Over the next few days it seemed like a rocket or mortar attack would weed out those K9 handlers who could not handle the stress which came along with war. Five men would leave in that first week at Checkpoint Two in the Red Zone and the other checkpoints of the Green Zone. Over the next several months we would lose several more. Some broke after just a couple of days, some several weeks while others several months. It seemed everyone had their breaking point.

These men would approach our K9 Director and exclaim, "I have to get out of here. I quit!" Some of these were good men who just did not have internally what it took to function in a warzone. Then there were those who only wished to do the bare minimum. There was no ill will felt for any of these men. I was glad they were leaving not because of any dislike for them but rather because their actions might have resulted in death for them or others. I could not afford to have men around who were not focused on the job and the care of their canine partner. The stakes were just too high.

Of course the immediate problem with these guys going home was that we had dogs sitting in kennels not working. We had these amazing highly trained canines sitting hour after hour with no handlers. This lack of handlers also meant that we had to cover the hours that were missing because these guys went home. This put added stress on everybody. I recall having to work a 17-hour shift once to fill the gaps created in the staffing. Less sleep, less rest and more time to get zapped on the searches was not a good environment but we worked through it with dignity and resolve.

Regarding fear and its lifelong ramifications I think Eleanor Roosevelt said it best, "You gain strength, courage, and confidence by every experience in which you really stop to look fear in the face. You are able to say to yourself, 'I lived through this horror. I can take the next thing that comes along.'"

In Baghdad of 2005 and 2006 we did not have to wait long for the "next thing that comes along."

I Lost My Finger

I had been working at the checkpoint for a couple weeks and was finally in the swing of things. The routine was down and I was happy with my team of men and dogs. One morning the director of K9 operations, Mitchell Raleigh, called me on my cell and passed along the news that I'd be getting a new K9 handler in a matter of days.

68

Mitchell could sense my apprehension, "Dennis, I know you like to talk with new hires, gauge them, feel them out, see if they are the type who can handle the stresses of your checkpoint." There was a pause but I said nothing so Mitchell continued, "I know what you're looking for Dennis and I assure you; you'll like this guy."

Mitchell was someone I respected and trusted immensely so I had a feeling I would like the dude but I still felt I needed to clarify my position, "Yes sir, I understand, however, if I don't believe he's right for Checkpoint Two I'm trusting you'll allow me to change him out. Is this correct sir?" His response was immediate and definitive, "You got it Dennis. If you don't think he'll measure up I'll move him for you."

Mitchell informed me that the new hire had been a K9 police officer in South Africa and possessed years of experience. The guy was in his mid-thirties and supposed to be very levelheaded, "His name is Milton Harrison[29] and his German Shepherd is a big male named Boss. After they clear processing they will be evaluated by Isaac Reynolds (our lead K9 Trainer) who'll insure both are up to par in their training and teamwork."

I was thankful for the addition of another K9 team as it would mean shorter shifts for the men, the dogs and myself. We'd had some men quit so there were some vacancies.

I always made it a big deal when we got a new team, you know, making sure they felt welcome. We needed the teams integrated quickly so there was no time for hazing or making someone earn their way through trial and error. In the war zone it was put up or shut up, which meant, if the handler didn't have "it" I would send him packing to another checkpoint. In some cases I would even recommend the handler be sent home.

---

[29] A pseudonym for handler security

In a war zone with lives in my care I didn't have the luxury of unlimited time. There was no grace period. No time to ease someone in. From day one the job is very lethal so the learning curve is practically nonexistent. In fact, there is no curve, it's a friggin right angle. Either you measure up or you don't.

So, a few days later here comes Harrison with his very large German Shepherd. As soon as I laid eyes on the dog, I remembered him from training back in Texas. Boss, yeah, I remembered him. This bomb dog had a very bad attitude and was not afraid to let a handler know when he did not agree. As I stood there focusing on Boss, I tried to recall information about his attitude, his strengths and weaknesses. I remembered that Boss mirrored the handler, which meant that if the handler got too aggressive or had an attitude problem, well, so would Boss.

I introduced myself to Milton Harrison, shook his hand, looked him in the eyes and told him I knew of him, his canine and was looking forward to working with them both. I then gave him a few assignments, "Milton, go ahead and put your dog up in the kennels and come back here to me. I'll have you observe how we conduct the vehicle searches." He was pumped and ready to get busy. His energy was awesome, "Sure enough! I'm ready to get into it!"

I was impressed.

Milton got right down to business and in no time at all had read the assigned materials and observed our checkpoint operations for the required amount of time. He was good to go.

At the beginning of his first shift I walked up to him and said, "Ok Milton, I'll be standing nearby in the event you feel you're having a problem. Begin when you are ready." He was so enthusiastic, "Thanks Dennis!"

Beginning downwind, which is a huge plus in any search for explosives or drugs, I observed as Milton walked Boss up to the left front bumper of the first vehicle. I scrutinized everything, from the brand-new rookie brown leash in his left hand to the placement of the loop. K9 handlers know that the loop is supposed to go over the thumb of the left hand and all of the fingers were to be clasped down over the thumb and the leash, for control. A slight smile showed at the corners of my mouth. It was all looking textbook perfect.

Milton reached down ever so slowly and with patience and respect ran his right index finger along the top of his bomb dog's head, between its ears. Boss looked up at Milton who gave a slight smile, and said, "Are you ready boy?" He then gave the command to search and made a deliberate gesture with his hand towards the left front passenger side bumper.

As Boss was moving in to sniff around the left lower area of the front bumper, Milton went to the next area he wanted Boss to search. Again, textbook, as Milton presented the next area up high, near where the radiator cap would be. You see, going from the lower corner bumper of the passenger side bumper, then to the area of the radiator cap area directs the bomb dog to cross all of this area that holds so many possible hiding spots in the engine. With the wind blowing through the engine block, the front wheel well areas and the undercarriage of the vehicle the chance of Boss picking up the odor of explosives was high. Boss had done this type of search hundreds of times in training and it was obvious to me that this was second nature for him to follow this structured search pattern. Milton and Boss had great chemistry together and were a well-oiled machine. They were as we say, "dancing together", it was smooth, it was obvious Milton did in fact have years of experience as a K9 handler in South Africa.

Milton was positioned at the driver's side, right front bumper, preparing to present the lower portion of the bumper, when all of a sudden Boss started vigorously wagging his tail. I instantly knew this was a signal that the canine was in the presence of explosive odor. Milton had his leash hand stretched out just a bit from his left side, giving Boss slack in the leash, when all of a sudden Boss sniffed the underside of the bumper and went into a hard and fast sit position, which was the position he was trained to take when he's telling the handler, "I'm in the presence of explosive odor."

Milton looked at me and yelled out, "There's a bomb in this vehicle!" The declaration caused everyone who understood English to turn their heads in our direction. I was furious, "Milton! Shut Up! Don't ever say that out loud! You don't know if there's a bomb in this vehicle! Relax!" I could see he was very stressed: his eyes were wide and he was breathing hard and fast. Milton knew he was in a real war, looking for real bombs and he was at Checkpoint Two, the most dangerous in all of Baghdad.

With a calm but authoritative voice I said to Milton, "Are you ok now?" Milton was losing it, "We're going to die right?" I had to nip this in the bud quick and make him think with the other side of his brain, "Milton, calm down man, we don't know if this is a bomb. It could just be residue from road dust where a mortar or rocket had blown up and the explosive odor has collected to the underside of this vehicle. Calm down. I understand you're shook up. It's your first day working in a war zone, I get it but you'll be just fine." This conversation all took place in a matter of seconds. I had to get him calm and I needed to find out in a hurry just what Boss was telling us.

I looked toward the vehicle and noticed that Boss was still in the "Final Sit" position, waiting for his ball reward. In training I teach that a handler must never reward his dog with a Kong alongside a vehicle because bad guys are watching and they will know that the explosives were detected. They just might decide to set off the explosive early hoping to at least take out a K9 team. This naturally leads to the second reason you don't reward alongside the vehicle because you need to get the heck out of there and let EOD find and defuse the bomb. It's not our job to find the bomb. We just need to alert that explosive odor is present.

So, here I am trying to calm down a frightened handler while hoping the bad guys have not seen this frantic display. Simultaneously I'm trying to figure out what Boss was hitting on. Standing five feet in front of the vehicle I conduct a quick visual scan of the bumper and engine compartment. There it is.

"Milton," I said, "Come over here next to me and look at the vehicle. Tell me if you see anything unusual." Milton nervously approached and stood beside me. After a few seconds he spoke up, "Dennis, I see nothing suspicious." After a few seconds of silence I said, "Here's something you can place in your learning bag. Look dead center under the front bumper. Do you see that drip, drip, drip of green fluid and how it's forming a pool under the car?" Milton leaned forward and hunched down a bit, "Sure, I see it, it's antifreeze. So what?" It was time for instruction, "Here's your lesson, antifreeze has a chemical in it which is called ethylene glycol. This is the chemical additive in antifreeze which prevents the water from freezing in the engine block. Now of course that is not a problem here in Baghdad however, the other benefit of this additive is that it increases the boiling point of water meaning it will keep these engines cool and operating during the heat. Now pay close attention. Ethylene glycol is also used in the manufacture of C4 plastic explosives, to keep it from getting stiff and hard. I'm convinced this is what Boss was responding to. I want you to rub Boss on the top of his head and praise him for this find, tell him 'Good Boy' and walk him away, a few feet. Then bring him back and give him the command to search, but this time I want you to present low, below the passenger's side bumper and then step to your right to your next presentation point, keeping slack in your leash. Let's see what Boss does."

He performed as instructed and Boss went to searching low below the passenger bumper area. Suddenly Boss did a quick jerk of his head to the right, and his tail started to wag in a frenzied manner. Yep, he was on the odor again. The amazing dog went low, directly below the center bumper, sniffed the green pool of antifreeze, pulled out and then went to a fast, hard sit. Milton was so excited over this, I guess he was relieved that he was not going to get blown up. His bomb dog had performed just awesome. The bonus was that Milton enjoyed the opportunity to learn a valuable lesson.

A jubilant Milton walked straight up to Boss to scratch him on the head and give him some much-deserved verbal praise. Leaning forward he stretched out his hand while saying in a high-pitched voice, "Such a good boy! Good boy! All right Boss!" Then it happened, Milton stepped on Boss's right front paw. Boss was known to have an attitude and he responded. In a flash the massive canine chomped down on Milton's right hand. I heard Milton shout and scream in agony, "Oh God! He bit my finger off!"

I could see Milton was holding his arm up but from my vantage point I could not see his hand; however I could see bright red spurts of what looked to be blood squirting over his shoulder.

Not good! I have a handler bleeding to death and a car that a canine has indicated holds the presence of explosive odor. I suspected the antifreeze but in reality, the car had not been entirely searched yet. I glanced over at Boss to see if he was chewing on Milton's finger but he was not.

I walked over to Milton, "I just checked, I see no finger on the ground, and Boss is not chewing on anything, are you sure it's gone?" The scene was surreal and you know, looking back, I really have to admire both Milton and Boss because Milton was still maintaining control of the leash and Boss was still sitting in the "Final Sit Response" position. Impressive.

I looked back at Milton who in that moment turned his hand and then exclaimed, "Oh my God, my finger is lying up against the back of my hand, swinging around! Oh God!"

I could still see the blood spurting so I knew we needed to get that under control immediately.

With so many critical things taking place at the same time I sprang into action. First, I took the leash from Milton placing Boss under my control as the handler was obviously in no shape to take the dog to the crate and secure him.

Meanwhile, Milton was already turning pale so it was imperative that I get him to the vehicle and seated. I assigned a couple handlers to escort Milton to the vehicle, wrap the hand and apply immediate pressure to the injury site.[30] As soon as Milton handed me the leash, I gave the command for Boss to start his search. Readers must recall that we still had this civilian vehicle that Boss had alerted on and had not finished searching. I was sure it was the antifreeze but it's not safe to assume anything so I started on the right front driver's side bumper area and worked my way around the car. As soon as we turned into the front left bumper area Boss caught the odor of the antifreeze, he went straight to it, sniffed and went to his trained "Final Sit Response" for the presence of explosive odor. I knew now that the vehicle was clear of explosives.

Since Boss was responding to a chemical compound which is found in C4 plastic explosives, I decided to reward him for two reasons. First, this was the third time he had sat on this odor and a reward was overdue. The last thing I wanted was for Boss to associate this odor with not receiving a reward. Secondly, and I must say the thought scared me, was the fact that Boss absolutely hated to be placed back into his crate. Every time he was placed in his crate, he would turn to bite whoever was attempting to force him in. I decided to give him a Kong, allowing him to enjoy it on the way back to the crate but also knowing it would give his mouth a different activity than biting my flesh.

As I'm running with Boss on the leash, I'm yelling at my other K9 handlers to, "Open the crate door and be prepared to close it once I get him inside." Everything is rolling, the K9 handlers are at the crate with the door wide open to receive Boss, and as I'm running towards the crate, I take a quick look down at Boss who thankfully is still enjoying the red Kong between his teeth. So far so good and we are almost to the crate. Suddenly Boss spies the crate and realizes

---

[30] Later I would remember a saying told to me by my son who worked in a Level 1 Trauma Center for over a decade. He said that in EMS and in the ER, there is a saying that goes, "All bleeding eventually stops." Very true because we have a limited amount of blood. Dark humor from folks who see lots of death. Before deploying to Iraq I had the opportunity to accompany my son on the Trauma Team and watch the experts work. I used what I learned there in Trauma on this day in Baghdad to help Milton.

the jig is up so he starts to put on the brakes, determined he's not going in; however, our momentum pushes us forward and I yell out, "Boss, Phooey That!" As we are running, I quickly raise my right leg and place my foot squarely up against his butt and push as hard as I can forcing him into his crate. He went headfirst into the crate sliding all the way to the rear, "Bam!" Then with nails scratching at plastic he turns and lunges but "Slam! Click!" the door is swung shut and the lock in place. Whew!

A highly displeased German Shepherd was chomping at the metal bars and cursing with that heavy bark, you know, the one that means, "If I could get out of this crate, I'd rip right into you!" The scene was reminiscent of the clip from the movie Jurassic Park when the Raptor was crated. Anyway, Boss's crate was shaking and tipping from side to side and everyone standing nearby could hear his teeth grinding against the metal bars of his crate door. Barking, whining and drooling Boss was letting his feelings known. Red tinged saliva dripped from the crate door and it was all over his muzzle.

I still had another emergency to deal with so there was no time to rest. Two minutes had elapsed from the time Milton had been bitten and his dog secured by me. In that time I had searched the suspicious car and cleared it. But now I am running from the dog crate toward the truck yelling for the next K9 team to continue searching the other vehicles, "I need to get Milton to the CASH[31] immediately!"

I jump into my vehicle, look to my right and can see that Milton is as white as a bed sheet. Not helping matters is the fact that he is staring down at his mangled hand. He barely acknowledges me when I sit behind the steering wheel. I need to keep him awake, "How you hanging in their buddy? Don't worry man, we're not far from the CASH, I'll have you there in just a minute or so."

The truth was, we were about five to seven minutes out from the CASH but I didn't want him stressing over it. I was floored when Milton asked, "How's Boss? Did someone give him water?" I smiled with admiration and thought to myself, "This is a good guy,

---

[31] Combat Support Hospital. Pronounced "CASH".

a true, full-fledged 150 percent K9 guy." His canine just chewed him up bad, and he's concerned about his dog's welfare. I was deeply impressed! I reassured him, "Milton, Boss is just fine, the guys are taking care of him. Don't worry about Boss right now. You just worry about getting better. We will handle everything brother." Milton responded with a weak, "Thanks Dennis."

I am driving and navigating the Green Zone while trying to keep Milton talking. Suddenly it became very quiet. Milton had dropped his right hand down into his lap and his head slumped against the passenger window. Crap! He's lost consciousness. I yelled, "Milton! Milton! Wake up! Wake up!" I vigorously shook him and was relieved to see his head lift away from the window and say, "Wake up? I'm not sleeping. I'm resting. I'm so tired right now." Not good, "Ok buddy, you may be tired but do me a favor and keep your eyes open. Lift your right hand up into the air. Do it now! Keep it up! Stay awake no matter how tired you feel! Do you understand me?" Milton responded with a tired, "Roger that Dennis."

I'm driving very fast through the Green Zone and thankfully traffic was light. I pulled up to the CASH and assisting Milton out of his seat belt. As I am helping Milton out of the vehicle, I'm reassuring him, "Milton, we are here at the CASH. The Doc's and their crews are going to give you the very best care. This is a war zone Hospital so they treat every kind of battle wound you can think of. You're in the best place for this type of injury."

Milton was talking in a hushed voice, "I believe you, thanks for getting me here." He suddenly perked up a bit and with a worried tone said, "Oh! Who's going to get Boss out of his crate and to his kennel?" I smiled and thought, "Yeah Mitchell was right, I do like this guy." As we slowly walked into the hospital, I answered his question, "Milton, you're amazing. You know it? You're one in a million brother. No worries about Boss, I handled him back in the States so he knows me. I will make sure he is taken care of. You concentrate on getting better because I want you back here. I need good men like you with me."

Once inside the CASH the Emergency Room doctors looked at his hand and then whisked him off to a surgical room. I was impressed with the speed the doc's and medical staff took charge, it was as if they were all connected together by their brains, each knew what each had to do, and they did it. It was like watching professional dancers on stage, it was an awesome sight.

Soon one of the doctors approached me and listed all of the tasks they had thus far performed, IV, x-rays, pain meds, IV fluids. He then listed other injuries that Milton's hand had received which included a large puncture wound that went all the way through his thumb leaving a good-sized hole. He also had suffered a puncture wound which went through the webbing of skin between his index and middle fingers. The middle finger was broken, snapped at the base of the finger, which caused it to fall backwards and lay against the back of his hand.

Milton was in surgery for about three hours. One of the surgeons found me in the waiting area and stated that his middle finger required the placement of a rod and the reconstruction of the torn flesh. It was doubtful if the finger would ever have sensation. The other bite wounds were expected to heal fine. The wounds had all been irrigated with saline and treated. It was a good outcome.

Once Milton was transferred to his hospital room and had some rest, I paid him a call. As I entered his room I smiled and said, "Hey Milton, looks like you came through this very well."

"Well, I have, but I was told by the doctors that it would be a good three to six months before I'd be able to work with dogs again. I'm being sent back home to South Africa to see more doctors and undergo rehab. I'll see if they can fix the finger to where it will be functional again. You know Dennis, this really sucks! I'll tell you this, I'll be back. I promise!"

"Milton, I'm praying all will go well for you and that you'll be able to come back. You take care and I'll see you tomorrow. Oh! By the way, your first day at Checkpoint Two looked just great. The first five minutes looked like you and Boss were flowing together just like two professional dancers. I got to say that I was also deeply impressed by the concern you showed for the care of Boss while you were going to the CASH. You're a true professional K9 handler and I can see you one day becoming an awesome trainer if you maintain this attitude regarding the canines in your charge." Milton was smiling and taking it all in but then his countenance changed and he asked, "Dennis, what's going to happen to Boss once I leave. Will he be reassigned to another handler? It will have to be a seasoned handler to be able to work with and understand Boss." I answered truthfully that I didn't know what would happen to Boss, especially since he had bitten a handler.

Milton lay still for a few moments in silence. I could see the wheels in his brain were turning. He looked out the window and sighed and then said, "Well, I'll miss him of course, even after this bite, he and I had a good relationship. We bonded well together. Man, if I had just been more aware of where I was placing my big feet." He was disgusted with himself and his current circumstances. I felt sorry for him and couldn't leave him in this state, "Well Milton, we will just have to wait and see what the future has in store for you. I sure hope to see you back here one day." I patted his bed sheets and said, "I'll see you later man. Take care." Milton smiled, "Thanks Dennis, I'll see you later, on my return back here."[32] I turned and smiled back at him as I departed.

As time marched on Boss did go to another handler and in that first week bit this man on the hand as well. He was fortunate the bite was not as severe as the one suffered by Milton a few weeks earlier. Then Boss, true to form bit an additional handler. Such injuries bring attention from the "higher ups" and they decided that

---

[32] Milton did in fact return. Three months later while conversing with a friend I felt a tap on my shoulder. I turned and there was Milton with a huge smile on his face. We laughed, shook hands and enjoyed a few minutes catching up. He really wanted to join me on Checkpoint Two but I had no openings. Mitchell our boss needed him elsewhere. Over the next months we would see each other in passing. We'd say hello and he would always ask if a spot was opening up but one never did. I would have loved to have him but it never worked out.

the days of Boss working as a bomb dog were over. He had to go. So, off went Boss to the kennel which housed the canines waiting for the return trip to the States.

One day as I was walking by the big break and play area for the dogs, I could see a rookie handler playing ball with, you guessed it, Boss! The handler, Bert Swamp, was tossing a Kong. As you may recall I knew the guy from training in Texas. He was one of those dudes that always feels that they need to puff up their importance and knowledge. It was obvious to the trainers that his knowledge was limited at best. All this guy had to do to succeed was follow orders but it seemed that he always had a problem with this as well. He was, shall we say, difficult.

I asked this rookie what he was doing with Boss, his answer, "I've adopted Boss and I'm taking him home with me in about a week. He will love being a family pet. I just know my wife and little girl will love him." I was astonished and for a moment at least speechless. I could not believe administration would adopt out Boss to a family and I could not believe such a supposedly skilled handler would desire to take a dog with such a history and demeanor home to live with family as a pet. It all sounded so preposterous. I just knew administration must have tried to talk him out of it but he was not hearing it because, after all, he was such a seasoned K9 handler in his own eyes.

I was trying to save Bert a lot of hurt when I said, "You have no idea what this dog is truly like. He's playing ball and having a great time with you now but trust me, I know Boss well, there are very few people that he likes. Sorry but I don't believe you are one of them. Boss knows you don't have the experience to control him and he's going to take advantage of you. I ask you to not take him home with you. One day you may deeply regret this." He was appalled, "Blocker, I know this dog very well, and you're wrong, I can control him, plus he likes me." I tried again to dissuade him but it was no use. I turned and continued on with my business shaking my head as I thought of the dangerous situation this guy was placing himself in.

Well, a few months later, a friend approached me with the news that back in the States the inevitable happened when Boss turned on Bert. At the hospital the doctors and nurses counted over 200 puncture wounds received from Boss. Of course this meant that Boss had to be put down. It was all so unnecessary and such a waste. It could have all been avoided were it not for pride. I wonder if Bert had ever thought back to the time I advised him not to take the dog home.

Remember this, good handlers become great handlers because they thirst for knowledge. They ask for critiques and adopt the practices of those they respect. Great handlers know that correction comes from a desire to perfect, not to tear down. Never get to the point where you will not accept constructive criticism because you will mark yourself as unteachable. Time is precious and trainers in a forward deployed area are typically strapped for time. So, honor their efforts to sharpen your skills by listening to their instruction. After all it might just save your life one day.

Two Lines and Cash

So, yeah, then there was the issue with the dog bite. Remember that? If you recall I had been bitten on my right forearm by Buffie when I first arrived in Iraq and attempted to push him back in his crate. Now I was suffering from terrible bouts of shaking, chills and sweats. One minute I was burning up and the next I was shivering under my blanket. My chattering teeth should have been a clue to me that something wasn't right.

Around 7am there was a knock at my door. I stumbled to the door shirtless as during the night I had soaked my shirt with sweat and tossed it alongside my bed. When I opened the door one of our handlers was standing there. "Good morning," he said as he extended his hand. I extended my arm to shake his hand and was about to return the salutation when he interjected, "Gosh Dennis! What is wrong with your arm?" I didn't know what he was talking about but when I looked down, I could see two very prominent red streaks that traveled from the dog bite wound in my wrist up to the top of my arm, near my shoulder. With a voice full of concern he said, "Dennis, look man, it crosses over your chest! You need to go to the hospital."

I knew he was right, and my body had been giving me signs all night long, but I was too sick to fully grasp what was happening inside of me. I immediately reported the infection to Mr. Raleigh, our site lead, who took one look at it and ordered me to the hospital immediately. Isaac Reynolds drove me to the US Army CASH facility, there in the Green Zone. I shook my head in disbelief for I had only been in Iraq less than a week and Isaac and I have been shot at twice and now an Iraqi strain of bacteria is trying to kill me.

Isaac dropped me and my infected body off and I walked into the Emergency Department to check in. After the paperwork was finished an Army Major took one look at my arm and the wound and said she was going to admit me for several days stay with IV antibiotics. The Major asked, "Mr. Blocker, why did you not come in sooner? I understand the bite was a few days ago." I looked up and told the hardheaded truth, "Ma'am, back home in Texas when I get bit, I just irrigate it with water and peroxide and it does fine, so I thought I would just manage it on my own." The Major crooked an eyebrow and said, "Welcome to Baghdad sir, this is not Texas and there are bacteria here in everything, the air, the soil and the water. Some of it we've never seen before. So, you have to be extra careful here." I knew she was right, so all I could say was, "Yes, ma'am."

A medic came in, started my IV and drew some labs and soon I was admitted to one of the floors. I was intrigued to discover from one of the staff that this hospital had been built by Saddam Hussein to tend to his extended family and elevated members of his political party. Now, here I am, a Texan with a strain of bacteria trying to kill me lying in a room that used to hold his family. The history of it all did not escape me.

Being laid up in the hospital for several days was not cool. It was a big bummer because I had come here to work, not lie around watching TV and reading books. To make matters worse I could hear the occasional explosions outside as IEDs and VBIEDs exploded across the city of Baghdad. I felt useless.

Anyway, the one bright spot of my stay in the hospital was my chance to interact with some of our soldiers and Marines who had been wounded in action. I noticed a young man walking the halls with the help of crutches and asked what had happened to him. As he spoke, I could see that one of his knees was bandaged and that there was blood that had soaked through. He gave me the short version, "Sir, we were driving thru a small town in the 'Red Zone' when I heard my driver yell out 'Oh No!' Instinctively I yelled, 'What?' Then there was this huge explosion. It was a roadside bomb. One of our guys has 3rd degree burns on his right arm from the flash, and another of my guys had three broken ribs. I took three shrapnel wounds from the 'IED'. The first thing I did was look to make certain my legs were not blown away. I realized they were there so I went to work on my men. One of my guys yells out, 'Hey sarge, you're bleeding pretty bad!' I had no idea I was bleeding! I just wanted to take care of my men."

The wounded sergeant fell silent, looked down at his knee and then said what was on his mind, "You know sir, my mistake was getting too comfortable and not paying attention to detail on the road. There was a tripwire over the road, but you know, we were just enjoying the country drive."

He bowed his head and looked down at his knee again. I asked, "Did you lose anyone?" He smiled and said that they were lucky no one had died. "I am glad to hear that Sergeant" and then I asked, "How many days do you have left?" His face and expression were the face of resignation to fate. The same face warriors of all ages make when they make peace with the fact that they are probably going to die but are resigned to it, "Sir, I have 60 days left prior to totaling out." I told him how proud I was to chat with him and thanked him for his service. He seemed embarrassed and smiled and continued on down the hallway. I watched him from behind thinking about his folks back home and how they must wish to be near him.

I thought of how lucky we are as a country to still produce such fine young people.

Later that afternoon while lying in my hospital bed checking emails and sending word of my progress to family, I experienced something unreal. The sunlight suddenly began to give way. I looked at my watch perplexed. There should have been several hours of daylight left. I walked to the window and was taken aback by the spectacle unfolding on the horizon. A giant Haboob[33] was moving toward the city. The sky went dark, base lights immediately started to switch on and the temperature dropped twenty degrees in a matter of minutes. It was one of the most impressive and scary things I have ever seen.

The second day I was in the CASH, two of our K9 team members came to harass me, which is always needed for a few good laughs. Of course they joked around about how lame it was that I was bit "ON PURPOSE" just to get a nice room with TV, internet, hot looking nurses, and good chow. They went on and on about how nice it was for me to not have to worry about anything other than when to wake up. We all laughed! It felt good to laugh.

A few hours later medical staff entered my room and began to move some of the furniture around as I was getting a roommate. He was a soldier, I forget from which state, but he said that he had been at checkpoint 12 on guard duty with a friend of his. This young man was in a lot of pain and from the bandages all over his body, it looked like he had suffered some traumatic injuries. He seemed happy to see me and wanted to talk, probably to distract him from his pain and private thoughts.

The soldier told me his story, "We had been standing guard at Checkpoint 12 and were tired. My buddy was bored so he decided to approach this small group of Iraqi men who were in a sort of

---

[33] Haboobs are known in North America as Dust Storms. The Arabic word "Haboob" translated means "blasting/drifting"

huddle talking. As my buddy approached a car drove up. We could all see the driver was jerking his right hand upward, kind of like he was trying to set the handbrake. Turns out he was trying to detonate the explosives in his car. Anyway, the explosion kills my buddy and some civilians standing nearby. That's when I was wounded."

You know, there is a release that comes from talking about such horrifying experiences but combat veterans will seldom talk with civilians because they have no idea how to relate and the soldier knows that most US civilians have no clue what war is like. I was honored this soldier wanted to speak with me. We had many nice conversations over the next two days.

All through the night I could hear the medevac[34] helicopters coming and going bringing in casualties to the hospital here. Between the hours of 0130 hrs. and 0830 hrs. five casualties were flown in. One of the soldiers succumbed to his wounds a few hours later. Hits you in the gut to know that there is family back in the States that have no idea their son, husband, dad, brother or uncle is now dead.

As I was walking around getting some exercise, I could see more casualties coming in. One of the soldiers had a pile of bloody meat where his face should have been. His vehicle had taken the brunt of a roadside bomb. Seeing the young soldiers coming through in their bloody uniforms reminded me of a time back in mid-December of 1989 when President George Bush Sr. sent US forces down to Panama. The casualties were flown in via a US Air Force C-130 to San Antonio where I was stationed at Kelly Air Force Base. I received a call, "Master Sergeant Blocker you need to report to the main hangar immediately." I was to be in charge of maintaining the security of the hanger for the protection and privacy of all the killed

---

[34] Medevac denotes those helicopters designated to care for injured or sick individuals. In the field soldiers call for them using the radio call sign "Nine Line" which informs the helicopter crew that the ground unit has a combat related casualty. During the fog of war it is easier to call for a "Nine Line"

or wounded in "Operation Just Cause", our country's effort to remove Manuel Noriega from Panama.

I was asked if I could find some room dividers and have them delivered to the hangar. In addition there was a request for black material which could be hung over the room dividers. It was hoped the material would prevent people from snooping around because the bodies of several dead service members were aboard one of the Air Force C-130s. I put the word out to get these materials and within a short time it was all in place, and with the deepest respect and honor, those killed in action were brought into this extremely well protected and private area for our battlefield heroes.

I positioned two base police officers (Enlisted) to make certain no one approached this private cubicle. Then I'd been asked if I would assist by observing the items being taken from the pockets of the deceased, most importantly, to watch for any classified documents, or maps which may be taken. I had a "Top Secret" clearance, so anything from "Confidential", "Secret", and "Top Secret" I'd be able to assist with. I strongly suspected there wouldn't be any such Top-Secret documents.

I entered the room, put on some medical gloves and observed as items were being removed from the deceased and placed in clear plastic bags, inventoried, and marked as to who it belonged and what items were removed from this warrior. Papers, rings and watches were all removed. There were no wallets as these war fighters knew being captured with such an item could direct an enemy to loved ones back home.

As I stood in silence, I could not help but notice that these men were all in extremely good shape and in the prime of life. Those watches. I will never forget the image of those military grade timepieces. The second hands kept ticking away time, yet, their hearts had all come to a halt.

With this task accomplished I stepped outside the cubicle and was immediately confronted by my Commander, Lieutenant Colonel

Johnley[35]. He was all business, "Master Sergeant Blocker, I need for you to take this man, a Navy Seal, to our clothing warehouse and get him into an Air Force uniform. He was on the mission and was escorting the deceased warriors back to Kelly. Can you get this done for me?" I answered in less than a heartbeat, "Sir, not a problem. Will get this going right now". I then saluted the Colonel and proceeded to assign another NCO[36] to take care of this request to get this Navy Seal into an Air Force uniform. This order was accomplished in short order.

I later ran into the Commander in the hanger and asked, "Sir, why did we have to put the Seal into an Air Force uniform?" His answer, "Sergeant Blocker, we don't want the news media knowing the Navy Seals had been in Panama conducting surveillance and intel for almost two weeks getting ready for this operation to kick off. The SEALS just do not want the news media knowing they were there." I nodded my head and added, "Sir, we have given him an Air Force uniform as requested, and I had him taken over to the Chow Hall to get something to eat, and he'll be back here right away, anything else Sir?" Colonel Johnley responded, "That's all for now Master Sergeant Blocker."

My attention was now drawn to yet another C-130 Hercules aircraft pulling up next to the hanger doors, which were open, I watched as the C-130's cargo ramp began to lower. Inside were stacks of stretchers affixed to the frame of the aircraft. There were IV drip lines hanging down from everywhere, arms hanging over the sides of the stretchers, blood smeared on the floor of the aircraft. Amidst all of these casualties were nurses and medics who had traveled the whole journey with these wounded tending to their needs, administering fluids and pain medication. They were so

---

[35] A pseudonym. I wish I could have used his real name for he was a great officer. Someone I highly respected.

[36] NCO is a Non-Commissioned Officer. In the Air Force of 1989 the NCO ranks began at Buck Sergeant followed by Staff Sergeant, Tech Sergeant, Master Sergeant, Senior Master Sergeant and then Chief Master Sergeant.

efficient and their faces were set with determination and confidence. They knew their business. I was impressed.

Waiting outside the plane were dozens of Air Force trainees still in boot camp who had volunteered to serve as stretcher bearers. One by one the casualties were taken out of the aircraft on litters by these very young and very new to the military Air Force recruits. The litter bearers were directed toward five to seven long tables that stretched from the front of the hangar all the way to the rear. Each table was at least 30 yards in length and each table had a team of doctors, nurses and medics who examined each warrior for injuries and then provided the appropriate interventions. It was impressive to witness such care and concern devoted to these wounded.[37]

The triage process lasted only a few seconds and those deemed critical were quickly taken aboard waiting ambulances and transported to Lackland Air Force Bases' Wilford Hall Medical Center[38] which was a Level 1 Trauma Center. What struck me, and I mean truly struck me, was the way these warriors looked. They were proud of the mission they just came from. They were proud to have shed blood for America and I was equally proud of them. America had called and they answered.

Now, here in Iraq, at the CASH in the Green Zone, seeing the soldiers come off the medevac in their uniforms with blood dripping on the tile as they made their way to the trauma bays brought all

---

[37] There were other witnesses to this scene as I had placed my children in a position where they could witness this piece of history. I wanted them to see what war really looks like. My son Dennis would later remember, "The scene is forever etched in my mind of the soldiers coming off the aircraft still holding their weapons as rivulets of blood streaked down their white sheets. I remember how calm everyone was. The soldiers looked stern and not at all like they had been shot. I was so impressed with the professionalism displayed and the strength of those who had been wounded. I was so grateful to bear witness."

[38] Now known as, "Wilford Hall Ambulatory Surgical Center"

those old visions back. I was struck by a sight I was not expecting, someone on the hospital staff had placed small American flags on the chest of each of these wounded warriors. This was very moving and it spoke volumes to my heart. I said a quiet prayer for these young men and turned to go back to my room. I needed to get better so I could get out there and keep people safe.

My stay in the hospital and my interactions with the wounded US servicemen taught me many things that would keep me alive in the months to come. Now remember, I had only been in Iraq for a short time and I was already getting a crash course on what life was like in this part of the world. It was eye opening.

From the wounded soldier covered in bandages I learned how suicide drivers act during an attempt to blow themselves up. My bandaged friend taught me to never get complacent, but to maintain vigilance at all times. My soldier friend on the crutches taught me the importance of knowing your environment, what looks right and what looks out of place. He amplified the importance of situational awareness. The importance of constant training was reinforced by watching the medical staff and trauma team who worked like a well-oiled machine as they efficiently and effectively saved lives day after day. The other wounded I met made it very clear to me that no matter how long you have been in Baghdad, or how short a time, death is lurking very close, sometimes a fingertip away and other times a city block, but it's always there seeking to snuff out another life. Vigilance, training, trust, dedication; these were essential if I wanted to keep myself, my dog and my teams alive.

By the end of my fourth day the antibiotics had killed my infection and the red streaks were gone. Cleared to return to duty. I said goodbye and Godspeed to the wounded warriors I had befriended and then thanked the medical staff profusely. I also thanked God for I felt that my stay in the hospital had brought people into my life who passed on information that I needed to hear. Information that would keep my teams alive. I walked out of that hospital a changed man, better informed and more determined. I was ready to get into this war.

Being Taken for a Ride by a Ten-Year-Old

I had not been in Iraq for a very long time and I was about to learn another lesson but this time my teacher was an Iraqi boy who looked to be about ten years old.

A good friend of mine who had arrived a month prior to my arrival asked if I'd like to go with him to a military facility where he had some business to take care of. "Sure," I said, "Maybe I'll learn something along the way."

My buddy smiled and said, "Sure, I'll tell you what you need to do. In fact, here's something about the place we are going right now. Every time you stop and park your K9 vehicle in the Green Zone you need to look around for Iraqi kids. They will try to sell you DVDs but they are all pirated and most are real poor in quality. However, some of them are really good and sometimes they're movies that have not even been released in the States yet. You can buy these movies for $5.00 a whack. You can also hire these kids for $5.00 to watch over your vehicle while you're away taking care of business. Just remember to tell him you're paying him $5.00 to make sure no one places explosives on your vehicle."

This sounded to me like some real golden nuggets of information and I thanked my buddy profusely for the intel. So, later that day I found myself in a K9 truck running some errands regarding paperwork for our canines. After I parked my truck, I looked around for a kid to pay five bucks. I wanted my vehicle safe and free of explosives.

There he was, with an eager look on his face and an even bigger smile once he saw me wave him over to my location. Sure enough he had a stack of DVD movies in his hands, "My friend, do you want to buy the best American DVD movies in all of the Green Zone?" I chuckled and said, "Not right now kid, another time maybe!" He was not too happy with my response. He then said, "I watch your truck for $5.00, make sure no bad guy put bomb on you truck." I reached into my pocket and pulled out an American five-dollar bill. When his eyes saw the money his big smile returned. He said to me,

"Not worry, I be right here protecting your truck, go, all will be ok, go!" So, I said "Thank You Young Man!" He responded with a thumbs up and I thought, "What a nice little kid!"

I walked up the sidewalk, opened the doors of the building and took a few steps when I remembered I had forgotten the all-important papers. I turned, went back out the door, down the steps and when I looked across the street, I could not see the kid I had just hired to watch over my vehicle. I looked to my left down the street, then right, there he was, running and laughing waving my $5.00 bill up in the air over his head showing it off to his friends who were trying to sell pirated DVDs.

I yelled down the street at him, "Hey!" He turned, looked at me, and ran harder off to the right side of the road and disappeared out of sight amongst the buildings and vehicles. I could hear him laughing even harder as he knew that I knew that I had just been taken for a ride by a ten-year-old kid.

I'm walking back to my vehicle and this thought hit me, "Did this little punk, this squirt of a con-artist, this shyster put explosives on my truck? So, there I was inspecting the wheel wells, scrutinizing the engine compartment, lying on my back looking under the vehicle, nothing! Well, that was good news! I got behind the wheel of my vehicle, started the engine and started to just laugh out loud. I had just been bamboozled by a kid. Then it hit me, I still had to go into this building and take care of the business I came here for. I got out of my vehicle, papers in hand, locked the doors, insured the windows were all rolled up. Walking toward the building I then noticed kids off in the distance with their arms outstretched in the air waving DVD's at me. Nope, I'm not being taken again by another kid.

I was suddenly hit by the realization that this same scene must have been acted out in every war since the dawn of time. Little kids trying to get by and make a buck to support their family when everything around them had crumbled and all they had known was gone.

The next day I'm riding with my good friend in his vehicle. We pull into the same parking lot I got ripped off at and sure enough a kid runs up with a smile as big as Texas. In his hands spread out like a fan are DVD cases. The kid yells out to my friend, "You want to buy best American DVD Movies in the Green Zone?" My friend matches the kid's volume and tone, "I don't buy pirated DVD movies from America, it's against the law!" My buddy then looked at me and said, "Why am I telling him that, he doesn't care about our laws?" I said, "Well, I was thinking the same thing." I then said to my friend, "Are you going to ask him to watch your vehicle for you while you're inside, you know, just to make certain no one places explosives on your vehicle?" I had a half grin on my face.

A smile creased his face as he responded, "I don't do that, they just run off with your money as soon as you disappear into the building!" My reply was quick as I feigned shock, "Then why'd you tell me to do that with my vehicle whenever I parked it?" His smile was stretched from ear to ear, "You're the rookie here buddy and I'm just passing on what someone did to me. Look at it like this, you're helping a poor kid take money home to help feed his family, and it gives the kids and myself a good laugh. Besides, now you'll have to do it to the next rookie you'll be escorting around the Green Zone when you show them the ropes."

I must have looked hilarious with total shock written all over my face because my friend burst out laughing. He started to choke and cough. He then looked at me with tears in his eyes and said, "You were burned by the kid and then burned by me!" Here comes the choking and coughing and laughing again. He was worked up into such a state of hilarity that he was bent over holding his stomach. He looked up at me sideways to his left and I looked at him, and now we were both laughing hysterically. We were slapping each other on the back laughing and choking. He straightened up and imposed a serious look on his face and asked, "What are you laughing so hard about Blocker?" I responded, "I'm thinking about the poor rookie I'm going to set up, the way you set me up, I'm going to pass it on!" We were laughing as we continued on our walk up to the doors. I'm sure those kids thought we were insane. If they only knew.[39]

Enter the South Africans and Laky

Having now been in Iraq a matter of weeks I began to feel like things were running very smooth. I was learning the way things operated and beginning to form a routine of work, training and sleep. It was exciting to be here in such a famed, historic city. I just wish the circumstances for my being here were different.

One day our senior canine trainer Isaac Reynolds asked if I'd assist him with evaluating the new canine teams who had recently arrived from South Africa. They were joining up with us in supporting the request from our government to provide EDD (Explosive Detection Dog) teams to locate explosives in vehicles, packages, fields, alongside roads and inside buildings.

When one receives such a mandate it is imperative to have the best handlers and canines to meet the mission. This meant we would have to put the new arrivals through an evaluation of their skills and deficiencies. To this end the senior K9 trainer assigned me to an area where he had placed eight cinder blocks that were buried in the ground; all in a straight line and separated by about three to four feet from one another. If you walked up to each block and looked down you could see the interior of each block and the dirt at the bottom. However, one cinder block contained a very small amount of explosive odor in a small glass jar.

My job was to evaluate the K9 teams[40] as he sent them over to me for this search exercise. Once I was finished with the team, I'd

---

[39] I never did set anyone up. We were extremely busy and I soon forgot all about this episode until years later writing down my memories at my home in Texas.

[40] A K-9 team is made up of a single handler and single canine

send them to an area where they were to be evaluated on vehicle searches. The senior trainer, Isaac Reynolds, would evaluate them at this station.

Now, with our mandate and mission in mind I need to find out just how much these dogs know regarding explosive odor recognition. Therefore, I will always start with the explosive odor in the first cinder block. Why? I'm watching to see if the handler has control of the canine knowing that most handlers would never expect the odor to be in the very first block. I'm watching to see if the handler can read his or her canine's body language when it enters into explosive odor.

Several points run through my mind at such evaluations, for instance, does this handler know what his or her responsibilities are as the handler, pack leader? Is he or she controlling the dog or is the dog controlling the handler? Over the years since I've been training K9 teams, I've learned one very distinct critical area which will make or break a team; whoever controls the leash, controls the team! If the dog is controlling the leash, doing what it wants to do, and not obeying the handler, this team is doomed to failure, especially if it's a bomb dog. Their working days may be very short lived. Literally.

Continued training and evaluations serve to circumvent the issues that may pop up. An issue during a real-life search is not the time to find out a handler has a dog with a bad habit. For these reasons we were conducting these evaluations with the newly arrived South African handlers. Plus, let's face it, we didn't know these guys. We had never laid eyes on them and thus had no history with them or their dogs. An evaluation of the teams at this juncture would tell us a lot.

The evaluations were going very smooth and I was impressed with many of the South Africans and their dogs. I didn't know it then, but many of them would be lifelong friends after the war.

Suddenly my attention was drawn to a walking disaster off in the distance. I see a handler, sweaty and huffing and puffing, being pulled across this open field towards me. Oh boy.

The first thing I notice is that the dog is a big German Shepherd, black and tan, with a very nice straight back. As I'm watching this K9 team approach it's very obvious who is working for who. When they both arrived at my location the handler was breathing very hard, his chest was heaving in and out, and he was sweating so profusely that it appeared he had just jumped out of the shower and thrown some clothes on. This poor guy kept wiping his face with one hand while holding onto this out of control canine with the other.

I kept a straight face revealing nothing, "What's your name?" I asked. I wrote it down, and asked, "What's your dog's name." He said, "Laky." I thought I sensed a touch of exasperation in his voice. I asked how he spelled the name and how it was pronounced. The frustrated handler took a deep breath and said, "It is spelled L... A... K...Y and pronounced 'LACK-E.'" My reply was crisp, "Ok." I jotted that down and asked how long he had been a handler to which he responded, "about nine years." Ok, Got it.

Reflecting back on the epic walk I just witnessed I asked, "Why were you not able to control your dog on that walk across the field? Tell you the truth, it's kind of sad to see such a lack of discipline. Why are you allowing this dog to control you?" The handler caught me by surprise when he honestly responded, "This dog is killing me. I've never had a dog who is so strong willed and bull headed."

A thought rang through my head, "How in the world was this dog cleared to assist in this mission." I then said, "You need to get it together. Get this dog to recognize that you know what you are doing, and that you're in control. Laky needs to know that he works for you, not you working for him."

My goal was now to see what they could do, "Now to my left, you can see eight cinder blocks which have been buried in the ground. Only one block has explosive odor, it's a small amount, so the odor will not be spilling out everywhere. I know that you and your canine have been certified as an Explosive Detection Dog Team at your training facility in South Africa, correct?" He answered instantly and with what I thought was a hint of military bearing, "Yes sir."[41]

I asked if he had any questions prior to starting his search and he answered that he had none. My arm swung in the direction of the buried cinder blocks and I said, "Ok, let's see what you and Laky can do together. It's all yours."

He gave the command to move forward and Laky did what I predicted, he shot off like a cannonball and there goes the unhappy handler being drug behind. Clouds of dust fly up as the handler is trying to reign Laky in. As the team approaches the search area at a gallop, I hear the gasping command for Laky to search. Inwardly I am smiling because the command was supposed to be given with the dog at the handler's side, facing the search area in a sit position. Well, Laky was pulling this guy at a mild trot and paying the handler no mind. It was almost comical when the shuffling handler desperately threw in the command for Laky to search.

Now remember, I had placed the odor in the first cinder block. I like placing it in the first block because this tells me how well the canine knows this odor. Will the dog stop and go to the "Final Sit Response" position when it smells the odor or will it blow by the odor because it's moving, running so fast up to and passing the odor buried in the block? This is why I like placing it in the first block. If the dog knows the scent it will immediately go to the final sit response or at the very least it will show interest.

Well, Laky blows by the first block, running his nose a few inches above it, meanwhile the handler is desperately trying to go to a shorter leash so he can get in front of Laky.[42] This of course is

---

[41] I later learned that he had served in the South African Police

[42] **Training Nugget:** A handler can make the decision to get in front of the dog and either just walk the dog by each hole hoping the dog will pick up the odor and respond properly or, he/she can present each hole with a non-leash

impossible because the handler is being drug from block to block. Laky makes his way to the final block and then reverses course almost tripping the handler who jumps out of the way of the excess leash so as not to fall flat on his face. Back and forth, back and forth the sweaty handler is patient but obviously embarrassed. Laky finally makes his way back to block number one and shows interest but does not go to the "Final Sit Response" so it's a fail.

Okay, time to make this a teaching moment. I tell the handler, "Redirect Laky to holes two and three and then turn him back to hole number one." The handler does as instructed and as Laky approaches hole number one he sniffs and I tell the handler, "Ok, now give the sit command and once his butt hits the ground reward Laky with his Kong."

The handler did as directed and Laky enjoyed gnawing on the Kong. This gave the handler the opportunity to switch to a shorter leash. I instructed this poor guy, "Ok, now do it again." The handler used the back of his hand to wipe the sweat from his forehead and gave Laky the command to search. Laky was now placing his nose directly over the cinder block holes, sniffing quickly, and then moving to the next. During this time I'm shouting to the handler to, "Catch up and present each hole with your hand!" The handler desperately tried but he was unable to present the blocks because once again he was being pulled everywhere Laky wanted to go.

Once they passed over block number three the handler redirected Laky back towards hole number one. As they turn back toward hole number one Laky first places his nose over hole two and then continues on to hole number one where he inhales deeply and just stands there. He wouldn't sit, he wouldn't move, he just stood there staring down into the hole.

---

holding hand for the dog to sniff. Once at the "Source Hole" and the handler can see the dog is actively sniffing this explosive odor the handler gives the dog the "Sit" command then rewards with a ball or Kong. It's a handler's choice how he or she would want to search in such a situation.

I direct the flabbergasted handler, "Okay, now redirect Laky to hole number two and give the search command." I watch as they head toward number two and then turn back to number one. Once Laky sniffs number one I yell, "Give him the sit command and then the command to wait and once he does reward him with the Kong." I could see it was starting to click, however, Laky was still dragging, and quickly sapping this handler of all physical strength he may have had.

I must give credit to this guy for he realized the evaluation had failed but he was all for making this a learning experience for both he and Laky. As tired and as sweaty as he was this handler kept at it. Running the exercise again the handler managed to stay slightly ahead of Laky and present hole number one with his hand. This time Laky got much closer to the cinder block and took in a good sniff. Laky was right over it and his nose was almost breaking the top plane of the block when he took in a nice deep sniff. The handler instantly gave the command to sit and Laky did! Immediately! The handler instantly rewarded Laky with the Kong and a lot of rubbing and patting and high-pitched praising which these working dogs just love. Laky was happy, I was happy and the handler wanted to be happy but he was too tired. He looked at me and smiled. It was enough. I smiled and said, "Good job."

My heart went out to this guy but I knew Laky had no business being here at this stage. The handler was a good guy and truly desired the best for Laky but his lack of experience was glaring. He stated he had nine years of experience but I wondered what kind of experience it was. I looked at the handler and said, "You have a lot of work ahead of you with this dog because he's out of control. He needs more work on imprinting the explosive odors. If this is not fixed soon in refresher training, you'll not be, nor will Laky be searching for explosives. This is too dangerous for you, Laky, and anyone else standing in an area where a bomb could be. You have no control of this dog which shows the dog has no respect for you. So, I'll recommend both of you for refresher training, but you've got to master this obedience control first."

I then pointed with my right hand indicating an area across the open field where he was to go next with Laky. From where we were standing you could see a large mud walled area that was a motor pool for Iraqi vehicles of various sizes. I informed the handler to proceed to that area where our senior K9 trainer was waiting for him and Laky. They would be the last K9 team to be evaluated before lunch. I mentioned to him that his next evaluation with Laky would be searching vehicles for explosives and car bombs. His response was a sarcastic, "Great!" which of course told me this handler had no confidence the next evaluation would go well.

A short time later I arrived at the testing area for vehicle searches. I noticed the senior canine trainer Isaac Reynolds was briefing the handler with Laky. I found a place in the shade along a solid mud wall in the vehicle compound. Placing my back up against the wall and keeping my eyes on the handler being briefed I then slowly slid down along the wall into a crouch position. It was warming up with the temperature already cresting 100 degrees Fahrenheit and it was not even lunchtime yet. Yeah, welcome to Baghdad.

I locked myself into a comfortable position against the wall, reached out with my right hand and picked up a few warm pebbles from the ground. Plunk. Plunk. I started to toss the pebbles slightly in front of me as I continued listening to the instruction and watching the handler being briefed by Isaac. The handler was hanging on to every word uttered, "be aware that not all of the vehicles have explosives planted in them. It is your job as a K9 handler to start your dog in the search, maintain control of your dog during the search and know what your dog is telling you through his body language."

While Isaac is explaining the test and the parameters, I'm watching Laky who is turning, pulling, sitting, standing, turning, and pulling. I knew the lead trainer very well, we were friends, and we had trained many canines together over the years; drug, bomb, patrol, and trailing canines. I knew this out of control German Shepherd had Isaac's direct attention and that he knew Laky was being handled by an inexperienced canine handler.

I watched from a distance as once again the poor handler was being pulled everywhere by Laky; here, there and everywhere. There was absolutely no control of this dog being exhibited and furthermore no demonstration of what a proper search should look like. Isaac was irate and yelling in a fiery, disgusted voice, "Take Control of Your Dog! Bring your dog back over here and start over!"

The sweaty handler desperately tried with all his might to make it appear he was in control on the return to the starting point. All eyes were now intently watching this unfortunate display of dog handling. Isaac and I were thinking the same thing, "Perhaps some of those eyes are insurgents who might be thinking that our checkpoints have poorly trained dog teams. Perhaps a terrorist might get the idea that entry through our checkpoint is feasible."

Then it happened, "DENNIS!" My head shot up as Isaac continued, "Dennis, take this dog and fix it! He's now your dog!" I bent my head down just a bit and leaned forward to lift myself to a standing position. As I was coming up, I yelled out, "Roger that!" I had a slight smile on my face for two reasons. One, I knew this was going to happen for Isaac and I had worked together for years and he knew that if the dog was salvageable, I would be able to do it. Secondly, I really enjoyed working with problem dogs for they taught me so much. I was looking forward to the challenge.

As I stood there along the mud wall in the Green Zone, I thought back to when I asked to be a dog trainer at the K9 Training Academy so many years before. The head trainer had worked with dogs for over thirty years and just seemed to drip canine knowledge. I knew I could learn a lot there. One day this master trainer called to me as I cleaned out the dog kennels, "Dennis, so I hear you want to be a canine trainer. The very best advice I can give you would be to try and work with and train as many problem dogs as you can. The dogs with attitudes, those with fears, and those who may have been abused by a 'Hard Handed' canine handler or trainer. These types are your professors. Every opportunity you get, gravitate yourself to these canines with issues." So as I stepped forward in that Iraqi vehicle parking lot watching this unruly dog tug and pull at the leash of his handler I smiled and thought, "Here in Iraq the professor is about to teach the student" and I couldn't wait to see what Laky would teach me.

Laky needed a handler who recognized his issues, and what needed to be done to fix them. Isaac knew this and decided the dog was now mine. Now remember, I already had a canine named Toris, who was also a big Shepherd with a long history of being a war dog in two countries.

You know what though, I was pleased with the decision, for having two canines in the war would keep me on a much fuller schedule. Grooming two canines, record keeping for two canines, feeding two, proficiency training for two, it was all my new life and I was ready for the challenge.

I conducted several testing sessions with Laky to establish what were his strengths and weaknesses. I discovered that I would have to start from scratch but after a few weeks of training Laky on explosives detection in vehicles, roads, open areas, and packages, we did certify him as an Explosives Detection Dog. It's still a mystery to me how he managed to get certified in South Africa.

Laky, my new German Shepherd!

What's for Breakfast?

It's about 1000 am at Checkpoint Two and it's been a good day; cool all morning and thankfully the traffic has been moving along better than usual. It's my time to start searching vehicles for explosives. Both lanes of vehicles are stacked in position, one behind the other, about five to six feet between cars. This distance gives the dog team room to maneuver during searches. Everything looks good.

We get the "Thumbs Up" from the guards who have conducted a search of the drivers and performed their visual search of all vehicles lined up. Now it's our turn to come in with the Explosives Detection Dogs who will sniff out any explosives which may have been hidden from the view of the guards.

My German Shepherd Toris and I step out into the first lane of vehicles and my other K9 team moved to their lane. We look at each other, give a nod of our heads and begin the searches. Everything is going smooth; the searches are flawless moving around the vehicles like a gently flowing current of wind. Toris is awesome and I am so lucky to work with him. He's enjoying the work and wears a happy expression.

Bang! A loud crack from my partners row of vehicles causes me to slightly jump. I turn, wondering what the heck this friggin noise was that scared the crap out of me. In that microsecond I thought for sure that we were all dead. To my surprise I couldn't see a thing, at least nothing that would explain the noise. Perhaps it was a sniper's bullet slamming into the side of a vehicle or concrete barrier but from my position I could find no trace of either having happened. There was no way I was leaving this spot behind the open trunk of this first car. I was not going to make myself a better target.

I spun around looking at buildings in all directions but could find nothing out of the ordinary. It was so strange! Someone must have taken a pot shot at us and then bolted. I thought that maybe a sniper was trying to distract us from finding an explosive in one of these vehicles. Of course this thought made me more determined than ever to conduct a thorough search of all of these cars.

If it was a sniper, I am thankful their aim was horrible. Having been a sniper myself I know how much discipline is required to pull off a long-range shot. It's not easy.

Well, I looked over at my partner who shrugged his shoulders. No clue. Ok, back to the task at hand. I turn back toward Toris to get him back into searching this vehicle when my eyes fell on a horrifying sight. Toris had his huge German Shepherd mouth wrapped around an entire beautiful brown glazed turkey! Saliva was pouring from the corners of his mouth and pooling in the dirt. Oh No! Toris had chomped down on this beautiful turkey that had been resting atop the most immaculate bed of white rice I'd ever seen.

In the trunk was an ornate silver platter atop a beautiful white tablecloth. The silver platter contained this gorgeous bed of rice and then an empty space where a turkey had once rested. A turkey which is now fully hanging from Toris' jaws. Crap! This was obviously meant for a special meeting in the Iraqi government building and someone had spent a whole lot of time preparing this amazing meal. I quickly looked up and could see the driver peeking over in our direction trying to see if Toris was destroying his turkey.

I smiled and waved as if to say, "Hey! I see your turkey here! No need to worry that my highly trained working dog will touch your beautiful bird that someone spent hours perfectly preparing." I knew immediately that from the angle there was no way this guy could see that Toris was holding the turkey in his jaws. Well, that was good.

"Toris! Drop it!" Nothing. Toris just looked at me blankly, like he conveniently no longer understood any of the words that were coming out of my mouth. He wasn't fooling me though, I knew how smart he was and how many missions he had completed, oh no, this dog was not going to pull one over on me. This time I said it with more feeling and well, desperation but all the while smiling because I didn't want this guy getting suspicious that something unspeakable was happening to his prize bird. With a smile and out of the corner of my mouth I pleadingly yelled, "Toris, DROP IT!"

Thankfully he let it drop into my extended hands. Meanwhile I am smiling at the guy as I bend down and gently plop it back onto the bed of rice. I can clearly see the puncture holes but I begin pushing skin here and plugging there with bits of hanging skin. I brush it off and peek over the open trunk at the guy and wave as if to say, "It's ok, I'm not going to let my dog near your food, relax."

After picking up loose pieces of rice that have fallen off the platter, I flick them back into the heap. This is a flipping nightmare. Within ten to fifteen seconds I had pulled off a masterful job of concealing multiple teeth impressions. I stepped back and performed another inspection of the trunk. Everything looked great and the turkey looked amazing. I hoped it would pass the test.

I completed the search of the turkey caper vehicle being certain the sumptuous bird was not a distraction and moved onto the others. Within minutes all lanes were searched and the drivers were allowed to return to their vehicles. I watched very closely as the concerned driver trotted back. I could see on his face that he truly believed he would find the skeletal remains of his prize bird strewn about the trunk. Within seconds he reached the back of his vehicle and bent down. Oh man, the moment of truth. He soon popped up with a huge smile on his face and waved at me. I could see he was relieved and thankful that I had such an obviously well-disciplined dog that had refused to give in to its basic instincts.

Thankfully my forensic skills had been up to the task. I waved back with an even bigger smile and thought to myself, "If this guy (and whoever else is going to eat this turkey) was aware that his bird was in the mouth of an unclean dog he would be rip roaring mad." The thought made me smile. I didn't have anything against these guys of course but their disdain for these amazing canines irritated me. Later that night talking to the guys about it we hooped and hollered with laughter. I couldn't help but say, "Imagine Toris out there disbelievingly asking, 'What's for Breakfast? Turkey!'"

Wonderful, Generous People

After getting settled into a routine in the war zone of Baghdad I began to notice that each morning my two German Shepherds were showing signs of stiffness in their joints. The evidence was subtle but when I entered the kennel area after sunrise Toris and Laky would gently stand and then slowly walk as they exited their kennels. Some mornings they even limped a bit.

This was a huge concern. I got to thinking about the other dogs so made a point to watch the other canines exit their kennels the following morning and sure enough, they were stiff. The dogs were displaying the same aches and pains from sleeping on a hard-concrete floor. These amazing animals could not be expected to perform their job of finding at the peak of their abilities while feeling stiff, sore and groggy from fitful sleep. Something had to be done, but what?

I mulled the problem around and even prayed asking God to lead me to someone who would have a solution. A name popped into my head, Lucy Cigna.[43] Lucy had adopted a Belgian Malinois from me back in Texas and just loved the dog. Now she was extremely active in the Belgian Malinois community in the United States. She was very serious about canine issues and prior to my departure for Iraq she told me, "Dennis, if there's anything I can do for you and the war dogs while you're over there, please let me know and I'll see what I can do."

I smiled when I recalled that after only having been in Iraq for a single week, she emailed me with the same message, "Dennis, if there's anything I can do to help you and your dogs, please let me know!" People make statements like that all the time but Lucy meant it so I decided that now was the time to ask for her help

---

[43] A pseudonym to protect her identity. She knows who she is and how much we appreciate her kindness and efforts on our dog's behalf.

That night I sat at my desk, opened my laptop and composed an email to this very dear and extremely kind lady. "Lucy, several times now you've stated that if I need anything for myself or my dogs to please let you know. Well, so here's what we need. It may be too big of a request and I may be overstepping too much here or perhaps stepping on your toes of generosity but our war dogs need eighty-five beds."

With the big opening statement out of the way my email continued, "My two German Shepherds, and all of the other dogs, are sleeping on hard, cold cement floors. Every morning I watch them get up and out of their kennels very slowly, walking as if they are sore and stiff. Just imagine what it would be like if we had to be forced to sleep on a hard, cold cement floor."

The following day I finished up my long hot shift at Checkpoint Two and then took care of Toris and Laky: cooled them down with a water hose, fed them, checked their kennel for any spiders or snakes and then it was lights out, another night sleeping on the concrete.

After a quick shower later that night I once again sat at my laptop and was thrilled to see a response from Lucy and I thought, "It sure is awesome to have such friends in my life." I didn't know what her answer would be but I knew she was taking it seriously and that meant a lot.

I clicked on the message, "Dennis, as I said prior to your leaving for Iraq, anything you or the dogs need once you're there, let me know and I'll see if I can work it for you and the dogs." It was short, sweet and right to the point. She was on it. My response, "This is awesome, praying. Thank You!"

About a week went by before I heard from her once again. Lucy stated she had put the message out to the Belgian Malinois Club and being a nationwide organization she felt the response would be great. It was. The response in fact had been overwhelming. She had undertaken some research and discovered a bed for dogs manufactured by a company called Kuranda which I hadn't heard of before. I liked the sound of the word. Kind of a war cry or something you would yell when swinging on a rope over a river. "KURANDA!" I loved it already and had not even seen the beds.

I opened the attachment and saw various views of the beds. They appeared to be lightweight but durable. It was an ingenious design using PVC pipe and a thick heavy-duty vinyl mesh weave that was breathable. Best of all it gave the soft, off the floor comfort and rest our dogs so desperately needed.

Now, the cost.

Lucy had been working the phones and her email contacts and in a matter of a few days had donations lined up to purchase fifteen of these beds. It was awesome to see this outpouring of love. This show of support gave her another idea. She got in touch with Carol Grandmougin a wonderful lady who oversaw Kuranda's program for donating beds to animal shelters.

After a few minutes chat Carol was enthusiastically on board and said she would meet with Mike Harding, the owner of Kuranda, to see what could be done to alleviate the plight of these war dogs in Baghdad. Mr. Harding immediately came on board and the decision was made to add our need for beds onto Kuranda's donation website.

In short order donations steadily rolled in. It was amazing! In a matter of a few weeks over seventy beds were purchased for our canines by caring people we didn't even know.

It's hard to describe how good it feels to know that people, who I had never even been introduced to, worked so tirelessly to ensure our needs were met thousands of miles away. Because of the diligence of Lucy Cigna and Carol Grandmougin of Kuranda beds I was able to remain focused on daily tasks in Baghdad. Most of the details were worked out by these amazing ladies but the final detail was mine, the part where I informed our director of the imminent arrival of eighty-five K9 beds paid for and shipped by amazing citizens back home in America.

I knew my meeting with Mitchell Raleigh would be a breeze because our director's one purpose in Baghdad was to insure the care of these amazing dogs. Mr. Raleigh knew I had been up to something when he saw the huge grin on my face. As I related the story in all of its detail his smile broadened. He was thankful for the effort and stated, "Let me know when they arrive. I want to check them out. These dogs are going to love this Dennis. Thank you."

I had one last hurdle which I now brought up, "Sir, this was the only address I had to give for the shipment, so the beds will all be sent to your office. I hope that is ok." Mr. Raleigh smiled, reached out his hand and said, "It's fine. Once again, good job on this." I couldn't take the credit, "Sir, so many people are behind this effort. I will accept your thanks on their behalf." With that I stepped out into the sun light and grew excited thinking about the beds that would soon be sent.

After a brisk walk to my room I fired up my laptop and sent a short email to Lucy, "It's a go!" Within a few days I received the welcome news that fifteen beds had been purchased and that Mike Harding verified that they had been packaged and were in the mail. I knew the beds would have a long journey from Kuranda in Glen Burnie, Maryland to Baghdad, but I still wondered if my nerves could take it. I was so excited for our canines.

Waiting was horrible, even for a patient guy like me. I would retrieve Laky and Toris from their kennel in the mornings and try to imagine where the beds were on the journey. Every day I placed a call to the office, "Are they here yet?" The reply was always, "No Dennis, not yet." A huge smile crossed my face as it was apparent, I was sounding like my kids on vacation after a long drive, "Are we there yet?"

One day, when least expecting it, word was passed that I needed to report to the admin office. I could feel the excitement well up in my stomach. The beds must be here! Walking up to the office door reminded me of the joy of Christmas morning. The expectation, the buildup, finally laying eyes on the gifts hoped for and dreamed of.

Mr. Raleigh came out from his office and was beaming from ear to ear, "Dennis you can relax, they're here!"

A couple members of the K9 office staff helped me carry the dog beds to my room. Obviously the first two beds were going to Toris and Laky. Toris, being the only seasoned war dog, out of the entire group, received the first bed. He was a veteran so he got preferential treatment.

The first batch of Kuranda beds had been fifteen so the first dogs to get them would be all of the canines from Checkpoint Two. Later that night, there were occasional knocks at my door as various handlers came by to pick up a bed. The men were excited about providing their dogs the first comfortable night's sleep they had ever had.

I knew for a fact that the thirty-five dogs that had come with us from Texas had only ever slept on concrete. I suspected it was true of the other dogs as well. So yes, I knew this would be the best sleep these dogs had ever had.

I was proud to know that our country produced such fine people who would spend their hard-earned money on animals they would never meet. I was humbled by their generosity and thankful God placed these folks in my path. I made sure to let everyone involved know what they had done for these war dogs.

The big test would be in the morning. How would Laky and Toris look when I approached their kennel? Would they be sleeping on the concrete or would they have tried out the new beds? It was a huge mystery that only time would reveal the answer to.

In the morning I slowly and quietly approached my two boy's kennels which were always side by side. It was time for the big reveal. I almost burst out laughing when I saw them. Toris was snoring and Laky was blowing slow, full breaths through his nose, obviously they were both in some deep, deep sleep. They had not even heard me approach the kennel. Unexpectedly I let out a slight convulsive laughter. It surprised me and the dogs who both opened their eyes and turned their heads. Seeing my form they both sprang to their paws, barked a warning and then realizing it was me began wagging their tails as they approached the door to their individual kennels.

They both looked refreshed and had actually sprung up to their feet. There was no aching or grunting as they stood. I instantly knew we had a winner on our hands and that these beds were going to make a huge difference. The vote was in and the canines loved the beds and this of course meant the handlers loved them as well.

These dogs were heroes to us and we felt blessed to know them, to walk side by side with them. They toiled in heat topping 120 degrees Fahrenheit, but never balked. Together we faced danger, fear and the unknown. Lives were saved every single day by these dogs and all they asked for was a pat on the head, a flip of a Kong and an occasional scratch along the neck. That's it. They were loyal to the core and were some of the most incredible canines I have ever known. The opportunity to provide them with a comfortable night sleep was important to all of us and I was proud of the generosity of my countrymen and thankful for these amazing Kuranda beds.

A City Erupts

Winter had come to Iraq and with it of course the cooler temperatures. I was hoping the comfortable temps would also signal a drop in the number of explosions around the city. Hopeful thinking.

It was December 10th, 2005 and things were business as usual as far as the explosions, mortars and RPGs went. Every time an explosion reverberated across the city; we knew that people had most likely just died. It was a sound that I never quite got used to hearing. Grating. Troubling. The ramifications of the detonations were obvious as the concussive wave of the explosion washed over the city.

This particular day was a Saturday and the traffic into the Green Zone was always lighter on the weekends. This was different though. Traffic wasn't light, it was non-existent. Empty checkpoints signaled an imminent large-scale attack by religious zealots. With the numbers of pedestrians walking through our checkpoint way down, and the shocking absence of vehicular traffic I knew something was going to happen.

I prepared for the worst and passed the word to all of my K9 handlers to put their battle gear on. I then made sure the men were wearing their Kevlar vests and protective helmets and that their radios were all on and functioning properly. With my men squared away and the Peruvian/Chilean guards likewise prepared we had nothing to do but our job and pray that an attack would not materialize. Was this the calm before the storm?

Suddenly it happened, the sound of a gunmen firing an AK47 on full automatic ripped the air. Then more joined in, and more, soon the entire neighborhood across the wall from our checkpoint seemed to be engulfed in weapons fire. Tracers arched across the sky zipping left and right and then in all directions. It was madness. In a matter of seconds the entire city was rocking with the sound of weapons being fired.

"Well, this is it," I thought to myself, "The whole city is moving in to wipe us out and here at the checkpoint we are going to be a speed bump, barely slowing them down."

I ran across the road to the firing positions warning everyone to be on the alert and to watch for anyone trying to scale the walls. I yelled out, "Stay under cover because these bullets are going to start coming down all over the place."

We all hunkered down in protected shelters and firing positions waiting for the first waves of attack.

I could only imagine what was happening across the city at the various American FOBs.[44] I figured Americans were being wiped out. I'm sure everyone thought the end had come as the entire city of Baghdad erupted around them. Minutes ticked by with no sight of approaching hordes of enemy combatants. Soon the weapons fire petered off and was gone.

Then, slowly, the word was passed around that Iraq's National Soccer Team had beat their rivals from Syria in the West Asia Tournament. The game had been tied 2-2 and had gone to overtime and then to penalty kicks. The erupting weapons fire was Baghdad celebrating their nation's victory.

I was immensely relieved to say the least but also wondered if Baghdad's population fully understood the concept that, "what goes up must come down." Evidently it was a concept not quite grasped in Iraq as hundreds of thousands of bullets shot skyward and then descended back from whence, they had come. At least forty-six people were sent to the hospital that day having suffered bullet wounds from these falling projectiles. Fortunately we at checkpoint two were safe in our shelters listening to the outside world go insane.

---

[44] Forward Operating Base. Imagine an old Western with the cavalry troop being stationed at Fort Apache in the middle of Indian country. Well, that's a good idea of what a FOB is. It's an American outpost in the middle of enemy territory. There were over a dozen in the greater Baghdad area.

Scenes from the New Checkpoint Two

The new and improved Checkpoint Two on a weekend.

Toris searching vehicles at Checkpoint Two

Christmas Morning in the War Zone

How do you respectfully celebrate Christmas in a Muslim land? We didn't lose our identity or our own traditions simply because we were in a foreign country. Christmas was fast approaching and almost all of us at Checkpoint 2 were thinking about our families back home and of the food that would be prepared and the decorations adorning our homes. We had to celebrate in our own way but we needed to be mindful of the customs of the country we were in.

Everyone participated and it was the Chilean and Peruvian guards who found the blue and white vase that would be perfect for the Charlie Brown tree we found growing alongside a road in the GZ. The tree was really a bush and it had definitely seen better days but the guys all thought that it most resembled a pine tree. I agreed.

Now, how to decorate it. I had been keeping pull tabs off of soft drinks for just this purpose. A week before Christmas I began to form these pull tabs into a streamer that would alight our tree. I sat in the shade at Checkpoint 2 and using my Gerber utility tool I began to link the tabs together. Every once in a while, a Chilean guard would come by and check on my progress. The fellas were skeptical but after I had a long strand prepared, they were believers and began scouring the ground for more pull tabs.

One of the guys from Chile or Peru had a family member send a strand of battery powered Christmas lights which really livened up the tree. Someone else acquired a Santa Claus tree ornament which brought some character to the valiant spruce. A couple of the fellas fashioned little decorations from various materials and foil and the next thing you know we have a good old-fashioned Christmas tree. We positioned the tree on top of a concrete divider where it would be seen by everyone. Perched atop the crooked tree stood a white four-pointed Christmas star reminding us that these events we were honoring unfolded not far from where we stood.

The insurgents had no respect for our holiday and on Christmas morning around 0820 hrs. two mortars were directed at us. At that

114

moment I and another one of my handlers were walking across the parking lot of CP2. We both heard the "Whump! Whump!" of the two mortars coming out of the mortar tubes somewhere in the distance. For some reason I knew they would either go over us or come down directly on top of us. Either way I knew it was going to be darn close. We would never make it to the shelter in time so we did what all wise men do in such circumstances, we hit the dirt, making ourselves as small a target as possible.

The first mortar smacked into the earth and exploded about seventy-five yards from us. The second was a tad closer. I vividly recall the ground shaking and the shock wave vibrating my insides as it passed through me. Pieces of shrapnel were striking cement barriers and peppering the ground all around us but we were safe. Our adrenaline was peaked and perhaps this is why we both jumped to our feet and shook our fists in the air yelling, "Come on you cowards! Bring it on! Merry Christmas!"

Later that night in my quarters I opened my gift from Debbie which turned out to be a new laptop which I desperately needed. In an email I was able to learn how all the family back home celebrated the holiday. It was weird listening to music about silent nights and peace on earth when in the distance the sounds of car bombs exploding and machine guns reverberated across this giant ancient city. Christmas in Baghdad. I never would have imagined it as part of my life story. Not in a million years.

Bring it on...or Not

January 6th began as a nice cold morning. We arrived at Checkpoint Two under the generator lights which were still on due to the semi darkness that was by now beginning to give way to the irresistible breaking dawn. The sunrise was beautiful this morning. The crisp cool air, the multi colors of the sunrise above this ancient city and the history of it all was just inspiring. I would often look at the beauty of the sun in the morning and the breathtaking colors which splashed across the heavens and wonder how something so peaceful and beautiful could have so much hate, destruction and death below it. I am sure that through history I am not the first foreigner to have such thoughts here in Baghdad.

However, the filth of the streets quickly reminds me that I am in a different period of time and that this city has seen better days. Sometimes I could not comprehend why people would choose to live here. I am sure there are nicer districts in this city but my area was not one of them.

The insurgents brought me back to the present in a hurry for they were starting early this morning. By 0800 hrs. three mortars had been launched in our direction. The first hit a long way off and made a loud boom which reverberated through our area. The second mortar hit closer but was still not in our danger zone. When I heard the third mortar fire off, I figured they were "walking" them in closer which meant this next one would be close. Sure enough, not seventy-five yards away on the other side of the T-wall the mortar smacked the earth and erupted into a huge ball of flame, dirt and sand. The concussive wave blew through us and stirred something in my soul. I can't explain why but I immediately jumped out from the bunker shelter threw my fist in the air and yelled, "Bring it on!" and then for some reason I started yelling, "USA! USA! USA! USA!"

Behind me I could hear cheering and shouting and turned to see the Peruvian and Chilean guards were laughing and shouting. The South African handlers were smiling and clapping. I noticed that they were all still under the cover of the bunker and I thought, "What the heck are you doing out here Blocker?"

I immediately headed back to the "duck and cover" shelter where my shoulder was clapped and slapped and fellas were laughing. I was terrified. I couldn't believe I did that. How stupid! My wife would kill me if she saw me do that. The thought made me laugh, that she would kill me for getting myself killed.

It's now lunch time and I decided to do something different; I would have lunch at the Al-Rasheed Hotel. A couple handlers said they would like to accompany me so we set off in our truck. We had been seated at our table and were preparing to order when my cell phone rang. It was one of our guys from Checkpoint Two reporting that an RPG had come in and landed in the parking lot next to our checkpoint. It had not exploded so EOD[45] had been called. I didn't waste a second, "We'll be right there."

My lunch guests were staring at me when I said, "Time to go boys. One of our own and our dogs could be in danger." We immediately rose and made way for the truck. One of the guys had a friend working at the main gate so he called ahead and told his buddy to make arrangements so we could scoot through. "My buddy says that when you approach the main gate to have your hazard lights on and they will open up for us."

I had my flashers on and as we continued forward the large black steel gate was rolled to the side and troops armed with machine guns poured out of a bunker heading toward the control point arm bar which further blocked traffic. The arm bar was lifted while more troops pulled a lever that lifted the steel spikes that had been deployed in the road.

In my rearview mirror I could see the large black steel wall was rolling back into place and the arm bar was coming down. We waved to the soldiers as we went by. We continued on to the next entry control point and identified ourselves as K9 so they let us pass through but only after they pointed to where the unexploded ordinance was located. Good thing they did because at that moment we were not far from where the explosive was nosed into the ground.

I knew we were still not out of danger because if the RPG exploded, we would find ourselves in the blast radius. This of course would have resulted in shattered glass, lacerations and ruptured eardrums. Not a pretty picture so I drove very discreetly.

---

[45] Explosive Ordnance Disposal. These are the highly trained technicians who disarm and neutralize explosives.

Thirty seconds later and we were pulling up to our dogs and Bill Swanson our South African K-9 handler. We all jumped out, ran up to Bill in a huff and stated, "Dude! We just risked our lives to bring you lunch! You owe us big time!" We all had a good laugh.

Being able to see where the explosive lay in relation to where our dogs were crated at our checkpoint I was fairly certain that we were out of danger. I made a check on the dogs in their crates and found all the dogs chilled out, wagging their tails as if nothing special was going on. It was too funny.

It was now 1500 hrs. and still no appearance by the EOD guys. Suddenly the whoosh of an incoming rocket could be heard. We had no time to take cover. Wham! The rocket impacted fifty yards away. Then whoosh and wham! Another rocket hit close by the other one. I was praying these rockets would not detonate the one stuck in the ground.

One of the Chilean guards yelled over to me, "Dennis! There's a guy over there staring at our checkpoint!" The guard points and sure enough I can see a dude on an upper deck of a building two blocks away. Highly suspicious. Is this guy a spotter?[46] The Iraqi police and military units are notified as is the US Army who all send units to investigate. No word on what they discovered in the building.

Finally around 1615 hrs. the EOD folks showed up. They stacked sandbags all around the RPG and then placed their own explosive device on the rocket. Detonation cord was hooked up to the device and then unraveled to a safe distance. "Boom!" The RPG was expertly and safely detonated in place.

It had been an eventful day. Bill was able to eat his lunch, no one was injured and the gates were now back open for business. Six

---

[46] A spotter is someone who works with a sniper or fireteam letting them know where their rounds are hitting and what corrections to make so that the rounds will be on target. This process is also known as "Setting up a range card."

mortar attacks and three RPGs. Man, it was just another rocking day at Checkpoint Two.

You Never Know

It was only the 7th of January and 2006 was setting a trend that spelled heartbreak and doom. The first thing this morning we saw a report about a young Iraqi boy, about five years of age, who had been killed by the terrorists and left like a piece of trash in the middle of a neighborhood street. I never could understand how these supposed warriors of Islam could feel any pride at killing a child. There were plenty of Americans, South Africans, Chileans and Peruvians at our checkpoint who would have loved the opportunity to get their hands on the people who committed this atrocity.

This really jacked our day. Let me tell you that I have never seen men so amped up to go to battle. I felt the same and could feel it in my inner core; the desire to have these supposed men within arm's reach so I could utilize my K-Bar battle knife that my son had purchased for me. Our blood was up. I was imagining the things I would do to these cowards if I were to meet them in the street. It would not have been a pleasant encounter.[47]

I was in a funk and as it had been a couple days since I had checked in with loved ones back home, I decided to give my son Dennis a call. We had a nice talk and I must confess that it was wonderful to have a connection to normalcy, to a place where kids didn't have to worry about some terrorist snatching them up and using them for a religious message on the television. I asked my son to tell Debbie that I was doing fine and would call her later on. It was time to get back to work.

---

[47] Horrifying memories are often blocked out by people. The death of this boy was one of those for me. I had completely lost all memory of it. However, I kept a diary and the story is there.

I had no sooner ended the call with my son when suddenly a horrific explosion erupted just a few blocks away. The shock wave was not that great but for some reason the sound was super amplified. I immediately called Dennis back so that he would know I was fine in case they reported the explosion on the news back home. Thankfully the rest of the shift was uneventful and soon it was time to head back to our living quarters.

As a team leader I had my own truck which was a necessity as Checkpoint Two was too far from where our kennels and sleeping area was located. It was just not practical to walk. Now, I chose to walk to most places because I was very conscious of the fact that I needed to maintain my stamina and strength. In a war zone I didn't want to be the guy holding others back because I was out of shape. I worked hard at it.

After the short ride to the kennels I parked my truck and offloaded Laky and Toris. I ensured they had ample water and made a quick trip over to my room where I picked up my laptop. It had been a long day because a random storm system had come through and soaked us. My clothes were still damp and my boots muddy and waterlogged. I was uncomfortable, tired and hungrier than an Alaskan grizzly in April but earlier in the day, while on the phone with my son, I'd asked him to let Debbie know I would call, well, it was later.

The best place for me to eat, work on my laptop and call my wife was within walking distance; Saddam Hussein's Presidential Palace. I loved eating there because the food was always great and the setting was spectacular. Opening the regal doors to this majestic facility brought to mind the fact that hundreds of historical figures (a few good ones but the majority detestable) had crossed this threshold.

Entering into the main hall I was immediately greeted by the sight of opulence; with great crystal chandeliers hanging from the paneled ceiling and marbled floors and columns heading in every direction. I knew that in my lifetime I would never see such a spectacle again.

Since the US had wrested this building from Saddam it had been home to dozens of US government agencies. It was a haven for American servicemen and women and for all civilian contractors. There were gardens that surrounded the entire palace and an enormous pool complete with diving boards and a towering fountain that sprayed jets of water high into the air. The lighting of the gardens at night was spectacular and made me temporarily forget this was a warzone, well that is until the occasional explosion off in the distance swiftly brought me back to reality.

On this night I grabbed a sandwich and a bottle of water. I sat watching the soldiers and airmen moving about and thought of their families back home and how thankful I was that our country produced such fine young people. The thought turned my mind back to my task which was calling Debbie. It was so nice to hear her voice and to hear the latest news from home. All too soon it was time to hang up and finish my emails to friends and family.

Walking back to the kennel area to feed Toris and Laky I decided to make a quick detour to drop off my laptop in my quarters. Lying my laptop on my bed I was struck by the sudden call of nature so I walked the 200 feet down to the latrine. Most days I lugged around my protective gear, such as my helmet and flak vest, because my family had hounded me about protecting myself. I knew it made sense but sometimes, especially in the summer months, I didn't want to haul this stuff around when I was so tired. Tonight though, I took the gear with me, even though it would be such a short walk.

So, there I am, taking care of business in the latrine with my gear stacked up around me when suddenly the air is filled with the sound of heavy weapons fire and it was close, danger close. I could tell that AIF[48] forces were firing automatic weapons from across the Tigris River into our area. From where I was, well, sitting, the opposite

---

[48] Anti-Iraqi Forces, AIF, was designation given by the US military and government to signify those various branches of extremist groups who targeted Iraqi government and Iraqi Police units as well as all US forces and contractors.

side of the Tigris River was six and a half football fields away. In other words extremely close.

I leapt back into my pants in record time, scooped up my equipment, felt for my sidearm and started sprinting for my room. I look to my right and I could see enemy tracers[49] zipping overhead and hear the familiar snap as they cracked the sound barrier. I could discern the heavy staccato of a .50 caliber machine gun and what sounded like an M60 firing controlled bursts back toward the enemy. From my vantage point I could not make out what they were firing at but I knew from my military experience that this was a full-on firefight.

The weapons fire and the tracers zipping through the night air reminded me of a time back in the early 1980s when I was teaching at the Air Force Police Academy. We were conducting night exercises at Camp Bullis with our students who were supposed to guard a weapons storage area. Everyone carried M16s with muzzle suppressors but of course we only used blanks. We instructors had discussed the possibility that one of the students would keep a bullet from the firing range and use it against us.[50]

The night exercise called for the instructors to assault the weapons storage area and the students, who had been instructed on setting up a proper defense, were supposed to defend this area. I had several of the instructors open fire from a concealed firing position with an M60 machine gun firing blanks. If you have never heard this weapon fire it is quite distinctive. The machine gun fires between 500 to 650 rounds per minute. In addition to the M60, we were firing

---

[49] Tracers are bullets that are manufactured with a small pyrotechnic charge that will illuminate the trajectory of the bullet as it travels towards the intended target. These rounds are usually every fifth bullet which of course means that between each tracer seen there are four others also flying through the air.

[50] I don't want readers to think this was a ragtag bunch of Air Force Security Police trainees. They were excellent young people but as instructors we all had heard stories of the occasional mentally disturbed student who would fly off the handle and keep a bullet, threatening the instructors.

blanks from our personal M16s and then throwing flash grenades to try and frustrate and terrify the students. It was great.

A buddy of mine was with me as we assaulted the weapons storage facility. We were in camouflage and had our faces blacked out with paint. Suddenly behind me a student kicked open a door, rushed out put the M16 in my back and pulled the trigger. A large tongue of flame and gunpowder erupted from the muzzle piercing my layers of uniform and then my skin.

The intensity of the pain was horrific as my skin burned and the flaming gunpowder entered my body. It felt like someone had taken a red-hot poker and shoved it into my back. I immediately dropped to my knees. "Well I guess a student actually blew me away," was my first thought. My buddy, convinced I had just been shot by a rogue student, unholstered his 38 pistol, shoved the barrel under this kid's chin while pushing him against the wall. I could hear his cold deadly voice, "If you move, I will blow your head off."

Flashlights came on and my fellow instructors began inspecting my wound. There was very little blood as the blast was so hot it cauterized the flesh. The students M16 revealed that he had taken off the flash suppressor from the muzzle. When I stood up and saw the rifle, I calmly asked why he had removed it. His answer showed his maturity, "Sir, I thought it looked cool to see the flame come out the muzzle."

Investigation showed the kid had just run out and fired not realizing that I was standing there. I will say that it was pitch black out and we had camouflaged ourselves very well. I could have made a bigger deal out of it but it turns out he was thankfully firing blanks and the fact that the kid had been doing so well in the school eased my anger. I also learned that he was from Chicago, had grown up in a tough neighborhood and was trying to do something with his life. I gave him a break. Having been a street kid just north of Chicago in Milwaukee myself, I had a soft spot for kids trying to better their lives. It was a chord that struck close to home for me.

The feeling of being shot, of having flame enter my body and then having my wife Debbie later squeeze the gunpowder out of my back as it ate away and agitated my open wound always stayed with me.

So as these rounds in Baghdad were flying around and the tracers zipped overhead, I knew one thing for certain, I did not want to get shot because when lead was involved it was going to do a lot of damage. I wanted no part of that so I had to be smart with what I did next.

Back in the moment, as I am sprinting low toward my room which is 200 feet away, I know I'm vulnerable because I am on the side of the building that faces the Tigris. Well with mortars coming in I have no choice. I have to keep running. Push. Push. Stay low!

Ahead, near my quarters, I could see a few civilian contractors rubbernecking trying to catch the sights. Not me. I'm not a rubbernecker. Most times I would be in the fight firing back but that is not my task tonight. My task is to let our soldiers handle the fight and for me to get to cover. So, as I near the contractors I yell for them to, "Take cover! Mortars are coming in!" To my surprise they ignore me and continue standing there. I can still hear the continuous mortar thumps in the distance and I can hear the snaps of bullets zipping overhead. These guys just stood there. You have to love civilians.

I couldn't believe it but I made it to my room in one piece. I threw open the door and barreled in. Usually I would have turned a light on but that would be inviting disaster. Why give enemy spotters a target. I slam the door behind me and take comfort in the fact that I have a concrete roof over my head and a heavy iron door. My side arm is out now in my hand and I ensure I have a full magazine. I grab extra mags and lay them beside me. If this is a full-on assault they are going to pay dearly coming into this room. I am 400 feet from the protective wall of the Green Zone. 400 feet from a possible infiltration by AIF forces.

Then it hits me, all I have been hearing are the initial thumps of the mortars as they are fired. I have not heard a single explosion. These bad guys must be using faulty ammo! I laughed out loud, relieved. I laughed picturing the frustration of these guys realizing they were sold worthless ammo. I laughed picturing the arms dealer who was about to die at their hands in a few days. I laughed with relief that no one was dying from a mortar tonight.

The ammunition used by many of these insurgent groups was outdated with much of it being several decades old. The stash they used against us this night was all worthless. Not one of the over 25 mortars that were fired detonated. It was a miracle. Such a barrage would have decimated our area with shrapnel and explosions. Even today I shudder thinking about how bad it could have been as our sector was the target. Considering the number of mortar rounds fired, gosh, who knows how many casualties in men and dogs we would have sustained. That night, after checking on Laky and Toris and feeding them I looked heavenward and said out loud, "Thank you Lord."

Smoke, Screams, and Terror

Checkpoint Two had been renovated to allow us to search more vehicles but also to provide better security for us as we searched. There was the addition of an office that had the luxury of air conditioning which would benefit the dogs should they become overheated.

This particular day was slightly overcast and not too hot. Bill Swanson and I were waiting for our guards to complete their initial visual search of the vehicles and the frisking of the drivers. I looked over at Bill and could not help but admire his German Shepherd aptly named Beauty. She was stunning, breathtaking even. She had always had a sparkle in her eye that hinted at her zest for life and the job she was doing.

One of the guards looked our way and gave us the thumbs up sign so I looked over at Bill and said, "You ready to roll?" Bill smiled and nodded his head. I smiled and then looked down at Laky who was at my side and expectantly looking up at me, "Okay boy, let's do this." I took one step toward the row of vehicles.

Boom! Then a second or two later Boom! Two enormous explosions smashed the calm of the morning. Birds filled with fright ejected from the branches of trees around the perimeter of our checkpoint. Two invisible concussive waves blew through our bodies. Laky jerked to the side and hunkered down to the ground, nervously licking his lips and looking in the direction of the explosions. This had been close, very close.

Two very large black and gray columns of billowing smoke began to broil up toward the sky. All around us could be heard the sounds of pieces of vehicles and indistinguishable fragments striking the ground. Metallic clangs spoke of the horrendous scene as the vehicular pieces slammed against the ground and roof tops all around. It was literally raining death.

Thankfully not one of our team was hit by the falling projectiles. I had to quietly thank the designers of the large erect cement "T-Walls" because they did precisely what they were designed to do; they protected us from the blast.

At one point I turned my head and looked skyward and remember seeing the bewildering sight of a car door spiraling through the air. Then a steering wheel was ejected out of the smoke plumes. I knew that there were bits of people flying through the atmosphere but thankfully they were killed instantly and most vaporized. They didn't suffer. Others, of which there were many, were wounded and suffered so horribly as flying metal removed limbs and chunks of skin.

Then came the fire from the gasoline and the explosions which ignited houses and store fronts. People found they had survived the blast only to be consumed in flames, screaming, dying slowly and horribly. I could hear it all. I could smell the smoke and the burning debris but I am thankful I could not see the scene on the street. Unfortunately my imagination filled in the missing pieces.

Instinctively, Bill and I had dropped to the ground in a kneeling position with our dogs at our sides. I looked over at Bill and Beauty, Bills eyes were wider than usual and he looked pale. Beauty was crouched down, almost lying down, but keeping her head up enough to inspect her surroundings and see what the heck was going on.

I looked down at Laky, his eyes were wide, his ears were about halfway down, almost flat against his head and he was breathing hard. This really shook him up. Bill and I were separated by the three-foot high "Jersey Wall" which separated the two lanes of traffic. Bill was kneeling at the portion of the cement wall where there was an opening. I looked at Bill and he yelled out to me, "Were those two rockets or mortars?" I yelled back, "I don't think so! I didn't hear the screaming of the rocket coming in and didn't hear the sound of mortars! Just wait!" Bill yelled out, "Wait for what?" I yelled again, "Just wait!"

About thirty seconds later we heard automatic weapons fire from what sounded like AK-47s. Immediately we could hear a crescendo of men yelling, women and children screaming and I'll never forget the sound of one woman in particular who was screaming at the top of her lungs, yet also crying. It was a mixture of intense fear and pain I had never heard before and hope to never hear again. The horrifying sound pierced me to my soul. I'm not trying to sound dramatic or trying to win a Pulitzer. I am telling you that the sound that woman made reached into a hidden place in my heart and soul that instantly shook me to my core. It was heart wrenching. Even thirteen years later, writing these words and reliving the scene brings tears to my eyes. I suppose the wails of that woman will be with me for the rest of my life.

For some reason another sound seared itself into my brain, the sound of sandals and shoes on the pavement. The smack of the sandals against the undersides of the soles of dozens of feet as terrified people ran for their lives was unnerving. You must remember that we could see nothing because of the high concrete T-

127

wall barriers around our checkpoint so our sense of hearing was what we depended on. It was heightened and working quite well as these small details etched themselves onto my brain.

I could hear car doors slamming and tires screeching as panicked people left the massive scene of carnage. Insurgent custom was to blow up an IED or VBIED and then attack the responding police and medical personnel with machine gun fire. This was now happening and the terrified screams, the pitter-patter of sandals and the squealing tires all bore testament to the scene just out of view.

It was weird to be so close yet safe. I knew we were protected by gun mount positions and I knew that at this moment our checkpoint was not the target. I was scared of course, only a fool would not have been. Yet, I did not feel that we would be attacked. I knew these blood thirsty ogres were after civilians and they were taking the lives of many.

With my head down and my hand scratching Laky's head and whispering encouragement to him I could do nothing but continue to listen. I glanced skyward and could see the wind currents had picked up the top portion of the smoke spirals and were now bending them parallel to the ground and moving them out over the city, bearing witness for all to see that another mass murder was underway in this ancient city.

I dropped my gaze from the pillars of smoke down to Bill and yelled, "We now know what this was! Two VBIED suicide bombers! Either they detonated themselves or were detonated by remote control!" After just a couple of minutes, the weapons firing had stopped and the only sound that remained were screams and then the far-off wail of sirens headed our way. I instinctively knew it was over.

I stood, patted Laky on the head, walked over to Bill and said, "Let's start searching and clearing these vehicles so we don't get them all backed up for a half mile or so. Let's not give these insurgents a juicy target." I didn't say anything about it to Bill but I put myself in the shoes of these Iraqi drivers and knew they must have been terrified, sitting there helpless, listening to the cries of the dying. I knew these folks would want to get moving.

Our Chilean and Peruvian guards sprang to action and began frisking the drivers. We began searching the vehicles and everyone was compliant. No one was in a mood to hassle us because everyone, and I mean everyone, wanted to get through the checkpoint as quickly as possible. Our K9 teams worked quickly and professionally cutting no corners for the sake of our own safety. We had a higher calling, the protection of those under our charge, but I can tell you that I had no wish to have to deal with smoke, screams and terror in the skies ever again.

What haunted me then and still does are the shrill screams of the women and children overcome with fright and pain. Even after all these years I can still hear those screams, mostly at night in my dreams. I know that my own father-in-law had nightmares of Iwo Jima to the day he died so I have accepted that this will be my fate as well.

There is a part of me that wants to remember, to never forget what happened to these innocent people. That desire to remember was a key reason to do this book so that history will not forget that evil men willfully, deliberately targeted women and children with the intent to kill as many as possible. They were the lowest of men, despicable in the eyes of everyone I knew yet they seemed to take pride in their work. Such men needed to be eradicated and I felt no pity for these insurgents when they died at the receiving end of Uncle Sam's explosives, lead and gunpowder.

Later that night, lying in my bed I glanced over at the pictures of my grandchildren. I thought of the boys and girls whose screams haunted me that night. I was trained to defend such innocents and to kill the wolves sniffing out these poor defenseless souls yet, I was powerless. A grown, strong, highly trained military veteran with the power of an entire nation behind me and I could do nothing but listen to the dying. Powerless. Stranded. Frustrated. Resolved.

Resolved that such men would not get through my checkpoint. Resolved that I would go down fighting. Resolved that I would work harder than ever before and keep my men and their bomb dogs sharp. Ready, Vigilant.

Shot Nerves

It had been a long day of checking vehicles and stories. All the guys at the checkpoint were looking forward to a shower and some hot food in their bellies. The weather had been cold, wet and miserable. Time for some relief. Two men drove up in a small car to the checkpoint and were instructed to exit their vehicle so it could be searched and their identification checked.

There was nothing extraordinary about these two guys. They looked average and their behavior was cooperative and calm. While the Iraqi policemen glanced at the identification of the two passengers they separated and approached the policemen. The passengers were instructed to stop but they did not. Reaching for their sidearms the police were blasted by a wall of smoke, dirt and concussive power that blew them off their feet.

The passengers each wore suicide vests and had fulfilled their mission at the Iraqi Police checkpoint located five miles from my location at Checkpoint Two. The explosion killed the insurgents but thankfully did not kill the policemen though they were, of course, wounded severely. Two civilians standing nearby had also taken the blast but were both expected to survive.

Word passed quickly among the Iraqi police and army units but truthfully such attacks were common and happened daily in Baghdad. This day's attack on January 8th, 2006 was only the latest. By the time we showed up at our checkpoint the following morning everyone had heard the report and the Iraqi police and soldiers had seen the news footage on television. The specter of death hung over everyone in this city of millions.

January was only nine days old and there had already been sixty-seven IED and VBIED attacks against Iraqi and US forces. The figure does not even count the daily mortar and RPG attacks we received. Everyone was on edge but at least we who lived in the GZ did not have to worry about masked men kicking in our doors at night and taking us to a field for a midnight execution. The Iraqi men who served at our checkpoint in the army and police had this constant threat on their life. They were on edge all the time.

My team of handlers and K9s arrived at Checkpoint Two on January 9th and made ready for the coming day. It was a Monday so it would be busy, in fact, traffic was already backed up with antsy motorists eager for the gates to open. I looked down the row of vehicles and wondered what lay in store for us today. I did not have long to wait for an answer.

The first few hours were the usual; staying in a heightened state of vigilance, watching everyone and everything going on at the checkpoint. The handlers and dogs were doing a great job. The dogs were happy and performing beautifully. The handlers were enjoying working with such amazing animals and the cool weather was delightful. Comfortable weather always seems to put folks in a better mood.

Then, suddenly Tat Tat, Tat Tat Tat Tat, Tat, Tat Tat Tat Tat Tat Tat Tat Tat! Automatic weapons fire was ripping the air within forty yards of where I stood. It was incredibly loud. I and another one of our K9 teams had been searching vehicles for explosives when the AK 47 machine gun opened fire. Everything came to a halt and we all crouched down. The gunman was only forty yards away but on the other side of the wall. The fact we could not see the source of the fire made the scene all the more maddening. Was it the good guys or bad guys shooting? Were the bad guys about to storm our checkpoint? The Chilean and Peruvian guards had their automatic rifles up and pointed toward the source of this action. The guard in the tower was moving his machine gun left to right looking for possible targets. Meanwhile, we handlers had drawn our semiautomatic pistols and were ready to defend our position. I had

Toris lie down beside me so he would present a more difficult target to hit.

Bill Swanson, the other K9 Handler, called out to me, "Dennis, what do you think's going down?" My response, "Your guess is as good as mine, just be ready for anything." Bill's German Shepherd Beauty was looking towards the entry point where vehicles would enter through a wide opening in the T-Walls. Her ears were erect, gathering information. Everyone had weapons ready, just waiting to spot insurgents running through this opening. If they did, they would be ripped to shreds in such a corridor. The advantage was ours.

Seconds ticked by, then minutes, then several minutes and nothing. Curiously after the initial burst of weapons fire there had not been anymore. Still, we waited to see what the next move would be. After thirty minutes my cell phone rang and it was our director informing me that the shooting was not insurgent related. The story was a sad one.

When anyone sought to enter into the Green Zone through Checkpoint Two, they had to first pass through an Iraqi Police and Army checkpoint. These Iraqis were the first to inspect the vehicles for anything or anyone suspicious. Explosions in Baghdad had increased dramatically over the past several weeks. Each day there were more IEDs, suicide bombers, VBIEDs, rockets, mortars and snipers who killed dozens of Iraqi policemen and soldiers.

This morning there were rookie Iraqi soldiers sent to the Iraqi Checkpoint Two entrance to conduct the initial screening of vehicles. These young soldiers were terrified of dying in an explosion. They had seen the daily reports on television and I am sure that many of their relatives counseled them not to join but these guys needed a job. Terrified and with no experience these, well, boys were tasked with searching vehicles.

On this day at our checkpoint a small car pulled up to the Iraqi inspection point. Behind the steering wheel of the vehicle was a young man who had recently been promoted in the Iraqi government. He was so excited to start work in his new job which would allow him to provide so much more for his family. I knew this young Iraqi man and every morning he came through our checkpoint he always had a huge smile. I could see he had a zest for life. He was going places.

As the nervous Iraqi soldier told the driver to reverse his vehicle I suspect the nervous government employee could see the soldier was edgy and irritated. The soldier had raised his gun and motioned for the driver to back up but my young friend panicked and placed the car in the wrong gear so instead of reversing he lunged forward. At that moment the two terrified soldiers lifted their AK 47 machine guns and fired their weapons into the front compartment of the vehicle. Dozens of rounds smashed through the windshield and smacked into flesh. My hopeful and cheerful friend died in seconds and his passenger would die later at the hospital.

It was a horrifying situation as everyone in this debacle reacted as humans. Terrified. Nervous. Unsure. Self-preservation had kicked in and these young soldiers thought they were in the presence of a suicide bomber. They didn't want to die so they took out the perceived threat. Later, as the story was revealed in all of its horrifying details, I could not help but feel sorry for everyone involved. I would miss seeing the smile of this young man, the future of this ancient land. Maybe he could have made a difference here. We'll never know.

The Foxy Lady Then Boom!

I don't know why but I never imagined that there were many animals native to this land. I'd only seen movies and a few documentaries about the Middle East and I only remember seeing a sort of goat and of course camels. It never occurred to me that I should research the kind of animals I might run across in Baghdad.

I knew that I would see stray dogs but even the dogs caught me by surprise in the way they all looked so similar. Like everything in Iraq they are sandy in color. Most of them were medium sized with

133

white fur and yellow patches. In addition they were extremely good street fighters. They had to be in an environment where the local population despised them.[51]

One day at my checkpoint by the Iraqi Prime Ministers gate I met a creature I never dreamed I would see. I noticed that Laky, my other German Shepherd, kept turning to look behind us. I was steadying him and trying to keep him focused on what we were doing but he would jerk around quickly and force me to snap his leash and tell him to leave it and sit beside me.

After the third time I turned around to see what all the fuss was about. I was stunned. A beautiful fox was taking gentle swats at Laky's tail with its paw. The tail would wag and this little fox would swipe at it. Laky would turn and the fox would bolt off. It was so quiet that I did not even realize it had come back until Laky began to turn around again. Its eyes were beautiful and its expression majestic. The animal's color was silver with a mixture of tan that served to blend with the environment perfectly. The animal was a descendant of a long line of foxes that had seen many kingdoms and dynasties come and go. If only this fox could talk what stories would it tell. It was surreal to see something so beautiful and unspoiled in this place of destruction, fire and death. I was lost in my thoughts.

Wham! A giant explosion south of us that looked to be across the Tigris sent huge columns of smoke billowing into the air. It was too far away to see what was happening but we could imagine. I looked back down at Laky but the fox was long gone. A survivor.

Later the pillars of smoke in the distance died down but then the sound of automatic weapons fire met our ears. It was coming from

---

[51] I did see once what appeared to be a pure-bred looking Border Collie running the streets one night about midnight, running with a pack of yellow and white patched dogs. He was rare. I was told by an Iraqi K9 handler that those Iraqi people who had a better status in their society had German Shepherds and had them for protection.

the same direction. We also knew what that meant. Gunmen were taking out the first responders.

The following day we were briefed that the previous day's car bomb had been detonated ten yards from the Iskan al-Shaabi mosque. Just as we had suspected gunmen had shown up and were executing people who had come to aid the wounded. It was a massacre with eight civilians killed and fifteen wounded.

As the blast involved a Sunni mosque, we knew there would be swift and bloody retaliations across the city against Shia populations. Over the next week more than a thousand people would die as retaliations went back and forth. Meanwhile, we tried to stay out of the way at Checkpoint 2, our little fox hole in Baghdad. We would have to learn from the fox if we were going to survive this place.

Conditioning & Routine

When a young man I would often stay up all night, sleep for a couple hours and then go hang out with friends. I recouped very quickly. I could go for days on very little food and be just fine. It's amazing what you can survive on when you're young.

As I got older, I required more rest and as I made a good living, I could now eat whatever I wanted, when I wanted. I could eat nothing but fast food if I wished or solely sweets. My choice. Now, granted, I would pay for it by putting on some pounds and becoming unfit. However, the point is that when you only care for yourself you can do whatever you want. However, being responsible for two highly trained war dogs meant I no longer had the luxury of doing my own thing. Lives depended on my canines being in top physical shape and at the apex of their training. There was no room for error and thus no place for indifference. I was taking care of German Shepherds not sloths.

We all needed to get toughened up. My dogs needed to be conditioned and in shape so I needed to be conditioned and in shape. Why ask them to do and be something that I am not. It would be a lie. Before coming to Iraq I would drive with my windows up and the air conditioning off. Sometimes I would even turn the heater on. In Texas this was intense. I was tempted to roll the window down and enjoy a nice breeze but I refused it. I was conditioning myself. My dogs would be expected to work in this sort of heat so I would learn to work in it as well.

It was essential to have a routine. Dogs love a routine for it is something they can depend on. Our canines had an internal clock and they instinctively knew when it was time for chow. At the same time every day they would all be lined up at their kennels anxiously staring at the door, barking, ready to eat, wondering where the food was. Take away the routine and the dogs are shiftless, lost and perplexed. Their behavior is affected and bad habits learned.

Routine in my daily chores reflected everything else in their lives. Through routine the dogs know that there is a right way to search, there is a correct way to sit and that it is unacceptable to bark while working. Working dogs thrive on discipline and order. In the K9 world this is known as "Conditioning your dog" and it is vital. They are professionals and deserve to be treated as such. To honor their service and devotion I took excellent care of them. My routine was always the same.

One of our first tasks was to line up all of the crates that needed to be loaded onto the trailer. Our trailer could hold six crates so the seventh was placed in the back of the suburban. We would then inspect the inside of our crates looking for spiders, scorpions or snakes. While we performed this duty one of the team members would retrieve our white Chevy suburban and back it up to the trailer onto which we had previously loaded our K9 crates.

Great care had to be taken with the alignment of the crates. We placed the dogs in their crates and then one by one lifted them up onto the trailer. The first two were picked up with the dog already inside and loaded onto the trailer and then pushed toward the back

136

so as to make room for the next ones. When the next crate was slid beside the other one you never placed the crates facing door to door.

One of my handlers did this once and only once. So here we had two war dogs facing one another, crate door to crate door within inches of one another. As soon as the crate was turned and slid into position, it was as if the gates of hell had just been opened up to the world on this trailer.

There was an instant eruption of wailing and gnashing of teeth, crates were shaking from side to side, you could hear teeth gripping and biting on the thick metal stainless steel cross bars of the crate doors, the sound of canine nails scratching on the floor of their crates, disrupted the norm of everything. Then the dominoes fall as the canine in the adjacent crate joins in on the action, he's gripping his crate door with his teeth pulling backwards, shaking his head from side to side, and his crate appears to be in convulsions, shaking, and tilting. Of course, all of the other canines in the kennels are going nuts, biting at their kennel doors, barking, spinning, jumping up and bouncing off their kennel walls. Then in the back of your mind, you can't help but feel bad for the many military personnel, civilian contractors, and DOD civilians who are bedded down in their sleeping quarters trying desperately to continue sleeping.

Needless to say, it only took a second or two for this K9 handler to figure out the mistake he just made. He was in a hurry, then realized all of this noise sprang forth because he placed the crate in a wrong position. He jumped up to his crate, pulled it back just a few inches, then spun it around so that the door was now facing the back of the trailer. It was as if my Handler just transformed into the movie character, the "Incredible Hulk." This was a big German Shepherd he just spun around in this crate; his dog went a good 80-90 pounds of muscle. Anyway, the crate doors were no longer facing one another and the gates of hell were shut down within seconds. A calmness fell over the kennel area so now our comrades in the surrounding buildings and trailers could go back to sleep.

One last inspection of the trailer would be made to insure all of the crate doors were properly secured and that the wood planks were seated properly into their slots at the tail end of the trailer to keep any crates from coming off the back of the trailer. This was especially important as we did not want to look in the rearview mirror and see a crate slide off into the broiling dust. Once this was accomplished I and all the K-9 handlers would return to the kennel area and spray down the dog living areas. My dogs, Laky and Toris,[52] were kenneled next to each other. There were plenty of water hoses so there was never any delay for want of equipment.

Next, just like the crates, we'd check under their Kuranda Dog Beds looking for any unwanted lodgers such as spiders, snakes or any other critters wanting to take up residence with our dog. Finding nothing I'd spray Toris and Laky's doggie bed down, then hang it from the kennel wall where it would quickly dry out by the time we returned several hours later.

Next, I would empty their water buckets, spray them out and then I'd take the double clip I had purchased from a "Five and Dime" store in Fredericksburg, Texas called "Dooley's Five and Dime."[53] It was a clasp which would clip at both ends. If you've ever seen the clasp you'd find at the end of a dog leash, or horse leash, this was the same type only two sided. I could clip one end to the water bucket handle, then clip the other end to the kennel fence, thus preventing Laky or Toris from knocking their bucket of life sustaining water over.[54]

After spraying out the bucket, I'd tip it over and clasp it to the fence so that the metal handle of the bucket allowed the bucket to air-dry all-day upside down. It was important to maintain this routine to prevent the buckets from accumulating a layer of mold or mildew. Most other K9 handlers did not have these clips so they

---

[52] Both German Shepherds

[53] Buying from them was like going back in time to the 1950's. Their inventory contained all of the old-time things from toys to wrenches.

[54] I still use them in my kennels in Texas.

had to set their buckets upside down on the cement floor, which I did not like for fear that some critter would crawl up under it for a place to chill out away from the heat of the day. I'd purchased several of these clips and made them available to my handlers, some used them and others were ok with the buckets on the floor.

The next chore was to spray down all the walls of my dog's kennels. After this I would hose off the floor cleaning out all of the poop, urine, fur and sometimes yellow vomit caused by stress. The importance of discerning canine body fluids on the kennel floor can't be overstated. As a handler I would always take this opportunity to notice such things for they were visual cues on how my dogs were doing, medically. Were there signs of vomit, blood, loose stools, very dark urine, anything that could reveal early signs of a potential medical issue? A sick or injured war dog is a critical issue, meaning we have one less valuable resource in the war to protect our men and women in uniform.

If we had a sick dog, we would take it to the base veterinarian who was amazingly competent. In fact, the veterinarian. Lieutenant Colonel Thompson,[55] would inspect our kennels weekly. He was very strict on kennel care because his personal mission was to keep the dogs healthy and doing what they loved which was working. This in turn kept the Green Zone safe.

Anyway, after my two kennels were cleaned, I'd do a quick walk through of my K9 handler's kennels, making certain they were clean. In addition our Kennel Master would do a walk-through of all the kennels, looking for discrepancies of cleanliness. His was always an unannounced inspection. If a kennel was written up, that handler would receive a verbal warning, the next time it would be a written warning of counseling, all this to protect our war resource, the dog.

It was now time to depart for our two checkpoints. The first stop was to the gate for those seeking entry to the Iraqi Interim

---

[55] He had operated on Toris and saved his life.

Government offices (IIG). Then there was a separate private gate 40 yards away which was used by the Iraqi Prime Minister Ibrahim al-Ja'afari, his bodyguards and close administrative staff. We provided a K9 team for this private gate as well.

After dropping off the teams at the IIG Gate and Prime Minister's entrance I would proceed to Checkpoint Two. I'd back our K9 trailer up to our little building at our checkpoint, one of my K9 handlers would direct me with hand signals as I looked into the side mirrors, backing the trailer up. Once in position, the spotter would clinch his hand making a fist, at the same time yelling out "OK", I'd place the vehicle in park, set the hand brake, get out of the vehicle and assist in unhooking the trailer hitch from the vehicle. Then we would unhook the safety chains, block the wheels to prevent an accidental roll and at the same time cranking down the arm on the front of the trailer hitch which levels out the front of the trailer so it will not tip forward. Then each of us would start to unload our canines.

The first two handlers to start the morning shift off, would be the first to get their canines off the trailer. They were always placed at the very spot where the trailer tailgate would be dropped so that all they had to do was open their crate door, hook up their canine with their leash, bring the dog out, and head towards the two lines of vehicles, which were backed up a good half mile, all waiting to gain entry into the "IIG" compound where they all worked or conducted business. No potty break for the canines here, not now, they had already been given a break when we removed them from the kennels preparing to bring them out here to search vehicles for the day.

This was our routine every single day and it worked perfectly. You do not have to be a handler or dog trainer to have a routine with your dog. If you have a house dog you should have a routine of when they eat, where they eat and where they sleep among other things. Dogs love routine and so should you. It will make your life with your best friend so much easier. It worked wonders for us in war.

The Chase
(When Idiots Take Flight)

Toris was not a social dog. Every once in a while, he would like something about a person and allow them to become his friend but this was rare and only happened on a few occasions. Toris was a fighter and had already been deployed to Afghanistan twice and Iraq twice by the time I had him in Baghdad in 2005/2006. He was a warrior and with his teeth had taken down three bad guys during his deployments. His dual training as an Explosives & Patrol K9 payed off many times during his deployments. Toris was bad to the bones and he knew it. Oh, and so did everyone else.

He wanted to fight every dog he'd lay eyes on and he wanted to chew on Iraqi men. I believe that this attitude toward the local nationals was formed on his prior missions to Iraq.[56] His dislike of Iraqi men became very apparent to me from the start. Toris did not trust them and as they walked by, I could feel a rumble in the leash as he growled in a low menacing tone. He would turn and watch to make sure they kept walking. He was impressively vigilant all the time. I can't overstate how safe I felt with Toris. I felt honored that he loved me and I did reciprocate his love. I was very fortunate to have such a seasoned battle buddy by my side.

While on duty and searching vehicles I would hear weird hissing, clicking and whistling sounds. I would turn and see Iraqi civilian men[57] a few feet away on the other side of the concrete dividers making these noises teasing Toris, trying to distract him. This was unwise and all civilians had been informed that interactions with working dogs was forbidden. Still, the teasing continued.

---

[56] I often wondered what Toris experienced on his prior deployments to Iraq and Afghanistan. Toris was a battle tested veteran. More so than most of the men and dogs in our group.

[57] I never had a problem with Iraqi women teasing the dogs at our checkpoint, they just never did it.

Sometimes, when preparing to search a vehicle, I would hear drivers make whistle sounds to Toris and our other canines as they exited their vehicle. This was not wise. Why bring attention to yourself? Was this an insurgent attempting to distract our K9 from finding something hidden? Explosives. Weapons. Who in their right mind is going to screw with a "War Dog?" I adopted a policy that each time someone tried to distract one of our dogs I would have our interpreter inform the man that I was going to have him detained for questioning to be sure he was not an insurgent trying to distract our dogs from their work. After a few detentions the word got around and the teasing ceased. Amazing how the word could spread so quickly.

Finally, one day, Toris had enough of these childish games. A group of three Iraqi civilian men walked by and one of them hissed at Toris. Toris went crazy, jumping up on his hind legs, lunging forward, barking, snapping his teeth in the air, dust clouds kicking up beneath his huge German Shepherd paws, thick strands of saliva flipping through the air in slow motion. Toris was letting them know, "You want to play games with me, well, let's get it on! I love games! Especially those where I can chase you down and get a bite!"

Today was the day I allowed Toris to send a message I hoped would get around. It was beautiful and Toris loved it. Here's what I did. I had Toris on a twenty-foot leash which was coiled up in my left hand; my thumb through the leash loop and my fingers grasping the leash tight. I allowed Toris to pull me towards this idiot.

Now I must admit there was some Hollywood involved here, for I would lean back just a bit and allow my feet to slide along the hot hard clayed surface of the road. The Iraqi jester is now observing this huge German Shepherd gaining ground on him, barking, snapping his teeth and this guy knows the dog is not playing around. Of course it was acting on my part, pretending as if I had a war dog so strong, I was not able to hold him back.

This guy now knows Toris is coming in for a bite. Of course I was well aware that if he bit someone, I'd be in big trouble so Toris most definitely was not going to get a "Real World Bite." There

142

were two parties who did not know this though, Toris and the dude who had been taunting my dog. Toris was in the zone, getting closer and closer to this guy and getting amped up for a juicy bite with 240 pounds of pressure per square inch.

It took everything in me to keep from laughing. The terrified look on the face of this guy who realized he had chosen poorly was priceless. Glancing over his shoulder as he high stepped out of there provided him an image of bared white teeth, furrowed eyebrows and swirling clouds of dust that I hoped would be seared into his memory banks.

Oh, and believe me, I was hamming it up as I wore a look of concern and pretended to lose control of Toris as he "drug" me down the street. Ok, now it was time to show how much discipline this amazing animal had. I gave Toris the command to come back along to my heel side, (left side) and he responded as always, with an immediate turn to the left. As he did, he would turn and look back in the direction of this fleeing man. I bet Toris had satisfaction with this image.

When he got to my heel side, he'd, as always, swing around and press the right side of his body up against my left leg. I'm not sure why he liked doing this but it was his trademark. For me it was not an issue since he continued doing all he'd been trained to do. I'd like to think he was coming back to let me know he had my back and that we were best buds. If I were to guess, I'd have to say that's what he was doing, letting me know he's protecting me.

I knelt down next to him, placing my left arm across his back and up on his right front muscled leg and shoulder. His muscles were as hard as rocks. I would work my fingers down into his fur, touching his skin. I would scratch him and tell him "Good boy!" He absolutely loved it. During this time his eyes are locked onto the fleeing Iraqi man as are mine.

Once this guy was out of view, Tori's turned and gave me a big wet lick on my face and I returned his show of affection with a big hug and kiss on the top of his head.

143

Ok, time to get back to work. I stood and told Toris, "Let's go buddy."

Toris stood and walked at my left side and every few seconds he would glance behind us to be sure our "six" was clear. As we're walking, I reached down with my left hand and with my fingers gently rubbed the top of his head and said, "Good Boy!" He loved this praise. He'd look up at me and flash me his special Toris look with his eyes and break out with a big German Shepherd grin. What a great partner.

Another interesting characteristic of Toris was that he never forgot who would tease or taunt him. His memory was an encrypted data bank. Once a face was imprinted on his mind, it was there to stay and then if he was able to catch a person's scent, well then it was a done deal. Identity locked in. I would know when a passing civilian had previously messed with Toris because I would hear a low growl and could feel my leash vibrate. Sometimes I would not hear the growl but feel the leash vibrate. I'd look and see a familiar face, ah, yes, the hisser who now was acting responsibly. I wonder why?

Deadly Friendships

Every morning we searched vehicles we'd have scores of Iraqi men tell us, "Good morning my friend." Other times they would say, "Mr. Dennis, my friend, good morning." Dozens and dozens of times I would hear people call me and my handlers "my friend." Commenting on this later my handlers would say, "I never knew I had so many friends."

Webster's Dictionary defines the word friend as, "A person who has a strong liking for and trust in another." There were many Iraqi men who were very kind in their greeting to me in the mornings at Checkpoint Two. Several had the countenance of someone at peace with themselves and the world around them. Though they appeared

144

to be friendly and sounded friendly I did not have a "strong trust" in them for we had no history. We had not helped each other move furniture into a new apartment or cover shifts at work. The Iraqi men and I had not gone fishing together or watched a football game on the weekend. We had no occasion to form such ties. We were cordial acquaintances and I definitely wished them a full, happy and productive life but I knew we were not friends.

Yet, morning after morning there it was, "My friend! My friend!" During this time and day after day we were searching almost 1,000 cars a shift. The only days we had a let up in the traffic was on their weekends which were Friday and Saturday. Every other day it was bumper to bumper with horns honking and people shaking their fists waiting for their turn to go through the checkpoint. "My friend! My friend!"

One Wednesday morning the traffic through our checkpoint was the usual bumper to bumper and hustle and bustle. Then, around 08:45 hrs. we noticed that the traffic began to thin out and by 09:00 hrs. there was not a car in sight. Every other Wednesday it was wall to wall people all day long but today was different. What was special about this particular Wednesday?

There was nothing significant about the day but my men were speculating about the various reasons there was suddenly NO traffic. I had my own idea about what might be going on but for the moment, kept it to myself.

The minutes continued to tick by and not a single vehicle came through. I looked at my men, it was 09:15 hrs. and I said, "Get your battle gear on. We are going to get hit." The guys could not believe what I was saying and a few sceptics complained aloud. I interjected, "This is not a request. Put your gear on. We're going to get hit with mortars or rockets."

As my guys began to don their Kevlar vests and helmets, I revealed my thoughts, "Guys, think about it. How often have we ever seen NO traffic at this hour of the morning?" My guys were mulling my comments around in their heads and a few conceded, "Never." I was quick and now in a hurry, "Gear up!"

Fifteen minutes later I could hear the sound of a low "thump" off in the distance. A mortar. The words burst from my mouth, "Here it comes guys! Take cover!" A few more dull "thumps" were heard and then several mortars impacted around our checkpoint. "Swoosh!" A rocket arched over our heads on its mission of death. Explosions were heard all around at all points of the compass but we had been fortunate with no injuries to men or canines.

As we nervously emerged from the bunker we could smell the aroma of smoke in the air. Our nerves were shaky but we took our posts and prepared to search vehicles if anyone should arrive. Within fifteen minutes the vehicles began arriving, one after another in droves. It was the typical traffic jam we dealt with on a regular basis.

As the drivers exited their vehicles and began walking toward the assigned waiting area I stood there, still wearing my battle gear. Then it came. I could hear the shouts from the drivers, "Good morning Mister Dennis! Good morning my friend!" I was seething. These people knew we were going to get hit so they stayed home until it was safe. They had been warned to stay away from Checkpoint Two. I was livid!

I recall this cream-colored Mercedes drove up in the search lane and parked right next to where I was standing. I recognized the lady behind the driver's wheel. She was dressed in nice expensive clothes. Covering her head was a silk scarf that looked silver and gray in color. It reflected the light of the day and was evidently expensive. It was obvious to me that she was from the "Upper Crust" of Iraqi society.[58]

---

[58] Someone once gave me the definition of "Upper Crust." Seems it's a bunch of crumbs held together by their dough.

I was trying to remember how I knew her but then recalled that this woman worked for the Iraqi Interim Government. She turned and looked directly at me. There was a warm, pleasant smile on her face. In perfect English she said to me, "Dennis, good morning my friend."

I was steamed. Wrong thing to say to me at this moment, considering, she knew what just took place. I looked directly into her eyes without a hint of kindness on my face and yelled, "You're not my friend! You're not a friend to any of us! You, and all of the others, who just pulled into the search lanes, knew this attack was going to take place, yet, knowing this, you and none of your people warned us! We could have been severely wounded or killed and none of you supposed 'friends' did a thing to alert us that this attack was coming. We search vehicles and packages every day to protect all of you who work here. Not one of you said anything to protect us! No! You are not our friends, nor will you ever be our friends! Now stay seated in your vehicle until the Security Guard gives you the signal to step out of your car."

She just sat there staring, with not a hint of emotion. I moved on to allow our Peruvian and Chilean guards to conduct their business with this lady. I was disgusted. Look, I'm a realist. I knew people did not want us there. Fine. I can respect that. However, to lie to our faces about a word so important as "friend" was too much to let slide. I had to set them straight and perhaps educate them on how friends interact with each other. I knew one thing for sure though, friendships with these people were deadly, deadly to the core.

Fuse Box Cell Phone

It was a beautiful clear morning at CP2 and our Security Guards had just opened up the huge twenty-foot metal gate at 0700 hrs. The giant metal gate creaked and moaned as the large roller wheels trundled over the tiny rocks and dirt. All of the Iraqi civilians who worked for the IIG (Iraqi Interim Government) were lined up in a

147

single lane, waiting for this moment when the opening gate signaled the start of another workday in the Red Zone.

The Peruvian and Chilean guards would approach the vehicles and ask for the driver's cell phones. Each driver was then directed to a designated area where they would be hand searched over their entire body. Such inspections were seeking hidden cell phones, explosives or anything else that might be secreted away. Once they were searched, they were shown the waiting area out of eyesight of the vehicles being inspected.

The guards would then take metal poles which had large twelve-inch round mirrors attached to them. The mirrors were positioned just a few inches above the ground and beneath the underside of the vehicle so they could view the undercarriage looking for explosives or anything that looked out of place. These men searched thousands of vehicles and became experts on the various makes and models of vehicles. Their knowledge of the undercarriage was phenomenal.

Once this search was complete, they would make certain that the hood of the vehicle was up about two inches, the same with the trunk, and then that the driver's side door was slightly open, just about two inches as well. The guards were very accommodating and willingly accepted and implemented my request that the vehicles be staged as just described.[59]

I did not want the hood of the vehicle, the trunk or the doors opened all the way because if the driver had been transporting explosives, and he or she had no explosives presently in the vehicle, then the chances are very great that there would still be explosive residue inside the vehicle. If the engine hood, trunk or doors of the

---

[59] I had learned early in my military career to treat people with respect and kindness. This has rarely failed me. I explained to the guards why I implemented different procedures at CP2. The Peruvian and Chilean guards were always willing to listen. Looking back I still get a smile when I think back to those security guards and how they thirsted for knowledge and appreciated being treated like men and the outstanding professionals they were.

vehicle were all wide open, and it took several minutes to get to vehicle number four in the line of cars to be searched, well then, the residual odor may very well be gone. With the vehicles staged appropriately our K9's would search those areas and it was like a vacuum of air blowing right into their noses.

Another instruction I gave to my guards was to have all drivers open and keep open their front driver's side door. The guard would then go up and move the door leaving about two inches of the door open. If the driver closed the driver's side door when they exited their vehicle they were instructed to go back and open the door and leave it open. The guard can then go back and move the door in the position described above.

My desire was for the word to get around the insurgent community that CP2 is a "Hard Core" Checkpoint, a place too hard to infiltrate. I was hoping we were so good at our jobs that insurgents would have to go elsewhere. Our message was clear, "If you come to our checkpoint, we will find your explosives and this is where you will die." We just hoped we would not be standing nearby when they realized their goose was cooked.

On this particular day, everything was running smooth and all the team members were performing their tasks expertly. The two lanes of cars to be searched were formed up perfectly by our guards with just enough space between vehicles to allow the dog and handler to work. There were two rows of five to eight vehicles and my K9 handler Bill Swanson with his German Shepherd Beauty were setting up downwind of the first vehicle in his row.

Our top-notch guards from Peru and Chili were instructing the drivers on the procedures when the driver of vehicle number one gets out and smiles at me. There was something creepy about it. He did a little wave with his hand and said, "Good morning my friend." Well, this starts all my alarm bells ringing and I think to myself, "This dude is way too nice. Keep your eye on him."

The guy's car was a small older one which had a hideous orange paint scheme that had been bleached out by who knows how many hot summers. The paint job was horrible but the vehicle itself was in really good shape. The engine ran smooth with barely a sound coming from the engine compartment. The windshield was crystal clear and the other windows were remarkably clean as well. I glanced over at the tires and they looked to be in very good shape with plenty of tread on them. The front bumper was actually shining, as if it had been polished. It was obvious this guy took really good care of his vehicle. I must confess, I was impressed at how well he maintained his car in a war environment.

Meanwhile, Bill gives Beauty the command to search their lane. Beauty goes to the lower left front bumper, sniffs around in that area for a second or two, then proceeds to move upwards to about where the radiator is located. The wind is moving through the engine and bringing invisible currents of odor from the engine block toward Beauty's amazing nose. As she inhales her 300 million olfactory receptors go to work analyzing and separating each particle into various elements: oil, dirt, petrol, radiator fluid, rubber and grease. However, her nose is so powerful it even breaks down these various odors into their separate elements.[60]

Beauty moves her search pattern to the lower driver's side corner bumper, again covering all the area between the radiator cap down to the lower right front corner of the bumper area. Bill is staying ahead of Beauty, allowing her to finish her investigation of the corner bumper and once Beauty is satisfied there's no presence of explosive odor, Bill tells her, "Check Here", he cast his right hand towards the driver's side wheel well area. While holding the leash with his left-hand Beauty moves in smoothly investigating this area. As she moves in Bill moves out towards his next presentation point which was the open hood area over the driver's side wheel well.

---

[60] This is why drug dealers have such a hard time concealing their cargo from the dogs. Humans have 6 million olfactory receptors compared to 300 million in the canines. For example, humans smell fresh baked bread while a dog smells the ingredients of flour, yeast, salt and butter. We had insurgents try to mask the odor of explosives (refer to my story Balls for Moths).

As Beauty comes out of the wheel well, Bill presents just above the wheel well of the engine area, the hood is slightly opened thereby containing any odor while also giving her a good place to inhale the odors of the engine. Beauty pushes her nose under the hood and lifts her head up as if she's trying to open the hood. She is on to something. Pushing with her muzzle this hard-working dog causes the hood to raise another twelve inches. Seeing the open space she has created Beauty leaps up placing her front paws over the fender and into the engine well. Bill helps her by securing the hood up.

Now she has got our attention and I can see some of the guards are now watching Beauty. They have seen the dogs work and these guys can all tell when one of our dogs is onto scent. Well, this was definitely one of those times. Bill is encouraging Beauty with a high-pitched voice, "Find it girl, good girl." She rears back to get some leverage and leaps up pulling herself deeper into the engine block area with her hind legs dangling just off the wheel well.

Beauty is nuzzling and pushing her nose around the various parts of the engine. She's between wires, by the brake fluid and then she pushed her nose down even harder and sniffs what we can see is a black box. She cleared her nose with a strong exhale and then pushed her nose hard against the black box and inhaled. As she let herself drop back to the ground, we could see she was going into the sit position but we could also see that the black box she nuzzled was slowly opening. Bill leaned into the engine compartment and said, "Dennis, check this out."

I was a feet away but I could see that Bill's face was quite serious and his jaw set. I walked over, leaned over the engine compartment and there inside the fuse box was a silver cell phone. Yes, you read correctly, a silver cell phone hidden in a fuse box in the engine compartment. Oh man! I was so proud of Beauty! She was sending a message with this phone, "You can't hide anything from us!"

I told the supervisor for the Checkpoint Two Search Team to get an interpreter and bring the driver of this car to the vehicle. As they approached, I instructed the supervisor, "Tell a couple of your men to keep their guns on this guy. This is way out of the norm." Ok, I am sure I am dealing with an insurgent. My blood was up and I couldn't wait to hear how this guy was going to try and explain away the presence of a cell phone in a hidden compartment in the engine block.

My years of training told me this could very well be a probe to check out our K9 teams, to see if our defenses were up or if we were lackadaisical. Was this an attempt to get a triggering phone into position? The scenarios were running through my mind as this Iraqi man walked up. It was the same overly nice guy who a few minutes prior had waved at me and said, "Good morning my friend."

As we are standing there, I notice the dude looks nervous. He is pacing back and forth and doesn't quite know what to do with his hands. While we wait for an interpreter various groups start showing up. The Iraqi Police show up and are shown where the phone was hidden. They are talking amongst themselves and flashing glances over their shoulders at the driver. Even they knew this guy was up to no good. Soon the US Army arrives and then the Iraqi Interim Government Director of Security walks up and with him is the interpreter. Wow, I made one phone call and suddenly had all the resources I could possibly need. Cool!

So, the obvious question was asked, "Why do you have a cell phone in a fuse box in the engine compartment?" The terrified guys answer is hilarious, "That cell phone has all of the numbers of my friends, this other phone I carry is for business only." Some of the guys are smiling at that one. We aren't buying it. Next question, "So why do you not keep it on the inside of your car, like the glovebox?" No response by the driver. He knew he was done. The question was repeated and again met with silence. It was over for him and he knew it. He would have been better off denying knowledge of its existence but to admit he knew the phone was in the engine compartment was perfect. Slam dunk case.

Someone in authority ordered, "Place your hands out in front of you with your palms up." The driver complied and his hands were sprayed with a chemical after which his fingers and palms were swabbed. The test came back immediately positive for explosives residue. Photographs were taken of the compartment, the driver and the cell phone. Then the phone was tested for residue and likewise popped positive for explosives.

We never saw this man or his burnt orange car again. He was whisked away for interrogations and who knows what after that. I was so proud of Beauty. She was tenacious and would not give up on the scent, pushing deeper and deeper into the engine. I was proud of Bill who patiently let his dog do what she was trained to do. They were a great team and were comfortable with each other. They "danced" well together.

I couldn't have been prouder for I knew that our team had just taken a bad guy off the streets. We will never know the intentions and evil deeds behind the phone in the fuse box but we were all certain that lives had been saved because Beauty found it. A cell phone, a fuse box and Beauty, what a combination.

This was exactly why I was hard on our K9 teams. There were no cut corners, no lazy searches, no distractions because the stakes were too high. I warned the handlers when they first arrived, "If I find you are here to just hold a leash and collect a paycheck, I will transfer you. If you cut corners, get lazy, fail to keep your dog excited, fail to maintain good grooming and care of your canine I will have you sent home. This is not a game. You may not like me but that is fine because I didn't come all these thousands of miles to make friends. I came here to keep our people and our Allies safe."

Bill and Beauty were a true professional K9 team dedicated to the job and task at hand. From the very first day I met them I knew right off that they were my kind of team. It was such a joy to watch them work. I Salute you both! Oh, and by the way, Beauty and Bill did finish a complete search of the rest of the vehicle and no explosives were found. Well done!

Here I am with Beauty. What an amazing bomb dog!

Balls for Moths

The Security Team gave me a signal with a "Thumbs Up" indicating they were satisfied with their visual search and it was now our turn. Toris, my German Shepherd, and myself began to approach the vehicle that minutes ago had been occupied by a driver with three passengers. I stop, stoop slightly down and grasp a few hairs from Toris' back and then lift my fingers with his fur to the wind and release it from my grasp. Slight wisps of wind catch the fur and cause it to float to my right. I now know the wind is blowing south to north so I position us downwind of the vehicle providing my partner with every opportunity to pick up on the odor of explosives.

I knew that explosive odor is heavy and thus the scent would drop to the ground and move along its surface with the currents of the wind. Odor always follows the path of least resistance so I just needed to determine where that projected path would lead.[61]

I gave Toris the command to search and he took off straight towards the left front passenger side bumper, got about halfway across the bumper, then stood up on his hind legs and began to sniff in towards the engine area. He then backed out of the engine compartment, came back down on all fours and finished searching the front bumper from center to the right front driver's side.

Winding around the vehicle Toris stuck his nose into the front driver's side wheel well, came out, popped back up on his hind legs and sniffed in towards the driver's side engine compartment. Nothing of interest there so he backed out.

Toris was extremely good at this job and had searched thousands of vehicles in his career and it was a joy to watch him work. I know I had a slight grin on my face as his motions were fluid and his

---

[61] This is why it's so important to be downwind of a vehicle to be searched. The position affords the K9 ample opportunity to pick up on odor. If it's a car bomb there is going to be so much explosives odor coming off the vehicle that the dog will definitely detect it.

purpose clear. I was there just taking it all in, watching the master at work.

Our searches were always very quiet and this was no different as he calmly and methodically moved from one part of the vehicle to the next. We were dancing together and it felt great.

Sniffing the driver's front door seam, he stood on his hind legs and stuck his head up to where the window was opened about two inches. Odd, he hung there longer than usual. "He's onto something," I thought to myself. His pause caught my attention. He was a master at his craft and rather than sniff at this location for just a second or two, he stayed hung there for about five to ten seconds. I did not say a word and I was very careful to put no strain on the leash for I had to let him do what he was born and trained to do. I gave him more room by moving to the end of my leash to the right of him. I didn't want to crowd him for he was in the zone and I wanted him to stay there. He could take as long as he needed during his investigation.

My action, moving slightly away from Toris made me smile because he and I both knew he could care less how close I was to him. He was a professional down to the fiber of his heart and once he was on scent there was no pulling him off or distracting him. However, as I had other handlers watching I always conducted myself as I had trained others, so as to lead by example.

Toris then came down away from the driver's window and was now back on all four paws. He sniffed the driver's door seam past the door handle and as the door was cracked open just a couple of inches, he sniffed really hard at this location. Suddenly he dropped his head down below the driver's side frame of this Mercedes and then plopped down on his belly and tried to go deeper under the car. Clouds of dust came flying out from under the car as Toris worked to get further underneath. I could hear his grunting and his nails scratching at the ground. Ok, now I was deeply concerned. When detection dogs go down and deep under a vehicle, it is often because the explosive is deep inside the car and toward the center.

Well, perhaps this is the day I look Jesus in the face. One thing is for certain, if this is a car bomb it is not getting past us which means the trigger man will detonate it here hoping to kill as many of us as possible. No time to dwell on such things for Toris was suddenly out from under the car, back on his paws and swiftly moving to the trunk area. He put his nose into the open trunk, sniffed all around, came out and once again plopped down on his belly and worked his way under the car. Toris was on a mission.

Scraping and clawing he backed out and quickly went around to the rear passenger door area not bothering to smell the door seams. I didn't correct him on this because he was on odor and a tried and true veteran. I trusted him with my life and trusted his judgement. He immediately went straight under the rear passenger door frame, trying to go deeper and soon all I could see was his rear end, short stubby tail and two back legs sticking out from under the Mercedes.

My eyes were on that tail. If it wagged it meant he was getting very close to explosive odor. The tail didn't budge so I knew he had more investigating to do.

Suddenly my nose picked up something, a strong pungent odor coming from the car. It was a very strong and distinct scent of mothballs. As we were at the rear passenger door area, I quickly looked inside to the rear back passenger seats and noticed a couple of white moth balls on the back seat and then looking down at the floorboard I noticed a dozen or more. About this time Toris emerged from beneath the rear passenger area and we then proceeded to finish our search along the passenger side of the vehicle, up to the front passenger side door, wheel well and engine area. Toris then turned and pulled me back to the rear passenger side area again and dove under the vehicle. Searching, sniffing, trying to locate the source of the odor he was onto.

Now, NOT once had Toris gone to a positive "SIT" position. He never indicated to me that he had positively found an explosive source. However, because I knew Toris so well and trusted his experience I knew that there was more to this vehicle than what could be seen. We had to find out what this driver and his three passengers were trying to hide. Why did they have mothballs inside the vehicle? There was only one legitimate explanation and that was to mask an odor. What was there that they did not want a bomb dog to find?

I informed the head of the security team that Toris gave me enough in "Behavior Changes" to warrant a deep search of this vehicle I also recommended that the four men who emerged from this car be questioned separately about the contents of the car. I explained to the supervisor everything Toris had done but that he had never given me a "sit" position for a "positive" indication of explosives. There was something these men were hiding. The supervisor agreed. Having seen Toris work and having known his history the supervisor needed no further information. He turned and yelled some orders and the car was given a deeper, more thorough search.

When questioned about what they were hiding the men erupted in anger. It was one of those situations we have all seen at one time or another where the anger does not match the situation. It was obvious that these guys were really hollering for dramatic effect hoping to intimidate us into forgetting the whole affair and letting them pass. They had underestimated our resolve and dedication to the mission.

We had purposely kept them out of view of their vehicle. This was the whole reason for moving drivers to the opposite side of the blast walls. They could not see what was being searched and thus would not know when to trigger a bomb (if one was present) in the event the guards had missed a triggering device in the driver's possession. We also knew they had no idea what we referred to when we said we had found something. As far as they knew, we had, for they could not see their vehicle. It was an important part of our mission to keep them away from their vehicles.

Meanwhile the security team started to look deeper into this vehicle. Their immediate priority was to look where Toris had shown so much interest and where the curious mothballs were laid out. The rear passenger side compartment was the focus of the initial search and it immediately provided results. Pulling up the rear, back seat passenger side footrest carpet, a door was discovered. When it opened there were handguns and ammo stored inside. On the driver's side rear passenger compartment floorboard there was an identical hidden space with handguns and ammo. Wow, this was huge.

Then it was discovered that the back seat actually lifted up and underneath was another compartment with machine guns and ammo. Now, in Iraq it was not necessarily against the law to have these weapons in a vehicle[62] but what was suspicious was that everything was hidden. Were these men trying to sneak through our checkpoint and go on a shooting spree killing as many Americans and Iraqi government employees as possible? This was an amazing find.

Another interesting point, and one that led the security supervisor to call his superiors, was the fact that the men knew the car would be searched by canines so they had sprinkled moth balls all over the areas where the secret compartments were located. They were trying to distract our dogs. To what end? This was a serious point and one that needed to be addressed.

Within minutes there were Iraqi police and US Army on site as well as civilians both American and Iraqi in obvious authority. These four men were all taken away and their vehicle removed for fingerprinting and further forensic investigation. We never saw those four guys again nor their black Mercedes.

---

[62] Iraqi citizens were allowed to have weapons and ammo in their cars because it was a violent city and people were getting gunned down all the time. Citizens were allowed to protect themselves. This fact created a bit of an issue because our dogs in the States had been trained to sit on the chemicals used in the making of gunpowder. When we first deployed to Checkpoint Two our dogs were sitting all the time because of the frequent guns. These "SITS" were causing long lines and delays because of their frequency. We had to train our dogs to not sit when coming across the presence of ammo.

Toris had done a great job and in all likelihood a terrible attack had been thwarted and it was all because of a dog; a black and tan "infidel" German Shepherd named Toris.

Shoo!

Flies have been an irritant to man for as long as history has been recorded. Even in the Bible when God wished to make life miserable on the Egyptians, he sent a plague of flies which drove people insane. In Iraq the flies were equally obnoxious. I would feel so bad for Laky, Toris and the other bomb dogs who sometimes would have ten to fifteen biting flies on their nose while searching cars and trucks for explosives and car bombs. We would have loved to try all sorts of ointments and sprays to thwart these pests but we could not cover their noses. It was the dog's nose that earned them a spot on the team. It was their whole reason for being there; to sniff out explosives.

I recall one day looking down at my bomb dog Laky's nose while he was searching for explosives. I could see several flies resting on his snout so I waved my hand over his nose and was shocked to see a dozen flies scatter. Looking closer I noticed blood pooling up all over his nose. Did I mention I hate flies?

I have been bitten by flies before so I know how painful it can be. I knew our dogs were suffering but they kept at their jobs as we tried to alleviate their pain and discomfort. Laky was an awesome bomb dog. Even though he was assailed by these vermin he continued to search. Ignoring the drilling into his nose he remained steadfast in his search for explosives.

At our checkpoint there was a light, well, sandy colored brick building off to one side. The small structure was about ten feet long, six feet wide and seven feet high. I noticed that when we were conducting searches on vehicles our bomb dogs would turn their heads in the direction of this small building, and "Air Scent."[63] If it had been explosive odor they would have turned and worked their noses to the source but they never once sought to approach the small building. One day I noticed there was a foul stench in the air and it seemed to be coming from this building. I asked an English-speaking Iraqi soldier what the building was used for and he said that it was a restroom for men.

The statement jarred my memory and I recalled when we were faced with establishing our presence at Checkpoint Two, I had taken Toris over to this building to sniff it out for the presence of explosive odor. He showed not the slightest hint that explosives were there. Curious, I poked my head inside this small building and noted two small holes in the floor with stones on each side of the holes.

I didn't really think much about it but I did notice that there were flies everywhere inside. There were dozens of empty clear plastic water bottles spread all over the inside as well. It wouldn't be Iraq without water bottles all over the ground. In addition there were hundreds of cigarette butts all around.

With the temperatures now warming up I knew this outhouse was going to get very ripe. Now that I knew what it was used for, I noticed that many men waiting for their turn to have their vehicles searched were running to the restroom making their contribution to the stench of this place. Once in a shift I saw several of our dogs turn their heads toward the offending building and air scent. My mind was made up, this building was going to come down. I could not have such a distraction in this place.

One afternoon I got some of my K9 Handlers together and told them what the building was. It stunk to high heaven and never seemed to get emptied. It was filling higher and higher and if I had learned anything in this country it was that native locals would not

---

[63] This is an action displayed by a dog that lifts its head up high and inhales deeply through its nose trying to pick up on an odor and the direction the scent is coming from.

show initiative by doing something constructive about this disgusting situation. I described to the handlers how thousands of flies were passing in and out of this building like aircraft at JFK airport in New York. These flies were landing and feasting on Iraqi urine and crap and then landing on our bomb dog's noses. Flies with filthy feet were landing on us and trying to alight on our food while we were eating a sandwich. Things were about to change.

I said to a few of my K9 Handlers, "We've got to tear that building down before one of our dog's or one of us catches some stinking Iraqi disease, plus I'm tired of seeing these flies biting our dogs on their nose and drawing blood." The K9 Teams were all in and our plan was set! We waited until Friday, a Holy Day. Being a day of rest and prayer meant there were very few Iraqi men and women working.

With the coast clear there was nothing keeping us from doing this community service which would make life and work much more enjoyable. A day without the stench of human waste seemed like a luxury. Skies not filled with filthy flies in our search area seemed like a dream. So, you guessed it, we tore that crapper house of disease down baby, down to the very ground.

We took pictures of one another standing atop the ruins of this festering heap. We were conquerors of old who had toppled a castle and as we stood atop the rubble with chest puffed out the cameras clicked and laughs bellowed. For fifteen minutes the war melted away. We were boys, all back home having fun, laughing about the surprise in store for the would-be squatters in the days to come. This was a great stress release for all of us.

We were looking forward to Monday, the start of the new work week, the time we would be able to witness the famous run to the latrine. We talked about it and speculated on the reactions. One thing was certain the building was down and there was no putting it back up.

Finally the day came and the highly anticipated fruitless jaunt to the restroom, aka Iraqi Crap House. The first customer provided

162

entertainment a bit after lunch. I can still see it, here he comes, running to his house of relief. We were all watching from Checkpoint Two, the pile of bricks a good forty yards from where we were. All of a sudden, this dudes entire body language changed. It was as if we were watching the famous "Change of Behavior" in one of our bomb dogs. We were all snickering among ourselves as we observed this running man suddenly change from running to shuffling. Now he's leaning forward looking intently at what used to be a solid yellow sandy colored brick building but which is now clearly just a pile of debris, strewn out in all directions. The guy begins to walk back to his car but stops halfway, turns and looks in our direction.

This was the moment we craved. This desperate guy raises his right arm up in the direction of the pile of bricks and his eyes begin to express a form of panic and he's looking at me for some sort of explanation. I provide him one. I raised my right arm up into the air, and brought it down like a mortar round, and I yelled out "BOOM!" This guy grabbed the back of his pants as if the action would help him control what his bowels were telling him needed to happen.

Now we are all snickering and tears are flowing and to make it worse we dare not burst out laughing for that would offend and give away our deed. Guys were crying with laughter. It was the funniest thing I have seen in a long time.

So here comes this poor guy in his mid 40s and in obvious discomfort relinquishing his keys and cell phone so his car can be searched. I could tell his mind was occupied with one thing, not losing control of his bowels. He was putting every bit of energy into this purpose and we could all see it.

Once the guy was cleared by our security detail, I had compassion on him and led him over to our sanitary portable toilets. The man was profuse with thanks as he entered. I just had to show some compassion to this guy for we have all been in situations where nature was calling but there was no place near to answer the call.

When he emerged, he had a smile as big as my home state of Texas. Once he entered his vehicle and drove off to begin his workday we exploded in laughter. The K9 teams and the Peruvian and Chilean guards all together just letting it out, tears flowing. Things had been so tense and so many were dying all around us. This laugh did us good. Oh, and this man would pass by every day and he always had a big smile for us. Perhaps we had won a new friend that day. I know one thing for certain, our demolition of the outhouse had definitely impacted the fly population.

My family asked if I could have been reprimanded for tearing down the building. Yes, I suppose. I was well aware I could have gotten into trouble for this, however, for the health of my dog teams, this was the right move. Another reason for such a decision was that it was a break from the same routine day in and day out. I needed to do something which would jar the men from their humdrum existence of routine. I had to make this particular day fun. I just had a gut instinct that morale was sagging and something dramatic needed to happen to get everyone laughing. I wanted them to have a story they could tell years later. I just needed my K9 teams to know what it felt like to act like "boys being boys.' Doing something they all would laugh about. Having been a leader of men in the military I developed an instinct for these things and I just knew I had to do it. The dogs needed it, the men needed it and so did I.

With the outhouse destroyed I had eradicated a breeding ground but I still had flies to deal with. I made a trip over to the Vector Control Office in the Green Zone. This office was responsible for dealing with pests such as rats, parasites and flies. When I stepped into the office and told them my problem they agreed to help. I was asked, "Where do you work in the Green Zone?" I smiled and said, "Checkpoint Two, in the Red Zone." The response was immediate, "There's no way man. No one will go out there! No one! It's too dangerous!" I guess he could see the frustration on my face or perhaps his manhood was embarrassed by his outburst because he then piped up, "Hold on, there's one guy who may go out. He's a crazy cowboy from Oklahoma. I'll give him your number".

Sure enough, about five minutes later I received a phone call from the cowboy. We got to talking about the problem and we clicked. A few minutes into the conversation with his Oklahoma drawl he asked, "Well Dennis, where you from?" I knew my response would get a reaction, "Texas! San Antonio, Texas!" We both laughed and he spoke up, "Well you know there is a lot of bad blood between Oklahoma and you guys DOWN in Texas so I ain't too sure I can help you."[64] He fell silent and hemmed and hawed as I laughed and then he continued, "Well you guys and your dogs are protecting us here so I guess I can come out and help you with YOUR flies." We laughed so hard.

About thirty minutes later he showed up at our checkpoint and set up several awesome devices called Magic Flytraps. Within days our fly problem was taken care of. I would no longer have to physically push flies off of my sandwich as I held it too my mouth. I no longer had to wave them off my dog's nose. Don't tell anyone from Oklahoma but I was and am very grateful for this cowboy!

The Weakest Link

Anytime you work with a team of people, you are dependent on their work ethic to keep operations running smooth. Unfortunately in almost every work environment there are slackers. Those who would rather sit around and do nothing than put in an honest day's work. I was not raised that way. My father taught me a lot of things, some bad and some good. One thing that always stood out to me was his work ethic. Even in his later years he was shuffling around his property at the crack of dawn with a screwdriver in hand fixing things.

---

[64] There has always been a huge rivalry between these two cowboy states that border each other. Especially during football season when Texas teams play Oklahoma teams. The culmination is always the famous "Red River Shootout" between the University of Texas and Oklahoma University.

I am the same way. I also have this old school code that your work reflects on your character and your family. I have always desired to honor my name by working hard and providing good results for my employers. Fortunately in Iraq I was in a position that I could have men moved off of my team if they were not men of good character.

I took full advantage of this perk and had several men transferred and some even sent home. I was in the business of saving lives not of making friends. Now I am a friendly guy. My family laughs about this because they say I never met a stranger. This is true. I love meeting people and feel quite comfortable initiating conversations with complete strangers who within minutes will be a new friend.

I say this to let you the reader know that I am not a surly guy who enjoys berating people. That is not who I am. I love people and am respectful of their lives and opinions. However, when given a task and directive to defend human lives I will see it through to completion. Those who would train little and poorly handle constructive criticism were given ample opportunities to change their behavior but if they refused to budge, they were let go. Our work was too dangerous and too important to be left in the hands of half-hearted sentinels.

Now, I had no worries about suicide bombers in vehicles blowing up the Iraqi government building because I knew our teams would detect them before they could get close. Traffic. Yeah, there was a lot of it. The vehicles through our checkpoint would vary from day to day but I had seven K9 teams working this checkpoint and we would search 800-1200 vehicles a day. We also searched packages with our canines.

With the vehicles being searched by our K9 teams, the drivers were being searched by our Peruvian and Chilean security forces. These guys did an awesome job. I would gladly serve alongside them anywhere in the world. They were extremely focused on their duties. Many had been policemen back home in South America and you could tell they were professional to the core. They put their all into making certain everything was done right. Equally important is the fact that they took instructions from me and their supervisor very well. This is not easy for men to do, especially in the Law Enforcement world where many egos are bolstered with pride.

With anything in life such an attribute varies from person to person and is not agency wide. However, having done this for such a long time, I discovered that many in Law Enforcement from the United States bristled under my tutelage. I never understood how a professional could assume they had reached the pinnacle of learning and were no longer open to learning new things. Let's face it, if you're a policeman you're an Alpha type and this can lead to a "no one is going to tell me how to do things" attitude. Many of these handlers were used to being the supreme authority, or at least representing that authority, and now I was telling them better ways to do things. Many resisted.

I felt bad for these guys and for their dogs because I knew they would never dance together and reach their full potential. Such a K9 team might truly die on the vine refusing to receive nourishment to grow.

Pride. The small word with giant ramifications.

There was one aspect of our job at Checkpoint Two that drove me crazy and it was the quality of the Iraqi soldiers and police. The majority of them had received minimal training but more importantly the vast majority of these men seemed to have little desire to do a good job. In fact, for most it seemed nonexistent. I can always bring someone up to a higher level of training if they have the desire, but I cannot do a darn thing with a guy who has no yearning to do a good job.

This lack of training and work ethic played havoc on my code of conduct. We had an important job to do and were protecting some very important people so why was our first line of defense so abysmal. I wondered, "Is this the best they've got?" If so, I knew we were screwed because it would not be long before a suicide bomber would reach my team of handlers. I knew they would not get through us so the likelihood of us getting killed was high.

This brings me to another point. In addition to the vehicle entrance we had a pedestrian gate for those folks who would walk to work. Many of the people walking through this gate carpooled with relatives or friends who dropped them off on the corner at Yaffa street and moved on to their place of employment elsewhere in the city. These pedestrians had to be screened like everyone else seeking access to the Iraqi Interim Government grounds.

It should be made clear that there was only one reason for someone entering our checkpoint, they had business with or worked for the Iraqi Interim Government. Our checkpoint was not another way for civilians to access the Green Zone. No one drove through our checkpoint to run errands on the other side of the zone. Our gate had one purpose alone, access to the Iraqi Interim Government.

After vehicles entered through our gates they parked, that was it. There was nowhere else for them to go. No driving around and shopping. No cruising around the International Zone taking in the sights. Once people passed through our gate, they immediately found a parking spot for their vehicle and then conducted their business with the Iraqi government.

This main fact was the reason Checkpoint Two was so dangerous. We were in the Red Zone. Meaning, enemy territory. There were many factions that wanted Iraqi leadership killed. This of course meant that those who worked for the Iraqi Prime Minister were likewise marked for death. It was deadly business and thus the reason I took security so seriously. There were many people who wanted us all dead and they were actively pursuing this goal, while I, on the other hand, was actively trying to keep us all alive. If I hurt some feelings along the way, I am sorry. I really am, but I would make the same decisions over again because some folks needed a reality check. I had been tested in battle and had smelled the iron stench of blood on the ground. I had seen the awful color of skin with no blood circulating and thus had no desire to see any of my men, our K9s, Americans or our Allies laid out in pieces.

168

To make certain we all remained alive I crimped down on toughness and alertness for our checkpoint. I wanted the word to spread on the streets that trying to get through us was pointless. Of course this meant that in keeping the Iraqi Prime Minister alive we were all most likely going to die. A suicide bomber, realizing the dogs are going to sniff him out will just detonate where he is and hope to kill as many of us as possible. It was the reality of our existence but we had signed the dotted line knowing the risks.

One of the things keeping us alive though was the search protocols that had been established. Everyone needed to be searched and the process started not with K9 but with the Iraqi soldiers and police a hundred yards away from us at the entrance to the Iraqi part of Checkpoint Two.

Here's how the process worked, well, was supposed to work. Those who were passengers in cars wanting to gain access through Checkpoint Two would get out of their vehicle at the Iraqi checkpoint. It was there that the Iraqi military would check identification papers and conduct a visual check of each bag or hand carried containers being brought in through the gate. These passengers were by the hundreds and sometimes thousands every day. Each person carrying a handbag, briefcase, backpack and other items all had to be hand searched at the Iraqi checkpoint. Once they were examined, they were told to continue down a walkway that was a half t-wall, about waist high, that funneled them into the Iraqi Government grounds.

In addition to the passengers of the vehicles who had now been screened there were additional pedestrians who had walked up to the checkpoint. Now, people tend to tire of monotony. This is why it is important to cycle through guards assigned to inspect baggage and persons. It is boring but necessary work. With the passengers and pedestrians being searched the Iraqi Army and Police had quite a job on their hands.

I had been a Master Sergeant in the Security Police in the United States Air Force with twenty-one years of experience and having

169

been a leader of men and women I knew full well the famous saying, "People don't do what's expected, they do what's inspected." So, knowing this fact, I made an inspection of the Iraqi military checkpoint to see if they were operating as instructed. They were not. Not by a long shot.

I witnessed their procedure with alarm. First, the Iraqi Army and Police standing at the pedestrian gate would wave up the individuals seeking access to the IIG grounds.[65] One of the soldiers would search a bag or backpack and then return it to the civilian and let them pass. Ok, no big deal. Good job. Then the same soldier would wave the next person up and then just move them through the gate. From my vantage point I could clearly see that the pedestrian had a backpack slung over their shoulder but it was never searched. I couldn't believe it. Such a lack of discipline was astounding. One after another the pedestrians were granted access without even a cursory glance being taken into their bags.

Another duty of the Iraqi army at this first station was to check the vehicles seeking access to the IIG grounds. First, as previously mentioned, the passengers were told to get out and stand in line for inspection. They were not allowed to return to the vehicle but rather continued down a walkway where they were searched as described above. The driver was told to remain in the vehicle and prepare to open the hood, the trunk and provide proof of identity. The Iraqi soldiers were then to look into the front seat, back seat, under the hood and in the trunk of every vehicle. I quickly discovered the same lack of professionalism displayed in this area as one by one the cars were merely glanced into. One soldier took an ID through a window and without searching the car at all simply waved it through. He looked bored out of his mind. Very rarely was a hood opened or a trunk popped and looked into. This was outrageous.

I walked back towards our K9 area of CP2 and grabbed the large steel gate on rollers and slid it shut. SLAM! With great flare I then fastened the lock on the gate. I now had everyone's attention and

---

[65] Iraqi Interim Government

they asked, "What's up? What's going on?" I explained to my guys and the South American guards what I had just witnessed, "I'm going to call on the Iraqi Prime Minister's Security Office and fill them in on the atrocious job performed at the Iraqi part of Checkpoint Two. This gets fixed right now!"

Cars were backed up; horns were blaring but I was NOT allowing another vehicle through when I knew what I knew. I made the call.

Concerned, I informed the head of security for the Iraqi government about the lack of control and professionalism displayed. I must say that another one of the perks at working this checkpoint was that I had exposure to many Iraqi officials and working relationships with them which always benefited us both. Shortly thereafter the Iraqi Minister of Security walked up to me at Checkpoint Two and said, "Good afternoon Mr. Blocker, let's walk down to the first checkpoint and see what they are and are not doing in the area of security." As we strode side by side, I couldn't help but contemplate the importance of what was happening and to tell you the truth I was sort of stunned. I knew the situation would be handled but I never expected the Minister of Security to handle this personally.

Of course I knew that the Minister had just as much an interest in security being tight as I did for there were many in this city who wanted him dead. As we walked, I leaned in close to him and said, "Let's keep our distance. I don't want them seeing us observe them. If they see you, they will alter their behavior." We continued forty yards beyond where our K9 teams were searching and stopped.

We stood there in silence for about fifteen minutes. He soon turned to me, looked me in the eyes and said, "Mr. Blocker, I've seen enough. You are correct. They are not doing their jobs properly. What do you suggest?" I had to digest that last part for it sounded like the Iraqi Minister of Security asked me for a suggestion. I took a deep breath and respectfully gave him my thoughts, "Sir, I recommend that those men in leadership positions be informed that you had personally observed their operations and were shocked at the lack of discipline displayed. I would tell these men that from this day forward you will be personally conducting surprise observations of not only this checkpoint but all of the various checkpoints[66] and that those not performing as outlined in the operating instructions will be moved to lesser paying jobs or fired on the spot."

Since I had his attention, I took the opportunity to inform him that not a single Iraqi woman was ever searched. "The men are not permitted to touch the women," was the Ministers reply. I then asked, "Sir, are their Iraqi women in the police force?" I could see he knew where I was going but I continued, "I would recommend that a portable building be brought in so that the women can be searched in private by other women." He mulled this around in his head for a few minutes and then replied, "It will be done. Thank you for bringing this to my attention." I warned him that many women would not be happy and that he might take some heat but he answered in an American way, "They'll have to deal with it or not enter." My answer was short and sweet, "Yes sir." I liked the way this guy handled business.

I knew the Minister of Security would handle this situation but I never expected what happened. Within three hours a tractor trailer was pulling up with a portable building. A tractor swooped in, pulled it off the bed of the trailer, set it where instructed and in no time flat Iraqi women were ordered in to be searched by Iraqi police women. Sure enough, from our area we could hear the yelling and complaining but also sure enough they, "had to deal with it."

The Showdown

Toris was a very seasoned War Dog. He'd already had two tours in Afghanistan and was on his third in Iraq. Toris was at New York City during 9/11 for five months. While there he was searching

---

[66] I felt that if they were this lax at our checkpoint, they were probably the same at all the others. So why not nip it all in the same bud now.

vehicles, boxes, and packages which were being delivered to the Empire State Building. Yes, searching for explosives or bombs in the protection of lives and the protection of one of America's most distinctive landmarks. Toris had America's back!

I was not his K9 handler at that time but a friend of mine told how Toris had done an awesome job. Of course this did not surprise me because Toris always knew what his job was and he put everything into it.

Toris was very tuned into reading body language of all people. People put off their own unique scent and folks from various parts of the world have their own unique odor they naturally emanate. Toris could smell this odor coming off the Iraqi people and in particular the Iraqi men who he had not the least bit love for. I long suspected that his dislike for Iraqi men must have germinated during his previous tours to this country but I had no way to know. I knew that Toris was dual trained as detection and patrol and that on a previous tour he had taken down three insurgents. One incident involved two men who jumped a wall into an American compound. Toris ran them down and then took them to the ground hard with his jaws. The second incident involved a suspicious man who refused to leave his vehicle. Toris persuaded him to leave.

I noticed that even at a distance of seventy-five yards and downwind Toris would pick up the scent of an Iraqi man and begin to show agitation. I'm not sure what food or seasoning was in their diet but it was either on their clothes or came out of their pores because Toris picked up on it every time.

I'd always know if he had the scent of an Iraqi man, an American or one of our allied forces. With the Americans and our allied forces, I'd see Toris air scenting, he'd lift his nose slightly upwards and take in the scent, I'd look in the direction he was air scenting, sure enough, someone would be walking towards us at a distance. Toris would then go back to what he was doing. Sometimes though he would pick up the scent of an Iraqi man and I'd feel my leather leash start to vibrate in my hand. Then came the sound of a low guttural growl. I'd look, sure enough it was always an Iraqi man. With Iraqi children or women he showed not the least interest, but there was something about the local men that he detested. Amazing. The science of it all.

In barking at these Iraqi men, who were short on brains, he was doing what he was accustomed to doing, barking at those I'm yelling at. He knows that when someone is being challenged by the K9 handler, it always involves the handlers voice being louder and direct. The Canine knows the distinct difference if things are good, or if the situation is changing. Patrol dogs then prepare to make things very awful for the bad guy.

Another thing that impressed me about Toris was his ability to pick out people from a crowd. Just a random person would interest him. I think most dog lovers will have noticed such behavior in their own dogs. For example, Toris would be working the checkpoint and we would have 500 people come through and Toris would not utter a peep. Suddenly, Toris would leap up, single out an Arab man in the crowd and just morph into a raging animal doing all he could to attack this dude. What made the man stand out? Was it a scent he put off or perhaps some sort of negative energy? It's an actual phenomenon I have seen many times. I know that you have probably witnessed this with your own dogs around a stranger at the park. Your dog is fine and friendly with everyone and then all of a sudden, a person walks by and your dog turns into a beast. Interesting.

Now, all of this came to a head during a three-day period and the way it played out was staggering. One day at Checkpoint Two I'd noticed Toris lift his head up and look intently down the road at four Iraqi soldiers. They were approximately fifty yards away and heading straight towards our location. As I'm watching them very close, I could feel my leash begin to vibrate, indicating Toris was not happy with either someone in this group, or all of them. I did not trust the Iraqi military, nor the Iraqi police. More than once while I was in-country, insurgents obtained Iraqi military or Iraqi police uniforms, dressed in them and killed Americans or our allies who mistakenly thought they were dealing with actual Iraqi military or police.

A case in point, on the 19th of January 2006 less than a mile from where I stood seven Iraqi food contractors were kidnapped and executed. Their bodies were discovered near the Indonesian Embassy.

Eyewitnesses stated that at least twelve men had been seen hustling the food contractors along. Testimonies highlighted the fact that all of the gunmen held weapons with silencers and that the kidnappers wore the uniform of the Iraqi National Police.

Stories like this served to keep us sharp and to make us wary of anyone wearing the uniform of the Iraqi Police or Army. If we saw a soldier or policeman we didn't recognize we became extra vigilant. We trust only those we knew. All else were suspect. Our survival depended on this level of awareness.

So as these four Iraqi soldiers drew within twenty yards, Toris was showing his teeth and not hiding the fact that he wanted to eat one, or all of them up for lunch. I quickly noticed which Iraqi soldier Toris had zeroed in on. This soldier scowled at Toris and I as he approached. He really stood apart from the other guys. He just seemed to drip hatred out of his pours. I kept my eye on this guy as each of the four soldiers showed their badges to gain access. The guard checked them out, no problem, and they were allowed entry.

The next day I see this same Iraqi soldier walking towards our checkpoint but this time he's by himself. Toris immediately detects him and again wants to do the Texas Two Step all over this guy's body. As the soldier gets closer, he lifts his AK47 just a bit, ever so slight, pointing it straight at Toris and myself. Toris picked up on this slight body movement and the weapon pointed directly at us and went nuts snapping his teeth together, lunging forward trying with all of his might to take this guy down. I could actually hear Toris' teeth snapping together. Of course I had control of Toris, but I did not make a correction because he detected something was not right, and he was correct.

Using our checkpoint interpreter I told the Iraqi soldier to point his weapon down to the ground. The surly soldier did not comply at first, but then his eyes followed my right hand which slowly dropped to the grip of my sidearm. He looked into my eyes and saw my resolve. His rifle barrel slowly moved down and was now pointing into the dirt at our feet. He moved through the checkpoint and was soon out of sight but not out of my mind.

The following day he came through the checkpoint again but this time in the back of a small pick-up. There were three other soldiers with him and it seemed like they had been on a supply run for there were bags of food lying on the floor. I had my eye on the idiot and moved up to tell them that they had to dismount so the truck could be searched. My interpreter then told them to also remove the food so that the search dog would not contaminate it. Well, these orders were not well received.

All four of the soldiers were yelling at me and I suspect cussing me out. They pointed to Toris and their food lying in bags on the bed of this small sized pick-up truck. They were gesturing wildly with their hands and I was fairly certain they didn't want the dog to touch their food. This fact was relayed to me and I replied, "This is why I asked you all to remove the food, so that the dog would not touch it."

During this entire interlude Toris was a real cool customer. He sat at my left side on his six-foot leash taking in the scene, looking for danger and waiting for the command to search. I made a compromise with these soldiers. I knew Toris would not be distracted by the food so I had the Iraqi interpreter tell these guys, "I'll keep the dog away from their food. He will be up near the food but will not touch it." While the men dismounted, I began our search.

The search was going smooth and I was just about to step to the rear of the truck, when all of a sudden Toris began barking and lunging towards the soldiers who had exited the bed of the truck and were standing to the side. I looked down at Toris and could see he was enraged and in battle mode. What had flipped his switch?

I glanced over to where the Iraqi soldiers were standing. Three of the men had their rifles shouldered but the fourth, the very same one we had issues with, had his rifle in his hands, at waist level pointed directly at Toris and I. Toris was jumping forward, snarling, barking and foaming at the mouth trying with all of his might to tear into this guy. This seasoned war dog knew what this weapon was used for and he knew the implications when it was pointed at us.

Here's something interesting about this situation. While Toris was searching this truck, for whatever reason, he turned his head around and looked back at these four men who had dismounted from the back of their small pick-up truck. Toris had never done this before. He's very methodical, disciplined and always very focused on his job. Searches like the one he was conducting had been completed thousands of times but on this day he either sensed a threat or heard something which troubled him. The fact is that Toris broke his tried and true pattern and cast a wary eye at these men because he sensed something was wrong.

Seeing the threat and its implications Toris sounded the alarm with his deep German Shepherd bark. I instantly recognized the vicious tone and knew he had switched modes from search to attack. Toris saw a threat to me and desired only to neutralize it.

I needed to nip this in the bud quick so I yelled out, "Shoulder your weapon soldier!" While I repeated this order, I acted out the action I needed him to take. The soldier didn't budge. He glared at Toris and I and all the while his rifle is aimed directly at us.

Directly behind me was a long row of vehicles waiting to be searched. The standoff had brought the flow to a screeching halt so drivers were poking their heads out of their windows and watching the scene unfold before them. What really bothered me was that the idiot soldier had a finger on the trigger of his rifle. The slightest pressure and it would have fired. This action would have caused our South American guards to open fire. The dominoes would have continued to fall as the three other Iraqi soldiers would have then fired. Soon it would have turned into the "Gunfight at the O.K. Corral."

In short, this was a bad situation. This was a friggin showdown. I yelled again, "Lower your weapon soldier!" I placed my hand on the butt of my 9mm, hoping this would suggest to this Iraqi soldier that it would be far better for him to lower his weapon and comply with my commands before he made a drastic mistake. I was well aware that my 9mm was no match for his AK47 with its 7.62mm rounds, BUT I had been firing expert for twenty-one years in the military. I was convinced I was a better shot than he was. I suspect his shooting would be everywhere considering he'd be moving around, breathing hard, all of which would throw his aim way off.

Suddenly one of my K9 handlers allowed his emotions to override his common sense. At a fast clip he walked right up to the Iraqi with the weapon and started yelling, "Point your weapon to the ground!" I have to admit, the handler had courage. Foolhardy? Yes. He was courageous though. He deliberately stood directly between me and the rifle which was now pointed at my handler's waist.

Now the situation escalated quickly as the three other soldiers swooped around my handler forming a circle around him. They are yelling at him and he is screaming at them. Making matters worse is the fact that all four soldiers now have their rifles pointed at my handler. This went from bad to worse in zero flat.

The soldiers have all forgotten about Toris and I who are only a few feet away. Toris is snarling and snapping, lunging forward hoping to sink his teeth into these guys. I'm holding Toris back and thinking, "How the heck am I going to diffuse this situation?"

I was on the outside of this circle watching my K9 handler blow this into something which is now almost out of control. This entire situation was but one trigger pull away from becoming a deadly international incident! I'm yelling at my K9 handler, "Get out of there! Do not reach for your weapon!"

It's funny how in this situation I could see that these soldiers, who looked to be in their late teens and early twenties, were actually nervous. It was almost like they didn't want to be in the situation either but didn't know how to get out of it while saving face.

Impatient drivers are blowing their car horns adding the obnoxious noise to a fiery situation. Toris is barking, the soldiers are yelling, my handler is screaming, drivers are slapping the sides of their car doors and I'm pleading for everyone to keep their heads. Of course I'm playing out scenarios in my mind and none of them end well. I could see that all of the soldiers had their fingers on the triggers of their weapons. One trigger pull and it would be a shootout. I would send in Toris who would neutralize one but then I would still have three shooters to contend with. Like I said, there was no good outcome.

In addition to the chaos was the fact that traffic was now backing up. I never liked traffic getting backed up because it quickly became a juicy target for an insurgent suicide bomber. For all I knew this idiot soldier I had been having problems with had purposely created a scene so traffic would become clogged and thus creating a prime target.

What was scary to me was that I could not come up with a scenario in which everyone walked away from this without bloodshed. These guys were all so hyped up that they were not using the rational side of their brain. It was all pure emotion and it was escalating past the point of no return. I could see my handler in the circle shouting so loud that his face was red and his eyes were actually bulging.

All the while I am yelling at my handler, "Shut your mouth and get out of there! Do not touch your weapon! These are young soldiers and they are scared! Do not touch your weapon!" Meanwhile Toris is spinning in circles, frothing at the mouth and frustrated that I will not allow him to enter the mix. Something is about to happen.

Out of the corner of my eye I catch some movement. Heading in our direction is the answer to our problem. Three senior Iraqi army sergeants are briskly walking side by side and in step heading in our direction. The men look sharp and exude confidence and control. They are silent and focused, never looking to the left or right but straight at the situation unfolding. Their feet hit the ground at the same moment as if they are on parade and the sound their boots make foretells their mission. Their purpose is clear to me, they are going to nip this in the bud. I recognize their bearing and instantly know we are all going to be ok.

As they were almost upon us, the sergeant in the center looked directly at me and gave me a reassuring look and slight nod of his head, which I took to mean "We've come to put a stop to this."

The four soldiers and my handler were so intent on yelling at each other that they had failed to notice the three sergeants descending on them. When only inches away from the group the sergeant in the middle shouted out above the noise a command that caused the four young Iraqi soldiers to stiffen, shoulder their rifles and immediately go to the position of attention.

I took advantage of the stillness and ordered my handler, "Get out of there and head over to the break area. Wait for me there." He immediately walked away without muttering a word. He knew he had messed up. As he passed by, I said, "Hang tight there and don't go anywhere. You got it?" He sheepishly looked at me and said, "Got it."

I turned my attention back to the four Iraqi soldiers who were being severely reprimanded by their senior sergeant. The other two sergeants were like wolves moving up and down the line of soldiers staring into their eyes, looking for even a hint of defiance. These sergeants definitely knew their craft.

I'm aware that traffic is really backed up and that we still have vehicles to search so I yell to the South American Guard Supervisor, "Get all of the drivers out of their vehicles so you can search them. I'll get my K9 teams ready to start searching the vehicles. We need to get things moving!"

180

I turned and ordered my handlers, "Once they complete the search of the drivers and their visual search of the vehicles go ahead and run your dogs. Let's get them moving!" One of the handlers yelled back, "Got it!"

As I was preparing to turn back around and watch the sergeants berate their soldiers, I noticed a short, well dressed civilian walking toward me. He had exited one of the vehicles in the line and was intently looking at me as he approached. I was impressed with his brown leather jacket and leather shoes. The guy had class and obviously money.

As he's getting closer, I recognize him as an Iraqi Army Major but I had never seen him in civilian clothes before. As the Major approached I ordered Toris to lay down and stay. An order he instantly obeyed. The order also caused him to cease barking. The Major nodded his head at me as he passed by and I returned the nod. I could see that he was heading directly for the group of soldiers.

One of the Iraqi NCO's now saw the Major walking up to them and called out an order that instantly brought the group to the position of attention. The senior sergeant spun around on his heel and faced the Major with a crisp salute. The sergeant was about to say something but the Major lifted a hand and the sergeant remained silent.

The Major walked among the men talking very calmly but I could see his words were striking fear into them. A couple flies landed on the soldiers faces but they dared not move as the Major admonished them. Suddenly the Major stood in front of the young surly soldier who had started the whole affair and with his face only inches away the Major spoke directly to him. Oh how I wished I knew what he said.

I have to admit I was impressed with the Major. He was sharp and through his bearing he projected authority, command and control. The speech was over and the sergeant saluted and took command of the small group. After screaming an order the group spun to their left and marched off to the government buildings.

The Major was now walking toward me and I was about to open my mouth and explain what happened when he cut me off, "Mr. Dennis, I was in the second lane of traffic and I was able to see and hear everything that took place. I could see this was a very dangerous situation you and your dog were in. I apologize for the unprofessional acts of my four soldiers. Mr. Dennis, I also know you will take care of your canine man, or whoever he was, who burst into this situation, making it even worse." He paused, looked down at Toris and continued, "I also know Mr. Dennis you and your dog were doing your job, and doing it correctly. I just knew if I did not come forward to help you reduce this explosive scenario that it was going to get deadly."

The Major took a second to take in a breath and at that moment I said, "Sir, I thank you for coming in and taking control of this situation, because as you stated, it was about to get deadly." I then asked the Major, "Sir, what is going to happen to the four soldiers?" He replied, "I told them that because of their unprofessionalism and for bringing shame on their country, each would be demoted by one rank and each would have one month's pay taken from them. The soldier who drew his weapon on you and your dog will be sent to a different assignment, one which most do not want. The other three are going to be assigned to different places as well. You'll never see these men again."

I thanked the Major again and he thanked me for what our teams were doing in protecting the IIG. We would have extended our hands and shook them but with Toris at my feet I knew this was a bad idea. We both smiled and the Major returned to the checkpoint to be searched by our guards. He knew the routine well. I walked back to our Checkpoint Two break area to chew out my K9 handler.

As I'm walking, I can see my two K9 teams have resumed searching the two lanes of traffic for explosives. One of the teams searched the pickup truck that had been occupied by the four Iraqi soldiers and fortunately the driver was not involved in their craziness. Operations have resumed and things are quickly returning to normal. I'm reflecting on how close we had come to an old-fashioned shootout and how thankful I was that God had sent the right people to defuse the escalating situation.

Random Death

It's one of those things and the famous saying, "If you weren't there it's hard to explain" truly sums up the specter of death in Baghdad. Every day from sunup to sundown and on into the evening hours there were the sounds of explosions off in the distance.[67] Many times they were not distant at all. With each one we knew people were most likely dying. In addition to the IEDs and VBIEDs there were also mortar attacks, rockets and RPGs fired into the Green Zone. These attacks were all point and shoot operations with the bad guys never sticking around long enough to be killed. These were frustratingly deadly.

Frustrating because our forces could not kill the guys who were firing at us and deadly because the business end of a mortar, rocket and RPG is lethal. Also irritating was the randomness of it all. Of course from the bad guys perspective this was exactly by design. If the insurgents had a pattern, they would have been killed by an Apache gunship[68] or US sniper team. Thus the mole like aspect of the attacks was effective as an irritant. However, as these teams were trying to stay alive to fight another day, they were not taking the proper time to zero in on vital targets. For the most part these mortar

---

[67] There were few explosions after midnight until around 0630 hrs. when the explosions would start up again. I was often reminded of the old cartoon of the sheep dog protecting his flock and the wolf trying to get them. The characters would actually punch in and out on a time clock. At night they would punch out and peace would descend over the fields until the following morning when the two would clock back in and the struggle resumed.

[68] The AH-64 Apache gunship is an attack helicopter in the arsenal of the United States Army. Equipped with rockets and a 30mm machine gun it is quite lethal. It was made famous by the part it played in Operation Desert Storm in 1990-1991.

teams set up, fired a couple rounds and split. These types of attacks were rarely fatal.

With anything there are exceptions, and one of these took place on April 23, 2006 when two rockets landed near an Iraqi Ministry building on Yafa Street, just a few blocks from our checkpoint. The explosions were plainly heard by us and were in quick succession to each other. Unfortunately the place of detonation was near a crowded early morning bus stop. Seven local nationals were killed and eight others wounded. Nineteen vehicles parked nearby were damaged. It was a scene of misery and chaos.

The presence of death reminded me of scenes from back home in the Texas Hill Country when the sight of dozens of buzzards flying overhead indicated something had died or that death was imminent. This is how I came to feel about the presence of death in this historic city. Of course in big cities back home in America death happened every day as well in the form of murders and traffic accidents. The difference in Baghdad was that bodies were being ripped apart daily in murders committed with explosives by faceless cowards who targeted women and children. These murders happened sometimes almost hourly. I mention such things because people of good character and morals think about such abominable atrocities in these environments and it really bothers them. Especially at night when the lights are out and people are in the quiet of their room lost in their thoughts. One could not help but ponder the lives and families dying so close. Yet, we, citizens of the most powerful country on the planet were powerless to help.

In my daily journal when I heard a far-off explosion, I would write little notes, "I pray only the suicide bomber died in that explosion" and things like that. Though I didn't know the Iraqi civilians being killed and wounded I prayed for them and hoped for their speedy recovery. Men and women seek to put on airs that they are battle hardened and "all together" but the reality is quite the opposite. Hour after hour, day after day and month after month the explosions, mortars and rockets went on and the civilian body count continued to rise. The numbers were staggering and though we didn't know true numbers at the time we could infer that many, many people were dying.

One shudders to contemplate the human toll of these indiscriminate explosions that were killing so many not only in Baghdad, but all across Iraq. 2006 would prove to be the bloodiest year in Iraq for civilians. January had started off 300 bodies higher than the previous January with 1,222 civilians killed in that month. The numbers in 2006 continue to climb from then on with 1,579 dying in February, 1,957 in March, a small drop in April 1,804 and then it continues up with May reaching 2,278, June 2,593, July 3,298, August 2,865, September 2,565, October 3,037 and November when I would leave would see 3,095 civilians die in Iraq. The religious fanatics and insurgents were deadly serious about their business and these figures demanded we remain steadfast and diligent.

This was indeed a dangerous city in a menacing land. Death was random here but it all had the same ultimate result for if it grabbed you, you were dead. The guy killed by a bullet is just as dead as the guy killed by an IED. The difference is in the way in which people died here. In the medical field it is called "mechanism of injury" and refers to how someone was injured. Was death caused by a flying piece of white-hot shrapnel or a super-heated fireball that consumed a body? It was these deaths by IEDs and VBIEDs that made headlines and left lasting impressions on everyone because the aftermath of such a mechanism of injury was so disturbing, so shocking.

Many times death by a bullet is quite clean, with a small entrance wound which nicks an artery and there is bleeding and loss of life. Not so with the suicide attacks and remote-controlled explosions for they left scenes of carnage that would terrify the first responders and the civilians standing round. The insurgents were effective at taking life and we had to make sure they didn't get through our checkpoint. The odds were against us surviving the months we had ahead of us but we would do our best or "die trying."

BOLO!

It was a very nice cool morning at CP2 and all was going well. My alert level was up because nothing's more suspicious in a warzone than a day that is going well. We had our usual stacked cars and trucks lined up in two lanes waiting to be searched by my K9 teams.

Everything was set in place and all drivers moved away from their vehicles and then hand searched by our Peruvian and Chilean security force guards. Within a minute or two we were given the thumbs up from the guards indicating we were clear to proceed with the explosives search.

I and my bomb dog Toris were standing at the front of our first row of vehicles, the beginning of a very long day I suspected. I looked to my left where my other K9 team was also standing in front of his row of vehicles to be searched. Both Toris and the other bomb dog are excited about starting out this day, they are hoping they'll be able to play with their rubber Kongs. I give the other K9 handler the thumbs up and it's time to set the day in motion.

I give Toris the command to lay down, it's something I always did with my bomb dogs. As soon as Toris was in the down position I'd focus my attention on his nose and body language. So, why this position? Well, in the down position Toris would be able to pick up any explosive odor which had fallen from this vehicle to the ground.[69] Having prepositioned us downwind these wind currents would whisk any explosive odor right into Toris' hyper alert olfactory receptors and he would in turn alert me to the presence of explosive odor.

Every dog has its own way of signaling to the handler that it is on to an odor it has been trained to search for. It's actually a fun topic of conversation among K9 handlers. With Toris he would slightly

---

[69] Explosive odor is heavy and falls to the ground. With the wind it follows the path of least resistance so it is vital to correctly preposition your canine.

lift his head and point his nose upward and then his short little stubby tail would begin to wag ever so slightly.

On this particular morning, with the search of the first row of cars of the day I noticed Toris was instantly on to odor. We had not even begun the search yet. All I had done was positioned him downwind, ordered him into the "down" position and watched his body language. After a few seconds staring at Toris I noticed that he lifted his head and began to sniff the air. Interesting. I looked at his tail but it was not wagging. Okay, I'm still intrigued though. I watch him for about thirty seconds and command him to "sit!"

Toris instantly jumps up on all fours and assumes a perfectly executed sit position. "Stay!" I then watch for a few seconds as he patiently sits there. All right. Toris is leaning forward sniffing the air and slowly wagging his stub of a tail, all the while obediently maintaining his sit position. I'm now taking quick stock, Toris is definitely air scenting and obviously onto something. There are eight vehicles in this row and one of them is about to be revealed as the source. Time to see what this workaholic canine has picked up on.

I give him the command to search and my boy is on the go, straight to the first vehicle and up to the left corner passenger side bumper. He sniffed below it a bit, then went across the front grill of the vehicle up to where the radiator cap was located and then sniffed around that area. Nothing. Swiftly he went down and across the front grill again and then to the driver's side lower front corner bumper area.

By this time I've noticed that he is searching at a brisker pace than usual. I've seen him go into overdrive mode before, but only when he's in explosive odor. I know and he knows that there is definitely explosive odor here. But where? Two questions are whizzing through my mind. First, is this just simply a residue odor, meaning the explosives have been removed but the residual odor is still present. Second, is this a VBIED and going to be detonated by the driver or someone else with a remote firing mechanism such as a cell phone?

As soon as he made the turn from the driver's side corner bumper, he went straight into the driver's side front wheel well. Toris is now sniffing harder but he was in the wheel well for only half a second before he is instantly out and now quickly sniffing the driver's door seams and then handle and then quickly jerks his head to the right and pulls back to the rear driver's side wheel well. When Toris did this I made a quick mental note that there had been a quick change in the wind direction.

Toris immediately went to the driver's side rear wheel well briefly, once again only half a second, enough time for him to stick his head in and inhale. Now he is out and moving along the rear driver's side bumper area. Rapidly Toris sniffed the outside taillights and moved to the trunk which was only opened about four inches.

Placing his huge German Shepherd paws onto the rear bumper he rose and stuck his nose down low enough to get it under the trunk lid and then with his muzzle he shoved the trunk open. Toris is now half in the trunk and half outside the trunk as he investigates the access hatch of the driver's side taillights inside the trunk compartment.

Standing up on his hind legs and resting his front paws inside the trunk he actually sidesteps his paws along the rubber seal of the lower trunk, moving from the driver's side to the passenger's side. It was an impressive display of agility and determination. As Toris is sidestepping I can see that he is air-scenting which tells me that he's still onto odor. His short stubby tail is slightly wagging, another indication that he's still on explosive odor. Ok, I'm still intrigued.

Toris is leaning hard into the passenger side of the trunk and about twelve inches from the access hatch of the passenger side taillight when I notice his stubby tail begins to wag faster. Then it wags even faster and faster. Oh boy! We've got something going on here. This is a huge "change of behavior" so I know he is getting into stronger odor. In his mind he is getting excited because he knows that if he finds the source, he'll receive high pitched verbal praise, pats and scratches on his head and the highly coveted rubber Kong.[70]

Now he's breathing through his nose faster and I looked down at his short stubby tail and see that it's wagging even faster. Toris turns his muzzle and his nose in towards the rear passenger taillights inside the trunk, almost touching them he promptly takes in a deep sniff and then instantly comes out of the trunk and goes to an immediate hard fast "final sit" position.

Toris is panting and wearing a huge smile[71] telling me he's in the presence of explosive odor and that he's at source, where the explosive odor is the strongest. I give him a verbal praise and a quick scratch on his head. My attention is now on the driver of this black Mercedes. I call out to the nearest guard, "Keep a close eye on the driver of this vehicle. Toris has indicated there's explosive odor in this vehicle."

The Peruvians and Chileans instantly take control of the driver. He had been searched previously and his cell phone removed but we were not taking any chances with this guy. The guards bring the driver out to where I can see him. He is about six feet tall and has red curly hair. His face is pockmarked making him quite distinctive. Not a good idea for an insurgent.

The Security Force team members looked into this taillight area, under the taillight and directly under the bumper of this light but they found no explosives. However, they did notice a suspicious white and gray powder substance, sort of a light film, that covered the inside of the taillight lens cover. It needed to be tested.

---

[70] The reward of the Kong is never given at the side of the vehicle that was searched because we did not want to alert an insurgent with binoculars to the fact, we had found the explosives. We realized they may have seen the dog go to a "Sit" response and guessed we found the explosives and thus remotely detonated them. Why confirm their suspicions by rewarding the canine at the scene. Get away from the vehicle ASAP and get behind the blast wall!

[71] K9 handlers and dog enthusiasts know what this smile looks like.

A special kit was brought to the rear of the vehicle and the lens of the taillight was swabbed with gauze. The sample would be tested for explosive odor by a machine that would reveal the type of explosive odor that was present. As we waited for the results on this swab, I watched the driver, his mannerisms, the way he was dressed and how he was handling the situation. If he was a bad guy, I wanted to have everything about him catalogued in my brain for future reference.

Well, for one thing, he was dressed very nice. I had to remind myself that not all insurgents were peasants. Some were well connected and had come from great wealth and used such resources to kill. I was aware of all of these things as I continued to take stock of this guy.

Wow! He wore what looked to be a very expensive black leather jacket. His dress pants appeared to be of superior quality as did his shirt. His leather shoes screamed money and of course his black Mercedes screamed leadership. This guy was up to something but what? We all stood patiently waiting for the results.

Within a couple minutes the technician who took the swab walked up to me and I could tell by the look on his face that I was not going to like what he had to say. "Dennis, the machine that was analyzing the sample taken from the taillight is broken. We walked the sample over and they said the machine has been sent out for repairs. We are supposed to get a new one tomorrow."

Ok, so in my mind I am thinking that this really sucks on many levels. First, it would have been nice to have been given this information beforehand in a briefing or an email. Second, I know this tech guy is only the messenger so I need to be cool. I looked the tech right in the eyes and he could see I was calm but also unhappy. He kind of half smiled and shrugged as if to say, "What can we do, life sucks sometimes."

I hated the words that were now coming out of my mouth, "Well, we have no other choice but to let this guy go since we have no proof that there's explosive odor on his vehicle." I could see the frustration on everyone's faces. We had a bad guy; we knew it but we couldn't prove it.

I informed the guard supervisor to make sure they took down this well-dressed guy's name, license plate number, and VIN number. I then said, "Make sure we document where this man works and lives. We need to know where to send the Iraqi Police when the results come back." I was sure the result would come back positive. Toris was not wrong.

Once all the vehicles were searched, we allowed all the drivers to return to their vehicles and continue on their way. I watched the guy in the black leather jacket closely. There was something irritating about his smug face. Almost a hint that he was thinking, "I got away with this. "He opened his car door, got in and drove off. I watched his car pulling away wondering if we had just lost our chance to nab an insurgent before he killed innocents. To say I was irritated would be putting it mildly.

The following day just before lunch I was standing with my guys at our checkpoint performing vehicle searches when off in the distance, I could hear shouting. It sounded like my name. I turned and could see the technician who controlled the explosive residue analysis computer running down to our checkpoint. He was shouting my name and waving a white receipt over his head. As he got closer, I could make out what he was yelling, "Dennis! Dennis! Toris was right! It was explosive residue in the black Mercedes!" As he reached our group he was gasping for breath, hunched over, lifting the receipt of the analysis print out for me to take and excitedly saying, "It...(gasp)...was...(gasp)...ammonia...(gasp)...nitrate! Toris was right! The guy was an insurgent!"

I was excited over this news because I knew Toris had busted this guy and he would soon be picked up. I looked at the technician and then the guard supervisor and told them, "Awesome! Now make the necessary phone calls to pick this insurgent up." A few minutes later the Chilean and Peruvians supervisor walked up and said, "Mr. Dennis I have bad news." I stood there expressionless as he continued, "The guard I tasked with taking down the information of the vehicle and driver said that he had forgotten to do it. He was busy and had become sidetracked."

It is not my personality to get angry and yell at folks. If the job requires me to yell at a potential threat that is one thing but to berate a coworker or employee is not something I do. Now, I do get angry and when I heard the news that one of our guards had failed to do the simple task of writing down numbers off of a vehicle and identification card. Well, I was fairly upset but I received the news in silence and very sternly responded, "You will counsel this guard, won't you?" The supervisor indicated that he most assuredly would. I replied, "Good and please make him aware that there is a terrorist associated with explosives running free in this city because he failed to do his job." The supervisor was ashamed that one of his men had failed at such a vital task. I could see it on his face and demeanor. It's why I trusted these men, because they truly desired to do a good job and when they failed, they felt it deep inside. Good men will.

Within minutes there was a BOLO sent out, "Be On the look-out for a six-foot-tall curly red-haired man with a pock marked face, black leather jacket, light blue dress shirt, black dress pants and leather shoes. Individual drives a black Mercedes and is wanted for questioning regarding the positive results of explosives scan of his vehicle. Suspected insurgent."

Perhaps the individual in question knew his "goose was cooked" because we never saw him again. We can only hope that he got spooked and decided to rethink his choices in life. We all hoped he had not gone on to create or transport explosives that killed any innocent people. Of course, we all kind of hoped that perhaps he had died making a bomb that blew up in his face. Or maybe he died from a drone strike while he manufactured the evil devices. We can only hope. What it all came down to though was that I truly believed this was a probe by the insurgents. On this day they discovered that our dogs and handlers were awesome and that they would be unable to sneak explosives through Checkpoint Two.

Part Two

Checkpoint Miami

Shocking News

Arriving back in Baghdad on March 11th, 2006 after some R&R (rest and relaxation) with my wife Debbie, I immediately made way to the office of our director of operations Mitchell Raleigh. Mr. Raleigh had a mountain of responsibilities yet when I entered his office, I could see he was glad to see me. After a few pleasantries he got right to it, "Dennis, I know you've done a lot for Checkpoint Two. I know you made it your baby but I need you for another assignment." He let that settle in for a minute and then continued, "The US is building a new embassy which when it's completed will be the largest in the world. All traffic going to the construction site has to pass through Checkpoint Miami. Some of the guys call it the New Embassy Compound Checkpoint or NEC for short. Anyway, I need you at this checkpoint."

Now I must confess that when I first heard I was going to be moved from Checkpoint Two I was upset. Being a professional I kept this emotion to myself and never let on I was displeased. I realized Mr. Raleigh was giving me a huge honor in asking me to protect the US Embassy. My thoughts were interrupted when my director continued, "I need you to lock down security at this checkpoint just as you did for Checkpoint Two. I know that you, more than most, will know what a huge responsibility this is. This is why I am asking you to do it."

I smiled, extended my hand and said, "Mr. Mitchell, I'd be honored and I will do my best. Does our arrangement still stand that I can have whoever I want or transfer out those who don't measure up?" Without a moment's hesitation he responded, "Absolutely." Ok, that was it and the new course for my time in Baghdad over the next eight months was locked in. Next stop. My boys Toris and Laky!

Walking toward the kennel I could see both Laky and Toris in adjacent kennels lying on the floor near the gate. I tried to sneak up on them but the wind changed and they had my scent. I knew because they jumped up and started barking their heads off. These guys were the best. I had a smile stretched from ear to ear and using a high-pitched voice said, "Hey Toris! Hey Laky boy! How have you guys been!" Oh man they were barking so loud, fussing at me for being gone so long but they got over their hurt feelings pretty quick and were soon licking me all over my face as I ruffed up their necks and buried my face in their fur kissing them. Oh it was wonderful to see my boys again.[72]

I gave Laky and Toris a quick inspection and was glad to see they had been well tended while I was gone. They had good weight and their coats looked great. Their kennels were clean and they looked very healthy. It did my heart good to see my war buddies. We all had a new job now and I was looking forward to the challenge. I knew these two were ready to work. Checkpoint Miami. Hmm. Sounded fantastic, sort of like a nice place to hang out. I knew better though; I mean this was Baghdad after all. Time to check out the layout.

First, the location was unique as it literally bordered the Tigris River. Standing at my checkpoint I could see the water gently rolling by and I could also see tall buildings on the other side of the Tigris. The buildings seemed very close and that's because they were. The fact that these buildings would make a nice sniper's nest did cross my mind. The distance from where I checked vehicles at Checkpoint Miami to the other side of the Tigris was only 700 feet. This had dire ramifications for us because doing the math one day I calculated that a 7.62 bullet fired from a Russian AK47 travels at 2,820 feet a second. This meant that by the time I heard the crack of the bullet being fired it had already passed by my head and traveled another two thousand feet. In a way this was a pleasant thought because I knew that if I was hit, I'd never hear it. There'd be sudden darkness. Another perk of the job.

Right up against the Tigris River didn't seem to be a good place to build the Embassy but yet there it was, going up. Fortunately the

---

[72] The reunion was done one dog at a time. My two alpha boys would have eaten each other alive if I put them together so while I hugged one the other was barking a jealous bark of protest. I loved every minute of it.

compound did have a sturdy wall that was quite tall. It surrounded the embassy of course but if insurgent combat swimmers decided to make a break for the compound, they would only have to dash fifty yards to reach the wall. We would often marvel at what appeared to be pure incompetence that placed the embassy here. I would joke with the guys, "I have no idea why it was built in such a position. Insurgents can take easy shots at it all day and night with a sniper rifle, mortars and rockets. They may as well paint a big bullseye on the side of it."

There was something we knew for sure and that was the fact that we would give our lives to protect this little piece of US territory. Of course I also had a little secret. Toris was dual trained as a patrol canine meaning all I had to do was say a single word and he would run down and subdue anyone I singled out. I kept this little secret knowing if an insurgent made a break for the wall, he would have to outrun Toris and that was impossible.

I soon discovered that at my new checkpoint we would be searching from one hundred to one hundred and fifty vehicles a day. The majority were long gravel trucks, cement trucks, dump trucks, cranes and other utility vehicles. The majority of the vehicles were directly related to the construction process so there were very few civilians at this checkpoint. There were also several food deliveries for the construction crews. This was a whole other experience compared to Checkpoint Two. I was ready for the challenge though. Checkpoint Miami/NEC here we come! Thank you for this opportunity Lord!

Checkpoint Miami aka Checkpoint NEC (New Embassy Compound)

View of Checkpoint Miami from atop a T-Wall

The Sandbox

When I was assigned to Checkpoint Miami, I took quarters closer to the new checkpoint, which was nice. Checkpoint Two had been quite a distance from our kennels and housing so the closer proximity during the coming scorching days of summer would prove to be a blessing.

This section of the Green Zone was called Camp Jackson and it, like our new checkpoint was located right up against the Tigris River. I would guess that the river was no more than 100 yards from where I slept. I was even closer to the Tigris than I was the night of the huge firefight outside our compound a few months prior.

A unique feature of Camp Jackson was a huge in-ground swimming pool fifty to seventy-five yards in length and forty to fifty yards wide with two entrances at each end of the pool. Rumor was that the pool belonged to one of Saddam Hussein's sons, Uday Hussein, who was known to be a sadistic torturer, rapist and murderer who enjoyed watching those under his power beg for their lives. The tale related to me was that Uday had crocodiles brought in and placed in the pool and then his enemies thrown to the starving reptiles. I could find no corroborating evidence regarding the story but that's how it went.

Turns out it was true that the pool had belonged to the Hussein family but the US had other plans for it. When our troops occupied and then created the Green Zone the pool was drained and then tons of sand brought in converting this pool to a rather nice soccer field complete with goal posts and night lighting.

I must confess that it was enjoyable to sit along the edge of this converted pool and watch the men below playing soccer, laughing, running, kicking the ball all over this homemade field and all the while forgetting about the cares and fears of the war and the dangerous city that surrounded them. I could just imagine the Hussein family gathered around sipping their drinks and lounging around never dreaming that Americans would own this pool one day.

At the end of a hot swing shift, I'd load up Toris and Laky and drive down to this converted soccer field, which I called "The Sandbox." I'd take my two boys there for a fun time at the end of their long day and these two boys absolutely loved it. We'd play what's called "The Exchange." I'd throw a red or black Kong as hard and as high as I could, Toris or Laky would peel off after it, grab it with their wide open German Shepherd mouth, turn quickly in the sand for a return back to me, knowing once they got within ten to fifteen feet of me, they'd drop the Kong on the run. While the Kong is rolling towards me, I'd let loose with another one thrown far off for them to chase. This exchange teaches the dogs, "You give me one, and I'll in turn give you back another." It works great!

Walking down the steps into this fabled "Pool of Death" was truly creepy. My imagination ran wild feeling sorrow for the unfortunate people who feared for their lives, knowing they were to be eaten alive by monster crocodiles. Once at the bottom of these huge steps, it was impressive just how large the pool had been. The walls around were ten to fifteen feet high. This had been no ordinary pool.

Once at the bottom of the steps, I'd walk about halfway across the converted pool looking left and right to make certain no one was resting in the sand leaning up against the walls. I'd then look to the opposite end of the pool, well, sand box, where the other steps were located, making certain no one was there. This was always my routine, I had to make certain that no one was down in the vicinity of Toris because he was also trained as a patrol dog with "controlled aggression" tactics. This meant that on command he was trained to take people down hard with his teeth. He was not a dog that would randomly attack someone, well, unless an idiot attacked me. Otherwise he would need to receive a command to attack. Toris was not a canine that people could pet. Every once in a while, he would surprise me by befriending a guard but it was an extremely rare occurrence.

I knew I was taking a chance having Laky and Toris off leash down in this giant sand box but I felt the benefits outweighed the risks. There were a couple of times I spotted men wanting to come down the steps but I'd intercept them and explain to them I just needed a few more minutes to let my two dogs unwind from a long day of searching for explosives and car bombs. Invariably these guys always understood, they would always say something like, "No worries man, your dogs are keeping us safe, take as long as you need." Very cool!

So, I'd bring Toris out of the crate, break him for a few minutes, and then we'd trot down the pool steps. The entire time we are trotting down the steps Toris is talking (barking) at me, he's been waiting for this fun all day. As soon as my feet hit the ground of our personal sandbox, I'd lift my right arm up high pull back as far as I could and then let it rip. Toris knew it was coming, so as I'm pulling back my arm, Toris spins around and is off running, fast. I'd let the Kong go as hard and high as I could.

It was fascinating to watch Toris running full force. When I'd throw the Kong almost straight over his path of running, his ears would turn slightly to the rear and he'd turn his head slightly upwards looking for the Kong about to fly overhead by a good fifteen to twenty feet above him. The Kong has a hollow center with openings at both ends, and because it's flying through the air wind whisks through these openings making a noise, which humans cannot hear. Toris could hear it just fine and he was on it. Soon his eyes lock onto the Kong as it's coming towards and then over him. Sometimes it'd be just low enough as it was about to go over his head that he would jump straight up and catch it with his big jaws. He would quickly turn towards me, crunching down several times as hard as he could to make sure it was dead.

Toris always ran up to me with this twinkle of happiness in his eyes. He'd lower his head while running full force towards me in preparation to release the Kong in my direction, knowing once he'd do this the toy would roll or bounce directly towards me, and then boom I'd throw the exchange Kong. Toris was off and running full force for the next catch. We'd do this for a good 15 minutes and then it was time to cool down. I'd stroke his head with my hand, pull out my dog brush and do some additional bonding and grooming, which we both loved.

Now it's Laky's turn. As we are now heading towards the pool steps to leave, I call out to the few who want to come down into the sandbox, "Ok guys, just about another twenty to thirty minutes. I need to get my second bomb dog so he can come down and play as well." The response was always, "No problem! Take your time! These dogs keep us safe and besides, were enjoying watching them play ball with you!"

By this time Toris is not running up the stairs, he's pooped. I let him carry his red Kong in his mouth all the way to the back of the truck, and of course the entire time he's chomping away on it. Once at the back of the truck I'd give him the command to "Sit" and then the command to release the Kong into my hand. Once he did this, I'd command "Hup!" and up he'd go into his crate. I'd give the command to stay, then close and lock his crate door, then say, "Good Boy!" Toris would plop down exhausted but happy.

Now it's Laky's turn, and of course, you guessed it, Toris is now having jealous fits, barking his head off, he wants to go again. As big as Toris is, he's turning circles inside his crate. The crate is shaking and every once in a while he gets his body wedged, stuck between the two side walls of the crate, but of course wiggles himself free and is at the crate door barking his head off and trying to get his teeth into the metal bars of the door to pull it open. Toris had a lot of heart.

I unlock Laky's crate door, swing it halfway open, grab his collar, attach my leash to the "O-ring" and once I know we are hooked up on the collar, I say, "Ok buddy, let's go have fun!" He jumps out of his crate as if someone shot him out of a circus cannon. Toris goes insane! Barking, feverish with jealousy.

As Laky and I are walking towards the break area I look over my shoulder at Toris in his crate, the dog crate is shaking, I can hear the loud scratching of his nails up against the plastic of his crate, it's as if there were five monkeys loose in his crate all fighting for one banana. I just shook my head in amazement that he still had all of this energy after searching for explosives during his afternoon and evening, then played hard for 15 minutes in the sandbox. I've heard dogs keep 10% energy in reserve as a backup when more energy is needed so I guessed Toris was using it all up this night. I knew he would sleep well.

Laky has finished his business and I pick up his and Toris' droppings and discard them into the trash can. Laky and I head towards the steps leading down to our play area. He is all pumped up as well, he's jumping two steps at a time to get into the sand. He looks back at me with this look of, "Well, are you going to throw the Kong or not knucklehead?" I'd laugh, toss the Kong in an upward motion with my right hand, yell out to Laky, "You ready Big Boy?" Bring my right arm back as far as I could then let it rip forward.

Laky was not like Toris. Laky would wait until he'd see the Kong leave my hand, then the chase was on. Sometimes I'd throw it at an angle to the wall. This would get the dogs thinking it was going to be near the wall when it hit, when in fact, it bounced off the wall, making them quickly turn their body to the center of the field. I liked throwing in this variable, it kept them thinking, and thinking quickly.

Guys waiting to come down into the sandbox would sit and dangle their legs over the side walls and watch Laky race by under their feet. I could see the smiles on their faces and hear their laughter, slapping the sides of their legs, taking it all in, perhaps thinking of their own dogs back home.

I ran Laky for a good 15 minutes playing this exchange game with the Kongs. When Laky was tired, he'd hold the Kong in his mouth and just lay down, right there and chew on his red Kong for about ten minutes. He'd prop the Kong between his paws and go to sleep. As soon as he laid down, I'd get after him and say, "No, come on, let's go to the truck." Sure enough, he'd get up. He knew the routine. Laky knew we were now going to the kennels where he'd be able to lay down on his canvas Kuranda dog bed, which he absolutely loved.

As we're walking closer to the truck, Toris is not making a sound, he's not even moving, he's just lying in the bottom of his crate with his big beautiful eyes looking at me, as if to say, "I'm beat, time to head to the kennels and tuck us in." I could not help but laugh out loud at what I was seeing, he wore himself out in his crate.

I gave Laky his sit command, his command to release the Kong into my hand, his command to stay, and then his command to jump up into his crate. I made sure both dog doors on the crates were safety latched into place, double locked, closed up the tailgate door, jumped into my driver's seat, and off we were to the dog kennels.

There they were, side by side, two war dogs who had served their country well this day, both laid out in their crates enjoying the cool breeze off the Tigris River as I drove them to a good night's sleep, and the bonus, still to come. They knew each night I'd pull out of the deep freezer a special treat for them. Once I got them into their individual kennels, I'd get the frozen bottles of water I had placed in the freezer at the start of my shift. I'd unstrap my K-Bar knife from my hip and cut the plastic bottle away from the ice. The frozen mold was in the shape of a quart sized bottle of water. I'd then place it on their Kuranda dog bed so they could lick on it through the night, just to give them that little extra for a great job well done for their country. Yeah, good memories were made in "The Sandbox."

Moon Dust

Everything was dirty or made of dirt. It blew in on the winds and settled on everything. There was very little grass to keep it contained so it just had free reign to go wherever it pleased. The only thing that made the place livable was that a lot of the city was covered in asphalt or pavement. Still though there was dirt everywhere.

It was a special kind of dirt, a fine almost dust that seemed to take flight with the slightest instigation. It reminded me of moon dust. The images of the astronaut's footprints in the soil of the moon showed how fine the dirt was. This place reminded me of that.

Every morning I'd dust off all of the flat surfaces in my room and by the next morning you could see a fine layer of dust once again on everything. I recall after I returned home from Iraq, my dear wife Debbie asked why I was spitting as we were walking to go somewhere. She said you've never spit in all the years we've been married. I was surprised as my answer revealed, "I was not aware I was spitting, I guess it's a habit I picked up in Iraq." Well, it was. Dirt and sand were always getting into my mouth so I was always spitting it out.

It didn't help that we worked all day on a route that was mostly a hard dirt road with a few paved sections. All day long cement trucks and gravel trucks and loaders of every kind and size were ambling through our checkpoint and each time they kicked up a miserable cloud of this fine dust.

At Checkpoint Miami or NEC, a white-water truck, just a bit bigger than a cement truck, would come by and spray water onto the road leading to our checkpoint. This truck had a large metal pipe which was just below the rear bumper and just as long. The pipe had several holes on the bottom which allowed water to spray out. Someone had decided to have this water truck come by a few times a day and water down the road leading to our checkpoint, and inspection area. Truthfully the effort did help but only for about an hour or so and then it was back to the billowing clouds of fine moon dust again choking us and making life miserable.

There was another bright spot to the arrival of these trucks though for I would wave them down and ask if I could use the hose on the side of the truck to cool down my dogs. With the temps pushing 120 degrees Fahrenheit the dog's energy was sapped after a while of searching. The driver responded with a smile and said, "I love dogs. In fact I have a German Shepherd at home right now. Use all the water you need." Toris was first and he absolutely loved getting hosed down. He would jump around, frisky and giving me drive by kisses. He was so animated and instantly revived.

Laky was the exact opposite. He would just stand there and let the cool water run down his sides and head. His eyes would close and he would just bask in the wondrous feeling of the cool water caressing his sides. All the while, ramrod straight with eyes squinted shut, enjoying the moment.

All good things must come to an end and soon the water truck was on its way and the effects of its passing by soon diminished completely. The clouds of fine dust would rise, our eyes would burn as we blinked the coagulated sand from our tear ducts. Our special sunglasses seemed to help but they made our faces so much hotter. It was one of those tough decisions in life determining just what kind of miserable we wanted to be.

Many of us took to wearing scarves around our heads like the locals because it worked. I felt bad for our dogs but there was no way we could cover their noses and mouths. Even if there would have been a way to do it the dogs would have hated it and pulled them off. We had to face facts though, the dogs were there to sniff out explosives so they would need to have their noses clear. There were some things we could do to assist though.

My routine was to tend to their noses during their break and to allow them to relieve their bowels. Prior to searching I'd get Toris or Laky out of their crate and I'd walk them to the break area, where they could relieve their bowels. This is critical to give your bomb dog an opportunity to unload prior to searching for explosives. We wanted our dogs focusing on searches not the needs of their bladders and colons.

Walking alongside Toris or Laky while on their potty break I'd look down at their nose to insure it was clear of any of this dust. Then we would head out to the search area and begin the day. One by one trucks would come through and the moon dust seemed to always hang in the air. During a search I would look down at Toris or Laky and see a fine tan cream looking mud slowly streaming down their nose. I would instantly stop the search, pull a water bottle from my pocket and have whichever dog I had go to a sit position. I would tip the bottle so the water slowly ran over his nose and then I would take my other hand and rub this disgusting ooze from his nose. I would purposely splash some up their nose which caused them to sneeze it out. Tan colored particles of saliva would spatter my pants. I was looking forward to the day I could get out of here and I hoped I would be able to take these dogs home with me.[73]

However, we had a few months left and I needed to protect the lives under our charge so we cleaned up as best we could and carried on. Of course the dogs never complained. That's why it was so vital that we, their handlers and buddies, were vigilant and very attentive to their welfare. Little things like sand and dirt building up in the nasal cavity could be so irritating and debilitating for a dog so I constantly monitored and cleansed their noses. It was a full-time job at this checkpoint and a task I did not take lightly. It's the small things. The attention to the smallest detail that makes or breaks a dog team.

---

[73] I was the handler and trainer of Toris and Laky. I spent day after day with them but in the end, they were not my property. The thought of leaving them behind created a pit in my stomach. I loved them.

Toris has the "moon dust" removed

Laky dove into a mound of moon dust for his Kong.

A Visit from Anisoptera

I challenged myself, that I would try to find something of beauty each day to remind myself that there was such a thing even in a war zone. It is so easy to get bitter surrounded by so much death and destruction. We humans build internal barriers so that we can deal with these things. My response was to challenge myself to find beauty around me each and every day. I was able to do it and sometimes it appeared at the most awkward times.

My new checkpoint was there to guard the grounds of the new US Embassy that was under construction. It was the whole reason I had been selected to handle this checkpoint; because of my strict adherence to detail at Checkpoint Two.

A glaring deficiency of security at the new checkpoint was the fact that any insurgent with the will to do so could have jumped in the Tigris, used some amazing skills at swimming and then come ashore only a few feet from our checkpoint. The obstacles faced by such a combat swimmer were nil. The only friend we had was the current which was swift. So, using all of my military training on base defense I set about improving our position.

I had the guard tower moved by crane to a position that would cover approaches from the river and both roads leading to our area. I then had camouflage netting placed over our rest area to provide shade for our working dogs. Shade would keep the dogs cooler and thus in their jobs much longer.

Additionally I had long strands of razor wire strewn all across the approaches from the river. Then down in the water, below the surface I had more rolls of wire strung so that unsuspecting insurgents would get caught and shredded in the current.[74]

---

[74] I had been puzzling over my necessity for razor wire. I had not the slightest clue where I could attain it. I knew that going through government channels was famously slow. One day while walking Toris along the Tigris River I spotted three large spools of razor wire lying along the road in the bushes. I smiled and thanked God for the speedy delivery and answer to prayer.

This was a task we had to complete on our own. There was no work crew we could acquire by filling out an order form. No, we were the work crew and I found the best way to utilize available manpower was to set the example by just jumping to work and let the others with a work ethic see my efforts and then decide on their own to jump in. This is what I did with the razor wire. I can't remember how many liters of blood we shed setting up the long lines of the accursed stuff but I can assure you it was quite a lot. One thing though, we knew it worked and seeing it spread along the banks of the Tigris filled me with a little more sense of security.

I was finishing up the distribution of the razor wire when my daily item of beauty made itself known to me. It was an 'Anisoptera," otherwise known as a "Dragonfly." It was large, at least three inches long and was resting its delicate body on the razor wire we had just finished laying out along the Tigris. I really wanted to see its face and get some photos.

Fortunately my camera was always by my side and I had an awesome zoom lens which I used to really zoom in and see the details of this insect. Slowly bringing my camera up to my eye I could see its face just as clear as crystal. Zooming in provided great detail in its eyes which were mesmerizing. It was looking straight at me and was not concerned in the least with my presence.

I began to shoot many pictures of the dragonfly. It's bright purple, blue, pink and brown body was magnificent. Its wings were transparent and crisscrossed by what looked like veins but it really reminded me of a stained-glass window. Each wing had sections partitioned off with crystal-clear paper-thin material. I was enthralled and totally removed from the war and the stench of death.

I was a student of nature and gladly studied this amazing creation. It looked away and then after a few seconds would look back at me. I kept my camera to my eye letting the zoom lens show me details I would never have dreamed possible in this place.

My son Dennis mentioned to me that the picture was one of his favorites that I had taken during my time in Iraq. The reason I took the photo was for the same reason it was so well liked, I wanted to convey to the viewer what I was seeing, a delicate magnificent creature in the midst of a war-torn land. Oblivious to the dangers surrounding it only knowing what had been passed on for thousands of years; to take wing, eat, procreate and then die. I knew it would only live a few months but, in a way, I was envious of its ignorance of its environment. How wonderful to just take wing and go wherever and whenever one wished.

It will sound crazy but I thanked the dragonfly for stopping by and visiting me. I was thankful for the display of stupendous beauty in such a horrible environment. I looked heavenward and thanked God for creating such a beautiful creature. I smiled, placed my camera back in my bag and walked back to the checkpoint. Beauty was indeed all around me. I just had to look for it and be wise enough to see it.

Anisoptera visiting me at Checkpoint Miami.

Two Antennas

It was hot! Friggin hot! This is a significant statement for a Texan to make because we know all about heat. Yet, I had to admit that it was ridiculously hot! In these temps Laky and Toris were only good for about twenty to thirty minutes of searching and then I would have to give them a rest.

That sun was merciless. I had been kind of spoiled because when I arrived in Iraq for the first time back in October the temps were actually quite nice. Reminded me a lot like Texas. Then through November, December and January we had to wear jackets as the temperature would drop down into the low 40s.

Well, now I was really being shown what heat was all about. Of course wearing a Kevlar vest, helmet, K-bar battle knife, 9mm and Kong bag didn't help with my own heat issues but the first priority for a K9 handler is his dog so I had to cool Laky down and I had a great idea how to do it fast.

Laky is walking along at a gentle smooth pace, just enjoying the peace, sniffing the ground at times and lifting his leg to leave his mark. I was heading for the Tigris River, great place for cooling down my dogs.

I'm enjoying the leisurely walk and every once in a while, I'd just lightly run one or two fingers of my left hand over the beautiful black and brown fur on his back. He'd always turn and look up at me with this happy look of approval. I would smile at him and ask if he was ready for a nice cool swim.

Suddenly Laky jerked his head up and turned toward the Tigris. His ears were pointing straight up, taller than I ever remember seeing them before. They reminded me of two tall antennas. Looking in the same direction as he I could see Laky was interested in an area across the river where a children's school and playground was located. Near the right corner of a large red bricked building stood a large tree which immediately was vacated by dozens of black birds in a hurry. For some reason in that flash of a second my mind

211

went to a scene from a war movie I'd seen years before in which a mortar had been fired and birds shot out of a tree in fright. My mind was instantly back to the present. Mortar!

I spin and dart for the duck and cover bunker at the checkpoint. At this point I have not heard the "thump" of the mortar being fired but am running on instincts. As I am sprinting with Laky, I know that if the mortar lands near our checkpoint I will be killed or wounded because there is no way I will make it in time but perhaps I can warn my guys. "In Coming! In Coming! Take Cover! Mortar Coming In!" I can see the guys all turn toward me, seeing me running and then they dart toward the bunker. At least I know they will be safe.

I could hear the quiet swish made by the fins of the mortar as it passed overhead, I knew right away it would pass us by, I've adapted an ear for them as so many have blasted over us in the past.

I am still running though for their may be other mortar rounds on the way. Wham! The mortar hit about a block from us in an empty field. I could hear a thump so I knew another was on the way but in actuality I knew there may be two. Sure enough I could hear the swish of air and I thought, "Oh man! This is going to be close!"

I'm not going to make the bunker, "Laky! Down!" My amazing partner knows me very well and he can sense something is not right. In an instant he drops to the ground and I cover him with my body trying to squeeze his vital parts under my chest and head which is fairly well protected with Kevlar.[75] Wham! Dirt, rocks and debris flying in all directions. Chunks of earth are peppering my back and legs but thankfully nothing metallic has slashed into me. I check Laky for any injuries and quickly discover that he's good to go so we continue on to the bunker.

---

[75] They make Kevlar vests for dogs but in the heat of Iraq they would kill a dog from hyperthermia

However, the insurgents picked the wrong day to fire on the "Green Zone." There must have been a passing Iraqi Police or Army unit or perhaps a US Army patrol because suddenly a huge gunfight broke out from the same area the mortars had been launched from. I had to be sure insurgents were not trying to swim the Tigris so I had to check on the situation. I took a deep breath and looked out from the "Duck and Cover Bunker" up at my machine gunner in the tower. He was looking down at the two roads approaching the NEC Checkpoint sweeping his big gun back and forth at the two approaching roads, waiting for insurgents to attempt to attack our checkpoint.

I yelled up at the gunner but he did not hear me so I took in a deep breath and ran with Laky at my side toward the Tigris River. I got to the corner back edge of our NEC Checkpoint building, ordered Laky into the "Down" position and peeked around the corner of the building. I'm sweeping my eyes along the road insurgents would have to cross if they were attempting to breach our area.

There was no one in sight and definitely no one in the river. However, on the other side of the river, just behind the buildings and the children's school there was an intense gun battle going on. Automatic weapons fire was shattering the air and from the sound I could tell it was taking place on Abu Nawas street and the battle was a running fight moving from right to left, block by block.

Soon the gun fight moved near the 14th of July bridge. If the insurgents decided to move across the bridge, they would pass 200 feet from me. Fortunately the bad guys stayed across the bridge and just kept backing down Abu Nawas block by block. Suddenly the weapons fire ceased and everyone looked West to the sky. A US Army Apache gunship was approaching. I could hear the very distinctive "Chop! Chop! Chop!" as the rotors swirled through the air creating thrust. The helicopter was so low that I could see the pilot and weapons specialist. I could see they were looking down at the neighborhood searching for targets. All eyes were on the gunship.

213

AK47 rifles were once again on full auto firing at targets on the street. I knew then that the bad guys were still there and could not help but wonder if they were aware of the gunship hovering above them. Suddenly "Bruuuuu! Bruuuuu!" the sound carried quickly from this distance and I could see the smoke wafting from under the helicopter as its main gun let loose a torrent of 30mm bullets. The force of the 30mm gun firing caused the Apache gunship to rise and slowly reverse momentum for a second or two. It was impressive to say the least and I was so glad they were on our side.

I could see the rounds punching down into the neighborhood and then silence enveloped the city. Not a sound other than the rotors of the helicopter, not a rifle, not a grenade and not a mortar, just nothing. The US helicopter then slowly turned and headed back to where it had come from. There was no more shooting and no more explosions. The Apache had finished the ordeal in a matter of seconds. I looked at my guys and we just stared in amazement. We knew then that the guys who had fired on us were dead and the truck they used to carry their mortar looked more like swiss cheese than a vehicle. It was such a great feeling to know these guys would not be firing on us anymore.

It reminded me of our frustrations at Checkpoint Two when day after day we would get mortars inbound but the shooters were never caught. Their standard mode of operation was to fire two or three and then load up and take off. As we sheltered in our bunkers we longed for the day when the insurgents would have that horrible feeling in their stomachs like we had the previous several months as we ran for bunkers, seeking shelter. Well, today was the day. These guys had fired their mortars at us, stayed longer than they should have and then run into a patrol who opened fire on them and then called in the gunship who ended their mortar firing days once and for all.

We celebrated for a few minutes and then returned to the business at hand; checking vehicles for explosives. We knew that another mortar team would be on the other side of the Tigris on the morrow but for now the air was free of the threat of mortars and we could strike one up for the good guys; the good ole Red, White and Blue! Finally!

I often wondered how many lives that Apache gunner saved when he eradicated that mortar team. It is certain he saved our lives and many others. Someone else had saved my life that day and it was Laky and his two antennas that sit on top of his head. Those ears had instantly zeroed in on the threat and where it came from. I had not heard the initial thump as the mortar left the tube but Laky had. I trusted Laky, so when I saw his change of behavior, I dialed myself in. I thank God for creating such amazing animals with such awesome hearing. As we say in the K9 world, "Trust Your Dog!"

Battling the Heat

Laky had to see the Veterinarian because of burst membranes in his nose caused by the intense heat that could reach over 130 degrees Fahrenheit.

I fashioned this "cool down pool" using a tarp and old cracked cement mixing bowl found alongside the road. After lining the bowl with bricks I laid down the tarp and filled it with 52 quarts of bottled water. The dogs LOVED it! One method of many used to cool them down.

Expect the Unexpected

Toris was lounging in the shade and I was watching children play at a school across the Tigris River. Boys who looked to be in Middle School were playing soccer in the school yard. This was the same school grounds the insurgents had earlier used to fire their mortars at us. I suppose I was thinking of my family back home as I watched the children play.

I heard the deep groan of a large truck in a lower gear heading toward Checkpoint Miami. I turned away from the sight of the school and walked toward Toris. When I saw the truck my heart skipped a beat. It was a long bed gravel truck and it had a peculiarity that we had been briefed about. In fact, it was only the day before that I had received the new information.

In an earlier incident a long bed gravel truck had pulled up to a target they could not pass up. Such a truck was a daily symbol of the ongoing construction in the International Zone so no one gave the truck a second thought. Suddenly the truck that contained almost 800 pounds of explosives detonated sending shards of metal and hundreds of thousands of small rocks flying in all directions.

The carnage was massive as almost everyone at the checkpoint was killed. An American M1 Abram tank posted nearby was actually shoved four feet by the concussion. Four were killed and even more wounded. Of those wounded several had been interviewed and asked to give any specifics about the truck or driver that might have seemed odd.

One after another the wounded were interviewed and no one had even the slightest bit of information that could help. Well, except for one individual who vividly remembered the truck pulling up. This civilian thought it strange that a long piece of rigid wire was protruding straight up from the center of the load of gravel in the trailer. Could this be a clue?

The information quickly made the rounds and everyone of course had their ideas on what this piece of wire or metal could have been

217

used for. The one thing everyone seemed to agree on was that it was most likely used as a receiver to take in the signal from a spotter who detonated the explosive by remote. Insurgents had found that many of their so-called martyrs were deciding at the last second that they did not want to die so they were not detonating their bombs. This problem was fixed by implementing the remote detonations.

You can imagine my feeling then when I looked up on this day to see a long bed gravel truck driving up with a long rigid piece of wire sticking out of a large mound of gravel. Well, this is it, I guess. "Toris, today is the day we see Jesus."

I noticed there was only one occupant and then glancing down at the front tires I noticed they were well worn. Suicide bombers had taken to purchasing new tires for their suicide vehicles because past attempts had been thwarted by the simple act of a flat tire while on the way to kill innocent people. Looking down at the tires of this truck I could see the tires had a lot of miles on them. Well, that is one good thing at least.

So now, for the obvious situation that has me worried. There before me, plain as day is a long section of rigid wire sticking straight up out of the center of the gravel. At this moment I looked down at Toris and he looked up at me panting, with his tongue hanging out the side of his mouth, ready to get to work searching the truck. He was blissfully unaware of our predicament. Well, at least this truck would not make it to the embassy grounds.

I glanced over at the Chilean supervisor and he shook his head slowly side to side. Yeah, he had seen it to and came to the same conclusion. We're going to die. I yelled to the supervisor, "Have your men point their weapons at the driver and tell the translator to instruct the driver to stop his truck and not approach the checkpoint any closer!" I then said, "Be sure to tell the translator to warn the driver, that if he fails to comply, he will be fired upon." The message was translated, the driver stopped his vehicle.

I had more instructions for the driver, "Have the interpreter tell the driver to put his hands in the air!" The message was being translated. I wanted to see his hands to see if he was holding a detonator. I also knew that the wire was most likely for remote detonation. I was hoping that if it was for remote access that perhaps the distance was too great. Then again maybe it was for the driver who would dial up the number to the cell phone connected to the antenna and bomb. At any rate we weren't taking any chances.

"Tell the driver to turn off his truck with one hand very slowly and to then exit his vehicle keeping his hands visible to us!" My orders were quickly relayed and the driver dutifully complied. As he did the Chilean and Peruvian guards moved up on the truck with their automatic rifles raised and aimed at the center of the driver's chest. One false move and it would be his last.

The driver was quickly searched and moved behind a concrete t-wall where he was interrogated further by one of the guards and the interpreter. Meanwhile I look down at Toris and am getting ready to begin the search of this truck. I hear some metallic noise and am horrified to look up and see the Chilean supervisor has climbed up into the bed of this truck and is walking on top of the gravel. I was dumbfounded. I didn't know whether to be outraged at his idiocy or to be honored to know such a brave man. Before I could tell him to get the heck out of there so we could search for explosive odor he grabbed the wire with his right hand and was pushing the gravel away from it with his left.

I couldn't believe this. "Get down from there! You're going to get us all killed! Toris and I will search! Let's see if he detects any odor of explosives!" The supervisor yells down to me with not the least hint of anger, more like, business as usual, "It is my responsibility to first search the truck for obvious signs of explosives. Once I have cleared it, I will turn it over to you and Toris." Well, he had a point. He was correct. That was the process but I could not help but smile. It would have been so much faster to run Toris around the truck.

What could I say? Technically he was right but I figured that since we could plainly see something sticking out of the bed of gravel I would just make a run through with Toris. I had to smile a

219

little. This guy was dedicated to his job and absolutely fearless. These guys did not want to look like sissies in front of us so these sort of demonstrations of courage were a normal thing for these amazing South Americans. You got to love guys like that, with such courage and devotion to duty.

My instincts were telling me to put some safe distance between me and this truck while he's on top of the gravel digging around with his hands. I just stood there though because with such a display of courage I couldn't let him face the danger by himself. I knew he had just been married before he deployed. He was just pushing thirty-two years of age and I was hoping he would have a long life but this demonstration made me wonder if we would not all disappear in a flash any second.

He then yells out, "Mr. Dennis, it's nothing! Just a piece of long wire! It's ok, no worries, no boom, boom!" As he is saying this he is waving the wire over his head and walking toward the cab of the truck which he scoots across, then steps down onto the hood and then slides down over the grill dropping down to the road all the while wearing this wide grin like he had just won a prize at the circus. He presents it to me, "See Mr. Dennis, nothing but wire." He had a huge grin on his face, but, I did not.

I keep my mouth shut as I begin my search with Toris, setting up down wind and then circling the truck just as we always do. Nothing. Not the slightest hint of explosives. I look toward our checkpoint and can see the embassy site security supervisor has arrived so I make my way to him.

We shook hands and he asked my opinion. I replied, "Sir, my professional opinion, this was a probe. This is the work of an insurgent who placed this wire to test us. To see if we would notice it. The driver of this truck may very well be an insurgent himself because he had to know how this wire got embedded into the center of his load of gravel. These insurgents wanted to see just how good we were, or to see if our security was lax. Today they found out that we are hypervigilant. Today they learned it will be impossible to get through us."

The Embassy Security Chief nodded his head in agreement. We exchanged a few more words and he walked away talking with some of his men. The driver, well his truck was taken away and he was never seen again.

I gathered all of my guys together and really hammered home what had just taken place. "Guys, this is the reason I am a stickler for detail. This is why I push all of us so hard. We were tested today and we passed the test. We may have just saved many lives, including our own. The insurgents might just think twice before trying to come through our checkpoint knowing we will find them out."

I then reminded everyone that we were guarding a high value target, the largest US embassy in the world. I let them know that our work ethic would keep our countrymen and allies alive. I stressed that we needed to not only do our jobs but watch each other's backs and insure no one missed a thing. One mistake and the consequences could be dire.

I told the fellas how proud I was of them, handlers and guards alike and that everyone had done an amazing job and had prevented a catastrophe. I was proud to know them and even more proud to serve with them. I then closed the teaching moment with this, "Now, let's not slack up. Let's be vigilant and when we train, we do so for real world situations. We do not train for the normal. No, we train and push above the normal, because if we ever get tested by an insurgent again, they will find that we will not fall apart, but rather we will overcome and come out the victor, as we did today."

I pointed over to the Embassy grounds and said, "Guess what guys. Those people over there are breathing a lot easier now and do you know why?" I paused and looked around at their faces and continued, "because they know that without a doubt they are protected by the very best team of men and dogs." I could hear a couple of the guys shout out approval and pride. Faces were beaming, slaps on the back and fist bumps all around.

The guys were proud of themselves and they knew that as a group they had just passed a huge test. Not a test designed by me, but rather a test designed by evil men bent on killing them and their allies. Tests in this life don't come with greater weight and stress than that. It was wonderful to see the look of pride on the faces of these guys, my men: Americans, South Africans, Peruvians and Chileans. I was indeed proud of them but I knew I would have to stay on them, train hard, work hard and above all else expect the unexpected.

Gold Rush Fever in Baghdad

Laky bunked with me in my trailer at Camp Jackson a few times a week; Toris would as well. I switched them out every other day. Laky loved the extra room to stretch out on the floor. When it was Toris' turn he would always start at the middle of the floor but end up sleeping up against the door. I suspect he felt he was protecting me.

Camp Jackson in a nutshell was where all of the Security Forces were housed in support of the world's largest US Embassy being built along the Tigris River. This included my K9 handlers. Camp Jackson is also where the huge in-ground pool was that I lovingly called "The Sandbox."

One morning I woke around 08:30 hrs. having enjoyed a restful night's sleep. Laky was still stretched out on the floor, sound asleep. He obviously enjoyed a good night's rest as well. Good, he needed it. Well, we would both need this good night's sleep because as usual, this was going to be another scorching hot day along the Tigris.

On this particular day Laky, Toris and I would be working a swing shift from 1500 hrs. to 2300 hrs. This meant we had a good six and a half hours before we had to be at Checkpoint Miami.

I swung my legs over the edge of the bed and as I did, Laky slowly rose, stretched out his long front legs and yawned. Then he

222

shook to reset his coat and rid himself of loose hair. Slowly he walked toward me and as he did, we locked eyes. It was a morning ritual which always led me to kiss him between his two beautiful almond colored eyes. I'd then give him a big hug and scratch him all over his body. He absolutely loved this.

After my morning rituals of brushing teeth and hitting the latrine it was time to take Laky out for his potty break. I'm standing there waiting for Laky's considerably large bladder to drain when my ear registers a new and strange sound.

I looked to my left in the direction of this annoying loud noise and noticed two Americans kneeling down behind their military vehicle. They were fidgeting with an object on the ground and it looked as if one was bracing it. Laky and I approached and then I could see that it was actually an old rusted up metal box. The other American had a large heavy hammer in his right hand and in his left was a large chisel. I put two and two together and figured they were trying to open this metal box with these tools.

As we drew closer the guys must have seen us in their periphery because they both looked toward Laky and I. The one with the hammer and chisel yelled out to me, "Hey man, is that a Bomb Dog you have there?" My response, "Yes he is!" "Would you mind if he checked out this metal box for us?" "No I don't mind at all."

As Laky and I close the distance there is something I have to get off my chest, "Let me ask you two idiots something." They looked startled by my statement but said nothing so I continued, "Did you forget that part of the briefing everyone receives which states, "If you did not place it there don't pick it up."

The two guys froze in place. I don't know if it was because of my nerve or because it was beginning to dawn on them that perhaps they should not be beating on a rusty old metal box with a hammer. Impressed by their silence I continued, "It's apparent to me you two either forgot that part of the briefing or you just don't care about rules and regulations or your lives and the lives of others." Ok, now I got something other than a blink. The guy with the hammer and chisel in his hands finally piped up, "Man, you just don't get it, do you, we found this box on the road, it could be full of Saddam's gold!"

My response to these two clueless gold rush idiots came swift, "Or, it could be full of explosives to either injure or kill both of you." I walked a few feet closer and noticed they had cut about a three-inch line into this heavy metal box, right along the upper left side. Laky and I were on the "Upwind Side" of the box so I knew Laky was at a disadvantage. I needed to move him downwind.

I instructed these two men, "Gently pick the box up and move it to the center of the sidewalk where you originally saw Laky and I walking when you called out to us." I reassured them that if there was a bomb inside the box, the hammering would have blown them sky high already. This of course did not eliminate the presence of explosives though so I told them to be careful. The two knuckleheads gingerly moved the box where I directed and then stepped a safe distance away.

Meanwhile I positioned myself and Laky a good thirty to forty yards downwind from the box. There was a nice cool morning breeze coming straight at us so I had Laky go to his "Sit" position and then watched his nose. Immediately he began "Air Scenting," lifting his head upwards into the air, and then he leaned forward into the wind. This was key for me because this was his nice "Change of Behavior," I instantly knew he was in the presence of explosive odor at this moment.

I released the tension on his leash, allowing him to go forward with no resistance from me. He headed straight for the metal box, placed his nose right over the hole caused by the chisel and hammer and then went to a fast "Sit" position. It was obvious the rusty old box contained a lot of explosive odor.

These two American idiots then asked me, "What's he doing?" I just looked at these two clowns and casually answered, "He's finished." They couldn't believe it, "Wait, what do you mean he's finished. He just got started." I smiled, "Yeah, he's done and he's

224

indicating there is a large number of explosives in that case of gold you idiots were pounding on."

I couldn't resist teasing them so I said, "By the way, you two can thank my boy Laky for saving your lives today!" I was surprised, but they actually walked up to Laky, looked at me and asked, "Is it ok if we pet him?" I smiled and said, "Considering Laky just saved your lives and you two truly seem sincere about wanting to thank him, go for it. He's very friendly." I watched as they both scratched the top of Laky's head and said, "Thank You Laky!" I felt good for my boy Laky, he just saved two American lives.

I then took my small camera out of my pocket and stuck the lens up to the hole they had punched in the old box. I made sure the flash was on and snapped a photo and sure enough there were explosives inside the box. I could see what appeared to be a well-structured wooden rack which protected several foam cylinders. It was the contents of these cylinders that had my interest peaked. I would say there were about sixteen of the projectiles in the metal box.

I told these guys they needed to call EOD and have them come out and secure this metal box of explosives. I told them to secure the area around the box and not allow anyone other than EOD to touch it. They said they would contact EOD right away.

Later that day I showed an explosives expert the photograph and he agreed they were very explosive. The fact that there were so many in the box made it even more lethal. The guy laughed and shook his head when I told him the story. He had the same esteem for these two jokers that I had, "They're idiots!" Yes, in that moment for certain but I hoped they had learned a valuable lesson that would keep them alive. I hoped it would discourage their search for the mysterious Hussein family missing gold.

Gold Rush Fever killed many Americans in California and Alaska back in the day and in 2006 it almost killed two Americans in Baghdad. Fortunately they were saved by an awesome German Shepherd named Laky.

An Insurgent, Sly as A Fox

It's around 22:30 hrs. and another shift completed. I worked the swing shift and because my relief showed up early, I decided it was a good time to conduct some proficiency training with Laky and Toris.

The moon was especially bright and the temps were already in the low 70s so it was quite nice. Even though I was now working in the Green Zone it didn't mean the danger level had dropped. Mortars would still drop in and rockets would still shriek their terrible intentions in our direction. Put another way, the Green Zone was the equivalent of a circle of wagons in "Indian Country." We had barriers and fortifications but were still vulnerable.

The danger did not negate the need for training. In fact, a wise trainer/handler takes advantage of any opportunity to instruct his or her canines. Therefore, it's important to conduct training at various times of the day and night, at different locations and in all types of weather. In this way the dogs are prepared for any situation.[76]

With this precept in mind I decided to use an open field just behind our "motor pool."[77] The area was ideal for training as it was enclosed by large tan colored cement walls that stood approximately ten feet high. There was only one entrance and it was guarded twenty-four hours a day by a machine gunner in a thirty-foot tower. I liked this because I knew there would always be someone watching my back. The only concerning item about the gunners was that they were members of the Iraqi Army and we all knew their ranks were infiltrated by insurgents. I always made sure to wave to him when I

---

[76] Sometimes back in the States I would train alongside a busy rural highway. The sounds of the cars flashing by creates a whole new environment for these dogs. Look for ways to be creative in this aspect of training.

[77] A group of motor vehicles centrally located, controlled (as by a governmental agency) and dispatched for use as needed.

entered hoping the trigger man would know I was a good dude and certainly not worth shooting.

A bright light flicked on and the machine gunner swung his spotlight around and zeroed in on me when I drove up. "Mr. Dennis! Hello my friend!" came the mysterious voice behind the light. I waved and yelled out, "Is that you Mustafa?" I thought I recognized the voice but I was blinded by the light.

The unidentified caller yelled back, "Yes, it's me Mr. Dennis! Mustafa! Your friend!" There was a pause for a second or two and then he called out, "Do you have Toris and Laky with you tonight?" I smiled and yelled back into the blinding light that had me fixed in place, "Yes! They have come to play in your field if that is ok!" The voice from the light bellowed, "Ok Mr. Dennis! You can come into my field and play with Toris and Laky!" I responded, "Thank you my friend! Coming now into your field!" Thankfully Mustafa swung his spotlight off of us.

Back in my truck I drove along the outside motor pool wall and parked in a corner. When I exited the truck I looked up at the guard tower where I saw Mustafa standing at the rail, "I'll protect you Mr. Dennis. Laky and Toris are good dogs and I will protect them to!"[78] I smiled, waved and yelled out, "Thank you so much my friend!" Like I said, it's important to cultivate friendships.

I had to get down to business so I surveyed the field and noted the five disabled vehicles that other K9 trainers had previously lined up in a straight line for training purposes. As I was surveying the field and the vehicles, my peripheral vision detected movement in the tall grass, five feet from the line of cars. I watched the tops of the grass swaying back and forth and followed the movement hoping to catch a glimpse of the animal. I suspected it was a cat.

---

[78] I asked Mustafa where he had learned his English. He stated that he had read books and practiced on anyone who could speak the language. He was a sharp guy and I liked him.

Then, near a black Mercedes I could see a figure emerge from the grass. A fox! It was small but absolutely beautiful. Majestic! The fox was golden colored with patches of white fur that was accented by a large bushy tail. I couldn't believe my eyes! How could something so delicate and beautiful exist in a place like this?

The graceful animal was moving its nose up and down. Air scenting! It suddenly looked in my direction, took note of my presence and then disappeared back into the grass from whence it had come.

I wanted to test Laky and Toris on open area searches so I unsealed the container which contained a block of C4 plastic explosive. Next I donned my non-scented surgical gloves so I'd not transfer my odor to the block of C4. I wanted Laky and Toris looking for C4, not me. After first checking the wind direction I found a good hiding place for the explosive under some overgrown bushes and covered it with branches. I was a stickler on this. My explosive training aids were always well concealed. I didn't want my dogs having any visual clues like the green wrapping of the explosives. I wanted them searching with their noses, not their eyes.

Now that everything was in place, I needed to establish four "marker points" so that I would know the exact location of the block of C4. Here's how I determined that. From where I was standing, I could see a tall telephone pole across the road at a distance of approximately fifty yards. This was my first marker.

I then turned to my right and could see a tall palm tree with its top blown off at a distance of about sixty yards. This was my second marker.

Making another ninety degree turn to the right I was now looking at the back wall of the motor pool. I estimated the distance to be about fifty yards. I noted that the wall had chunks torn out by what looked to be bullet or shrapnel strikes. This was my third marker.

One final ninety degree turn to the right and I easily spied what would be my fourth marker; a stack of four old truck tires which I estimated to be sixty to seventy yards in the distance.

Readers might ask, "You had bomb dogs, so why take the time to establish four markers?" Of course I had my bomb dogs who I was sure would find the explosives but I learned early in my career to always expect the unexpected. Have a backup plan.

It was now time to get Toris out and give him a pee and poop break. I didn't want him thinking about his bowels when he was supposed to be searching. During this time the explosive is sitting and emanating its odor which catches on the wings of the wind and moves through the bushes, the grass and dirt.

After about thirty minutes[79] I positioned Toris downwind of the hidden explosives and gave him the command to search. True to form Toris made wide sweeps of the field until he picked up the odor. I actually noticed a slight change of behavior on his second pass across the field. This told me he had picked up the weakest side of the "downwind side" of the C4 odor. I knew that the next time he turned he would be ten to fifteen feet closer and the odor would be stronger.

Sure enough on his third turn he displayed a stronger interest in the odor and was zeroing in on it. Toris was incredibly fast in these searches. It was impressive to behold.

Getting closer to the source I noted his stubby tail began wagging faster and faster and then he plopped down on the ground, crawled under a bush, placed his nose near the source, inhaled, scooted back

---

[79] I would mix the times up. Sometimes I would wait thirty minutes and other times I would wait for only two to five minutes assuming that sometimes the bad guys are in a hurry when they cross our paths. Perhaps they had only just met up with their contact before approaching our checkpoint. I trained with various amounts of time for this very scenario. Never assume. Always learn. Incorporate new methods. Become better.

out and went to an immediate "final sit" position. "Good boy!" I instantly rewarded him with high pitched praise, retrieved the large red Kong from my pocket and launched it across the field. Toris took off like a jet, clouds of dust billowing behind him.

I heard loud noises coming from up above and could see Mustafa in the gun tower hooping, hollering and clapping his hands. He really respected these dogs.

After launching multiple Kongs and continued high praise it was time to put Toris back in his crate. Laky boy, who had been patiently waiting in his crate, was ready and eager for his turn. As I'm walking I glanced up towards Mustafa but he was not visible up in the tower. Usually when we conducted these searches, Mustafa would pull the netting and have it draped across his back so he could watch the dogs conduct their searches.

I conducted a quick scan of the area with my eyes; first left to right and then for depth as well. Everything looked good and as I'm walking, I checked to see if the wind had shifted. It was still blowing in the same direction at a gentle five miles per hour or so. Perfect!

On this open area search I ran both dogs using my twenty-foot leather leash that gave them both plenty of room to separate themselves from me so that I was not right on top of them, crowding them, hurrying them. I felt like Toris and Laky preferred to be separated from me so they could search quickly. I liked for them to feel as if they were alone and not concerned about me at all.[80]

---

[80] There are times that K9 Handlers get too involved with their dog when it's searching, especially rookie handlers. I've "been there, done that" speaking from personal experience folks! Give the dog the freedom it needs to do what a dog does best, search with its nose. Keep slack in your leash so there's no tugging or jerking on it. Your dog may think you're putting a correction on it. Give your dog room! Of course, if you know your dog is goofing off, and not searching as it should, then yes, without question, get involved and make a correction, get your dog back on task.

I was now downwind with Laky at the starting point. The wind was still good so I gave him the command to "Sit." I praised him for the, "good sit" and as I did, I looked down at his nose to see if he was showing any signs of picking up the C4 odor. No. Ok, here we go. I scratched the top of his head and gave him the command to "search."

Working crosswind Laky made his first turn back across the field; nothing yet. Laky then made a second turn across the field; nothing, no change of behavior. After his third turn across the field Laky displayed nothing. I did a quick check to gauge the wind, thinking that perhaps Laky's trouble was due to a shift in wind direction.

No, the wind was still gently blowing from the same direction as before. Ok, this was strange. Laky made his fourth turn to cut across the field and picked up not the slightest trace of odor. At this point I was getting concerned because Toris had previously picked up on odor after making his second turn. We continued on and Laky made his fifth turn across the field and STILL NOTHING!

It was then that I began to question Laky. I hated doing this, but what else could I do? His reliability in searching for explosives in this warzone was suddenly in question! I knew he had been showing signs of K9 PTSD and perhaps he had regressed in his training. This work was life and death so the stakes could not get any higher. One thing for sure, I needed to nip this in the bud.

By this time we were right up to the bushes and branches and it was only when we were within twenty INCHES of the hide site that Laky finally showed an interest and change of behavior. Crap! This really sucked! Why was Laky shutting down on me?

I began to question my placement of the C4, "Am I in the right place? Perhaps this is the wrong location." Bushes all look the same at night, but with the K9 nose this should not have been a problem. Laky was supposed to find the C4 by odor not by my recollection of the hide location. So many questions were running through my mind.

I was really doubting myself so I checked my four markers and discovered that I was in the right spot. I thought, "Ok, I'm where the C4 should be but Laky is not showing anything other than the slightest interest. Weird. What's going on?"

I pulled out my flashlight, bent down to look under the bush and sure enough, there were the broken branches I had used to cover the C4. Pulling the branches away I saw nothing but dried needles from the bush. Wait! NOTHING?!

The panicked thought, "Where's my C4 explosive?!" pulverized my brain. In that instant all of the flood lights went out and I was instantly consumed by darkness. The rod cells[81] in my eyes were trying to adjust but this would take time. So, there I was, under a bush, with a flashlight on, showing bad guys where I was located. Perfect!

I turned my flashlight off and remained quiet and still, listening for the tell-tale sounds of humans moving about. My right hand dropped down to my 9mm and I pulled it from the holster. At that moment I was longing for an M4 or M16 over my shoulder. If this was an insurgent attack I was in a very bad predicament.

I looked up into the gun tower and was surprised to discover that Mustafa was not in sight. This was unusual because he always enjoyed watching the dogs train. I looked toward my truck knowing that Toris would alert if danger was near but he was quiet. I looked back up to the tower, took a deep breath and an even bigger chance and called out, "Mustafa?" No response, only the sounds of the night. So I tried again, "Mustafa? Are you ok?"

Then came a voice from the darkened tower, "Mr. Dennis! The generator has stopped running. Our men are inspecting it right now.

---

[81] Rod cells are photoreceptor cells in the retina of the eye that can function in less intense light than the other type of visual photoreceptor, cone cells. Rods are usually found concentrated at the outer edges of the retina and are used in peripheral vision.

Thank you for checking on me." I called up to him, "Mustafa, did you see any men out here in the field when I was giving Laky a potty break?" Mustafa quizzically asked, "I don't understand, what is a potty break?" I smiled, "It's when I take my dogs out in the field to go pee and poop." Mustafa laughed, "No Mr. Dennis, there was no one in the field." Relieved, I responded, "Ok, thank you!"

Satisfied that the area was free of insurgents I returned my 9mm to its holster but I still had to deal with the startling fact that my block of C4 was missing. This was a huge problem that could potentially cost me my job. I knew the ramifications of a missing block of C4 could be catastrophic. Worst case scenario; it would be used against our own people or allies. Allies and civilians could die.

What was so infuriating about the situation was the fact that I had shown proper protocol and had insured the area was clear of human traffic. It was the whole reason I picked this location. It was isolated and guarded.

A block of C4 does not just sprout legs and walk away. So, if it was not picked up perhaps it just vanished. Yeah, right. Impossible. So what could have happened to it? I had a huge problem on my hands and to make matters worse it was dark and with the flood lights out I had to use a stinking flashlight. Man I was feeling the pucker factor.

It was time to do what I'd been dreading. I pulled my radio out and called my Green Zone area supervisor. I explained that I needed to see him right away and gave him my location. He replied, "Heading your way in about twenty minutes." I felt a pit well up in my stomach as I replied, "Roger that." Well, it was a done deal now. I could picture myself packing my bags and heading home. How could this have happened? It was impossible.

As I was standing there, I kept feeling my leash tugging in my hand. I looked down at Laky and he continued to pull forward. Laky was sniffing the ground, lifting his head and then sniffing the ground again. It hit me, "You knucklehead! Your bomb dog is working explosive odor!"

Sure enough, Laky had the answer. Whoever took my C4 had to walk out of here with it in their hands, pouch, or backpack. They would have left a trail of explosive odor that Laky could follow. Mustafa stated that no one had been in the area but he may have missed something. I didn't believe Mustafa was in cahoots with whoever took my C4 but I could not dismiss the possibility that he had not seen everything going on down here.

I could feel the first swell of hope rise within me. Perhaps there could be a happy ending to the caper of the missing C4. I couldn't delay anymore. Time to get moving. I gave Laky the command to search and he was off in the direction he had been pulling. He was definitely on odor and moving fast. I pulled my 9mm because it was still dark and if I dislodged a hiding insurgent there would definitely be a gunfight.

As I headed in, I looked back to the moon lit tower and could just make out the silhouette of Mustafa leaning out over the rail watching my progress. Well, at least someone had my back. I hoped.

As Laky was searching, I put some downward pressure on his leash, which placed pressure on his collar. It was not a jerking or a tug but rather a smooth, slow downward pressure. If Laky was working odor the pressure would not make him slow but would in fact make him pull harder.[82] There it was, a pull from Laky and then an even harder pull from him. He was definitely on odor.

The glow of the moon was now reflecting off what appeared to be a worn footpath in the grass. Laky was leading me down the path and I couldn't help but speculate where it would take us. The thought made me swallow hard and sharpened my senses. This was for keeps.

---

[82] If he was goofing off and not following explosive odor, when I put the downward pressure on the leash to his collar, he would turn and look at me. In this case and story he did not. He was on odor.

Laky was now leading me into a corner of the enclosed field which was home to a copse of trees that stood about twenty feet tall. I could see there were about four or five of these trees all tightly grouped together. The branches of these trees blocked the glow of the moon and thus dampened my vision. Crud! I hoped to avoid this moment but now I had no other choice, it was time to turn on my flashlight and give away my position. If there's an insurgent in there with my C4, ambush here I come.

I quickly asked God to protect us as we entered the small grove of trees. I clicked on the light and braced for the hail of bullets. Nothing. Silence. I moved forward and was shocked at what greeted my eyes. There before us stood a large mound of dirt with a neatly excavated hole. Laky pulled me in closer and placed his nose up to the small hole and began sniffing hard. He was showing signs that he was on odor but he never went to a sit position.

Suddenly it hit me, "The FOX!" It must have been the fox that stole my C4 and then brought it down the well traversed game trail back to its den. My first thought was that I needed to retrieve a shovel and dig for the C4 but then I stopped in my tracks. Laky was not indicating that the explosive was here. The odor was strong but not in large enough amounts to cause a sit. So I turned Laky around and told him to "search." Off he went, back out of the trees. As we emerged back into the field my night vision returned and I could see the grass and the various game trails. At this moment I thought, "I trust you Laky, but you are the rookie bomb dog and I can't take any chances with this C4 loose. Time is against me. Sorry buddy but I need to get the most seasoned bomb dog in the Green Zone out here."

I bent down and gave Laky a big hug and told him, "You did a great job Buddy, you were on the trail, you got me this far." I will admit that at that moment I was not trusting him 100%. I knew he would eventually take me to the C4, but how long would it take? I felt horrible putting Laky back in his crate. Deep down I knew Laky would find it but time was critical and I needed it found NOW!

Toris was barking very loud. I think he could sense that something was amiss. I took the barking to mean, "Don't worry Dad, I can do this for you!" That's what my ears wanted to hear anyway.

As I was passing the gun tower to my left I looked up and yelled, "Mustafa! Any word on the lights coming on?" His response, "Mr. Dennis, we are told it will be another thirty minutes, maybe longer." I recall thinking, "It will be longer, I'm sure of it, it's just the way it is here."

So, now it's Toris' turn, "Search" and Toris sets out on his grid. As he runs back and forth dissecting the area, I slowly let out the twenty-foot leash. I kept my arms above my head thus preventing the leash from snagging on the bushes and underbrush.

Toris made a third crosswind turn and nothing. The first time we did this Toris had discovered a hint of odor on his second turn and now at this moment on his third turn, nothing. Fourth, fifth, sixth and nothing. Crap! This is not looking good.

Toris was now within twenty inches of the original C4 hide position and began to show a change of behavior. This was identical to the way Laky had performed only minutes before. Toris was onto odor. He then made a quick right turn and also like Laky he began to take me down the game trail. I gave a little downward pressure but Toris only pulled harder. Awesome. He was on to odor for certain.

I could feel the intensity of Toris' search through the leash. He was pulling hard and suddenly stopped dead in his tracks. The wind had changed direction. I could feel it on my face. I didn't budge. I stood there like a statue, waiting to see what Toris would do. His nose was in the air, definitely air scenting. His head turned into the wind and suddenly he leapt into the air clearing a large clump of bushes. I could no longer see him but the leash was slack.

In the light of the moon I saw something rustle in the bushes. I looked over the bushes and in the moonlight I could see Toris silhouette, sitting proud and erect! He was in his "final sit" position!

236

I turned my flashlight on, pushed my way through the bushes and there was my boy with that huge German Shepherd grin all over his face. I swear I could see a twinkle in his eyes. I gave the command to stay because this was a warzone and it could have been another explosive and NOT the C4 I was searching for.

I panned my flashlight around and there it was, that big beautiful green package with yellow lettering, marked "C4."

Ok, now I made it the 4th of July in Baghdad! I was throwing Kongs one after another and praising him with high pitched yelps. Toris was loving every minute of it and so was I. Wow, that was a close one. This amazing dog had just saved my butt.

I turned my flashlight in the direction of the C4 and noted the fox gnawed on a corner and had actually eaten a small portion of it. I hoped it would not die from ingesting the explosive material. Sweeping the ground with my light I discovered a leather glove that had been chewed. I also discovered various small bones of animals the fox had dined on.

Well, time to go. I packaged up the C4 and returned back to the truck where Toris enjoyed some cool water and a bit more praise. Once in his crate I looked back at the field, exhaled a sigh of relief and stepped toward the driver's side door, Bam! All of the flood lights came on! I laughed and said, "Figures." I looked up toward Mustafa and called out, "It was not an insurgent, it was a sly fox."

I called my supervisor and informed him that his presence was no longer required as I had taken care of the problem. The following morning I dropped in on my boss Mitchell Raleigh and told him the story in all of its detail. I then revealed the damaged C4 package with the small corner chewed off.

I asked, "What's next sir?" Mr. Raleigh stood there with a huge grin on his face and after a few seconds responded, "Well, you got the block of C4 back and as far as that little piece of missing C4, well, it looks like normal wear and tear to me. I don't think the fox will use it to blow anything up, do you?" I laughed. What a great guy. He could have caused a stink about the damaged C4 but he stated it would be logged as "normal wear and tear." We laughed and then he asked, "Oh, Dennis, did you thank Toris for saving your butt?" At this he burst out laughing and slapped me on the back. Of course now I'm laughing. As I left Mr. Raleigh called out, "It's ok Dennis, no big deal, nothing to worry about. Have a good Baghdad day!"

This is the field the fox called home. You can see the line of disabled vehicles to the left. We used these for training purposes.

The other side of the fox's domain. Note the tower on left occupied by Mustafa on the night of the C4 incident.

Remember Who's in Charge

It's critical that you build a bond with your 'Working Dog", well, it's critical with any dog you are attempting to build a relationship with. It's twice as critical that you have an understanding with your dog that there is a "Pecking Order" of rank. Your dog must realize and accept that he or she falls under you in the role of leadership, that you are the "Alpha" in this team.

If it's a household, say a family of four, husband, wife, and two children, the dog is ALWAYS at the bottom of the pecking order. If not, well, you're going to have issues with the dog not wanting to obey you. In fact, it will attempt to control you. I often will say this to my K9 students, "Who is working for who? Are you working for your dog, or is the dog working for you? Who is the Alpha in this team?"

Having written all that let me tell you this story.

My seasoned war dog Toris and I are standing along the side of the road at Checkpoint NEC waiting for trucks to be lined up in preparation to be searched by our Security Search Team. As the Peruvians and Chileans go about the task of removing the drivers, searching them and then performing the visual search of the trucks we stood in the blistering heat, patiently waiting.

Toris was panting fairly heavy so I removed a bottle of water from the side cargo pocket of my pants, pulled out my K-Bar knife and poked three holes in the top of the bottle cap. I turned the bottle towards Toris who then moved his lips to the upturned cap and as soon as he was in contact with the water bottle cap, I started to squeeze the bottle forcing water through the three holes. Water was shooting out and into his mouth. Toris absolutely loved this routine and he'd always flash me these happy eyes while he drank from the water bottle.

After he got his fill, I reached down and touched the top of his head and neck, his fur was very warm to the touch, so I poured the rest of the water over his head and neck. While doing this he turned his head enough to lick my hand, as if to say, "Thank You!" I put the empty bottle back into my side cargo pocket and looked over at the Security Search Team to see if they were about finished. I was expecting to see the "thumbs up" from one of the guards when all of a sudden, my mind seemed to freeze.

Something was happening to my body and I was trying to process the feelings I was having. Keep in mind, this is all happening in microseconds, but it seemed like I was processing everything in slow motion, what the heck is going on? What am I feeling right now? I had never experienced this at any of these checkpoints before and it was bewildering. I had a warm, almost hot liquid feeling moving down along my left leg.

For a moment I thought maybe I had been shot, and the pain had not yet registered or arrived but I was only feeling the warm blood flowing down my left leg. So I looked down at my left leg expecting to see the worst. I couldn't believe it, my highly trained veteran war dog Toris who I just gave a cool water break is now emptying his bladder onto my left leg. I couldn't believe it. He even had his leg lifted high as if he was peeing on the side of some tree. Well I could not let this stand so I started yelling, "Phooey! Phooey that! Have you lost your mind?!"

I popped the leash a few times on his collar with my loud verbal corrections and he knew I was very upset with him. By popping the leash and yelling at him in direct low tones I was letting him know, "I'm the 'Alpha' and you are NOT!" I could NOT let this go without a correction. That would have been a huge mistake, for he would have done it again, and who knows what else.

Well, of course, because I'm yelling at him it drew attention to myself by my Security Search Teams and everyone else standing around. It was obvious what had just taken place because I had my left leg lifted up in the air and I was attempting to shake my pant leg to get rid of as much urine as I could. I'm stomping my left boot on the ground because the boot has soaked up this dog urine like a sponge. Everyone is laughing! Everyone but me, of course, but then I realized just how funny this must have looked to everyone watching, so then I started laughing and then seeing this everyone started laughing even harder. This was a good stress reliever for everyone.

The Security Search Team Supervisor wore a huge grin on his face as he gave me the "Thumbs Up." It was our turn to search these trucks for explosives and bombs. I shook my head in acknowledgement as I was still shaking my left pant leg. I then looked down at Toris and said, "Remember Who's in Charge!" Toris gave me a side glance, panted and we walked on to finish the job at hand, searching for explosives!

Splish Splash Then Death

During the heat of summer there was a daily routine that I enjoyed with both Laky and Toris. It would cost nothing but time yet the rewards were immeasurable. I would take my boys down to the Tigris river to cool them off. Now even just typing that sentence seems crazy, like it was some parallel universe. I still found it hard to believe, the ancient renowned Tigris river and I was strolling its banks while my dogs splashed in its historic waters. All really quite surreal.

Now of course I could not take these two male dogs down at the same time for they would have ripped into each other. So, I would have to take them at separate times. When I did, I would use a thirty-foot leash which would afford them plenty of length to jump into the river.

I always had fun with them on these occasions and they loved it. I would let them jump into the river and then I would begin the search for a good stick. I always drew this process out and my boys loved it. Laky or Toris would stand in the water sometimes up to their necks and other times up to their elbows patiently waiting for me to find the stick. Their patience was on a timer though.

I loved watching their excitement build and build for when they could not take the waiting game any longer, they would start barking at me with those big deep German Shepherd barks, which sounded like they were "demanding" me to hurry up and find a stinking stick. I could just imagine what they were saying, "Do you need me to come over there and show you how easy it is to find a stick?" I'd turn and with a high-pitched voice say, "What?! What's up?! What's going on?!" This just drove them nuts. They'd give me a couple deep barks, followed by one more quick bark, putting so much effort into them that their front paws were coming up off the bottom of the river. Water was splashing all around them as we played this game of "Can Dennis find the stick?" It was all good fun and with the infernal heat the chance to wet their coats was something they relished.[83]

I'm laughing inside as I'm pretending it's so difficult to find a stick. I'm also very happy, as happy as they were, because at these times, I was allowing each of them to just be dog's, no restrictions. These two war dogs deserved this afternoon treat, a nice cool swim in the Tigris River after spending hours in the Iraqi heat, dealing with the blowing swirling dust and sand, the sniffing of the oil and gas from each vehicle being searched, the list of all the various smells with each vehicle being searched is endless, day in and day out, month after month.

I'd finally find the right stick, pick it up quickly, and throw it a good fifteen to twenty feet out into the river. If Toris were standing up on the shoreline and not in the water waiting for the throw he'd leap as hard as he could and hit the water like a whale who just rocketed itself up out of the deep. Once he got his sights on the fleeing stick, he was like a shark zeroing in for the kill, he'd bite into the stick with his huge canines, turn back towards me with this happy look on his face and twinkle in his eye that resonated sheer

---

[83] The heat was so intense that the "O" ring on their collar that I would attach the leash to was too hot to handle without gloves. The "O" rings were positioned in a way that they never touched my dog's skin or I would never have used them.

happiness. Once ashore we'd play a little tug of war, and of course, I'd always let him win the tug, which made him feel so confident and much stronger than I. For a moment the war was a thing of the past.

Looking back on it I know without a doubt that these sessions down on the river were therapeutic for not only Laky and Toris but for me as well. I would laugh watching them jump into the water with a huge splash and then swim, snatching the stick or chomping at floating debris. The stress of hearing explosions around you all day and knowing that your job is to actively search for the very substance detonating around you is, well, stressful.

I could see a visible change in the two boys. As I'm reading their body language, I noticed they both seemed happier, had more spunk, searched with more intensity. As for myself, I felt more relaxed and happier, the fun in the sun along the shoreline of the Tigris with my two bomb dogs was helping each of us get through this war. It took the edge off.

Now I must say that I never really truly relaxed on the shores of the Tigris for I knew that there was a bounty on my head and my dogs. We heard in our briefings that informants had stated there was a bounty of $20,000 for anyone who could kill a working dog. I also knew that the buildings across the river afforded great observation posts and sniping positions and that taking a shot at me or my boys would be an easy thing. Hitting us from that range would be another matter but taking a shot was easy. With this in mind I was always moving along the river, never standing still in one spot too long. I was crouching and running and bending and doing all sorts of moves that I was incorporating into my interactions with Toris and Laky but these movements also served to make a shot that much harder. A moving target is much harder to hit.[84]

Once Toris and Laky were out of the water they acted like young puppies, full of energy, bouncing around, spinning, barking. They

---

[84] I also made sure to never have a routine. In other words I never went down to the river at the same time each day. I would alternate times.

would charge towards me, slam on their brakes and slide almost up to my feet from a dead run and then crouch down with their front legs stretched in my direction, their butt high up in the air shaking from side to side, barking. Spinning around they'd make a mad dash for the river once again, jumping back into the water, swimming out about five feet, turn and bark at me once again, displaying that big German Shepherd doggie smile. I could see that twinkle of happiness in their eyes. With their barking they were yelling at me to throw the stick back in the river and how could I refuse these faithful friends who each and every day give above and beyond.

Of course, everything has an ending and they knew that once I brought out my leather leash, it was time to get back into the realities of war, fun at the beach was over, until the next day. Once back at the checkpoint, they both knew it was "Game-On." I was in full control, it was never a problem, we had a job to do, to protect our own, and our allies from insurgents attempting to bring in a VBED.

During one of these particular beach days I was once again struck with the realities of this environment.

On this day I'm walking Toris on a six-foot leash. He's out in front of me and he's in a hurry because he knows all too well what's about to happen, "Beach Time!" It's another hot blistering summer Baghdad day. It's so hot that even the wind is uncomfortable and brings no relief. I know Toris is going to have a blast in the water and then in about thirty minutes I will get Laky down here for his turn.

As we were walking to the river, I can see Toris stubby little tail is going crazy with anticipation of the cool water and the fun we will have. Suddenly Toris quickly snapped his head to our left, lifting his nose upwards in the direction of the "Fourteenth of July Bridge" which was less than 800 feet to my left. I could see his nostrils were flared wide open, they were opening wide and closing down smaller, then I heard him blow out the air in his nostrils and then suck in more air, he wanted more samples of whatever this odor was, then WHAM, I got a whiff of it, and it almost made me vomit. This of course was not the smell of explosives; it was the distinct stench of death.

I quickly turned my head in the same direction Toris was pointing his nose, to the left upriver. I'm determined to find where this foul smell is coming from so, I reach down into my backpack and bring out my binoculars. My suspicion is that the horrendous smell has to do with the pilings holding up the 14th of July Bridge. I am sure the dozens of pillars are catching bodies that were drifting downstream so I scan this area but surprisingly I came up empty. Strange. Very strange.

Finding nothing I check the opposite shore slowly moving my binoculars left to right inspecting every square foot of the beach. Soon my sweep pulls me to several buildings, one of which is a school. I can see children having a wonderful time in the playground and soccer field. Boys compete for lopsided and ragged metal swings supported by red iron posts. Smaller children careen down an aged and haggard yellow slide. I can see the smiles on their faces and I can imagine the sound of their laughter. Laughter in a place like this. Amazing. Older schoolboys were playing soccer while girls of the same age stood around in little groups chatting away. I could tell from their mannerisms that the children were all at ease. I took this to mean that the source was most likely not near the school.

The playground scene was unusual in one regard for off in the distance I could hear the sound of gun fire. I knew that if I could hear it then most assuredly these children could but they paid the dangerous sounds not the least bit of attention. It was actually very sad that these children could count gunfire as a common occurrence. So familiar in fact that they did not even bother looking up. Such a depressing place.

Without question, it was something dead and it was large whatever it was. The stench of rotting flesh will always be with me, how unfortunate. There are many things you want to forget about war but some things will stay with you the rest of your life, smells are one of them. I gave up trying to find the source of this decay, so it was back to getting Toris and then Laky their turns at playing and cooling off in the Tigris.

It was several hours later that one of the Peruvian guards informed me that the source of this terrible odor had been located. Several local nationals were discovered jammed up in a drainage system that emptied into the Tigris. A large drainage pipe designed to take water from the city streets had been used as a dump site for these executed civilians. I was to learn their story and it was heartbreaking.

Jewelry store patrons enjoying their day were blissfully perusing the various watches, necklaces and bracelets and engaging in friendly barter with the owner. Vehicles pulled up outside the store and several armed religious extremists emerged brandishing AK47s. In less than five minutes the owner and customers were all kidnapped and forced into the waiting vehicles. The man who owned the establishment had been warned not to sell his inventory to Americans or her Allies. The owner, a proud man who had worked his whole life to make the store thrive was not about to be intimidated by these thugs. Though courageous he did pay with his life. Unfortunately the bodies of these people indicated that they had been tortured. Electric drills had been used to bore holes in their feet and various other places on their bodies.

Finished with this heinous deed the bodies were discarded like trash into the drainage system. The terrorists had hoped the bodies would wash into the river but they had not counted on the grates covering the pipe openings. Unceremoniously. Unfeeling. Dastardly. It was a jumble of these rotting and putrefying bodies against the bars of the grates that Toris and I smelled that day.

I must say though that such horrendous acts only served to instill an anger and determination in all of us, K9 handlers, Peruvian and Chilean guards alike, that we would show no mercy should insurgents attempt to overrun our checkpoint. It's difficult to describe the fierce anger one feels at such a waste of human life. That these insurgents could so callously extinguish the light in these people who were only guilty of shopping is outrageous but truthfully it was just another regular day in this city.

It seemed executions were a daily occurrence and kidnappings in the middle of the night so commonplace that citizens slept with machine guns beside their beds. Motorists drove with AK47s in their front seats for car-jackings were a daily occurrence.

All of these stories served to harden our resolve that we would stand and fight should the time come. In addition to the 9mm I always wore a K-Bar battle knife on my hip. The amazingly durable blade was given to me by my son before I departed for Iraq. I will never forget when my son Dennis presented it to me, he looked me straight in the eyes and with intense seriousness said, "Don't be taken alive." We both knew that captured Americans were tortured and then beheaded in front of a video camera. My son's message was plain, "When your bullets run out and you see you are going to be taken, pull the knife and kill as many as you can. Make them kill you on the spot." Now I know this sounds dramatic but it was the reality of the city of Baghdad. There was no way I was going to end up on Al Jazeera having my head sawed off with a blunt dagger. It was stories like that of these nameless victims stuffed in a drainpipe that served to solidify an already rock-solid resolve that if I was going to die it would be on the spot and I would take as many with me as possible.

Tears Along the Road

It was another blistering day along the Tigris River at Checkpoint NEC. The sun was just a bit off center of being directly over us and standing in the shade with Laky at my side I watched phantom shimmers of heat dance across the compacted gravel road. I was tired. Tired of the constant sweating. Tired of the ominous presence of death that hung over every second of every day. I was tired of the drab surroundings, everything tan or a close shade thereof; the walls, the bricks, the roads, the dust clouds, the rocks, the homes, the concrete barriers, our pants and boots, everything the same color. Did I mention I was tired?

My attention was drawn to a large group of individuals off to my periphery. I glanced and could see United States Marines with full battle gear moving down the road preparing to leave the Green Zone on a mission. They were decked out in gear; backpacks, flak vests, Kevlar helmets, automatic weapons, grenades strapped to their utility vests. They were strong, fierce looking and obviously highly trained and disciplined. I was impressed and proud that our country still produced such men.

One Marine looked back at my German Shepherd Laky and then his eyes slowly tracked to me. He held this gaze for several seconds and then returned his attention to his group of warriors. Again and again this young Marine turned to look at Laky. I could see this young man yell something to another Marine who I took to be his Sergeant. I saw the other man's helmet nod up and down and a clinched fist with an extended finger pointing at Laky and I. Suddenly the young Marine broke ranks and was sprinting in our direction.

Panting and sweating this young man pulled up short of us and stopped. Knowing this was a working dog he was going to close the distance cautiously. I made a mental note that this Marine had some good knowledge of dogs, especially working dogs to act in this way. A young voice beckoned, "Sir, do you mind if I pet your German Shepherd?" I said, "I'm not supposed to." Our orders and protocols strictly forbade canine fraternization with anyone other than K9 handlers but there was something about this kid and what I knew he was facing that made me continue, "but he's very friendly and I'm not worried about you getting bit by him so go for it!"

The young Marine smiled and tossed his backpack onto the ground as if he were in a wrestling match in High School and just thrown his opponent to the mat. He then placed his M4 across his backpack, leaned forward just a bit and taking the back of his right hand moved it up slowly towards the underside of Laky's chin. Ever so softly this young man stroked Laky's fur. He then looked up at me and asked, "What's your dog's name?" I replied, "Laky". He then turned right away towards Laky and said, "You're such a good boy Laky, you're a beautiful boy Laky, good boy, good boy." This young Marine had the perfect dog voice. It was obvious he probably had German Shepherds back home.

The battle bound Marine then moved his right hand upwards and flipped his hand so that now his palm rested against the black and brown fur of Laky's face. Stroking my war dog's face the young warrior praised, "Good boy, good boy Laky, your being such a good boy." Laky was squinting his eyes closed, truly enjoying this special attention by this stranger. Suddenly the Marine did something I was not expecting and would never have recommended, he leaned in even closer to Laky and wrapped his right arm around Laky's shoulder and neck. This was the most dangerous position to take with any dog, especially by someone the canine does not know.

This Marine buried his face into the fur of Laky's neck and it was then I noticed tears from this Marine were rolling down and off the side of Laky's neck into the sand along the road. The Marine then turned his head up towards me, still holding onto Laky's neck and said, "Sir, please don't tell my Marines you saw me crying." My response was immediate, "I didn't see a thing and even if I had I still wouldn't say anything." I paused and said, "It's ok to cry sometimes. This is one of those times." The young man turned his face back to Laky was hugging him and gently caressing his side. I stated, "I'm guessing you must have a German Shepherd back home?" "Yes Sir. Not just a German Shepherd, but one that looks identical to yours Sir. I mean identical. He has the same sweet disposition too." He chuckled and his eyes sparkled as he said, "Sir, I thought you had my dog here with you."

"Awesome, so where is home for you?" I asked. "Sir", he said now getting his composure back, "I live with my parents and my dog on a farm in Minnesota, I sure miss them all." He then turned slightly and looked back in the direction of his disappearing fellow Marines. Still holding onto Laky's neck his voice changed in that moment when a man alters gears to the task at hand, "Well Sir, I'd better catch up to my guys." I smiled, "Sure! But before you take off, go ahead and give Laky one more hug." The young Marine smiled from ear to ear and did just that, but this time, he tossed in a kiss on the side of Laky's face. Laky in turn gave him a quick lick (Doggie Kiss) on the side of his cheek. The young warrior broke out with a huge smile as big as the State of Texas. The Marine looked at me and said, "Did you see that Sir, he kissed me?" I said, "Yes I did see it, and I'm jealous because Laky is not a kisser. In the ten months we've been here Laky has given me a kiss only one time. You've known him for three minutes and got one. He really likes you."

Just then a huge cement truck pulled up next to us wanting to gain access through our checkpoint and with it came the hot swirling tan dust from the tan road. The Marine jumped to his feet, reached for his weapon, strapped on his backpack and then snapped a smart salute to Laky and I which I proudly returned. He then bolted off to join his guys and the unknown dangers ahead.

You know what, I wasn't tired anymore and I didn't care about the dust, the heat, the shades of tan or the rivulets of sweat that coursed down my forehead. A young Marine showed me how important the little moments of life are. How, even in a far-off land, there are opportunities to make an impact on someone's life. As I watched the Marine sprint off, I noticed he kept looking back at Laky and I wondered what dangers he was running to. What hidden traps awaited him on this day? I immediately prayed for his safety and that of his fellow warriors. I prayed that he would make it home to Minnesota, wrap his arms around his parents and then sit on a lovely bed of green grass and hold his precious German Shepherd that held such a special place in his heart. It's been thirteen years since that meeting along that hot, sandy and dusty street but I have not nor will I ever forget those "Tears Along the Road."

The Gift of Giving

When in Iraq we often had children walk up to our checkpoints and ask for cold bottled water, and candy. I guess I'd watched too many war movies growing up where the kid would have explosives or hand grenades attached to them and then once close enough, Boom! Facts are facts though and there were many instances in Iraq involving young children being shot because they were pointing rockets and machine guns at American soldiers and Marines. Warning shots were fired but if the children attempted to bring the weapon up for a site picture they were taken out as a combatant. It is the reality of waging war against an enemy with no scruples regarding civilians.

In the Air Force I had many friends who had been stationed in Vietnam at flight lines protecting American aircraft. Several told of children slinging grenades at their pill box positions. These stories and briefings were in my mind as I stood vigil at Checkpoint Two and Checkpoint NEC.

One day, it finally happened to me. I was standing in the shade waiting for a cement truck to get cleared when off in the distance I could see three little girls walking our way. Oh boy, here we go. I hate being mean to kids but I already knew I would shoo these kids away as I had instructed my other guys to do.[85] My strong will was about to be tested.

With these kids bearing down on us I called my interpreter over and was about to instruct him to tell these girls to beat it when I got a glimpse of them up close. The three girls looked to be between the ages of six and ten years of age. The dresses they wore were haggard and worn. I could see that not a single girl had shoes or sandals to

---

[85] This was a policy I softly enforced. Basically I told the men to use their judgement with children. If they wanted to hand out goodies it was their call but I told the guys it was best if we just made the kids stay away.

protect their feet. I don't know why. I guess I was a sucker but I let them approach me.

One girl who appeared to be the oldest never looked up. She just had a continuous shrug. I guessed she was extremely shy. I said hello to the young ladies and they responded with a greeting and a request for bottled water. I told our interpreter that I would grab them some water. I went back to our cement walled office, opened our ice chest and pulled three ice cold bottles of water. I smiled knowing these little gals would love this.

I handed each one a bottle and their faces beamed with pleasure at the sight and the thought of the cool water in their parched throats. I handed the last bottle to the shy little girl with the shrug and then noticed that her "shrug" was due to her neck being fused to her chest. She had the most beautiful smile and it made me feel guilty to see her joy because her scars were a mirror that showed me the folly and insignificance of my own pathetic needs. I felt so guilty for complaining about meaningless things. Here was a young girl who had experienced such horrific pain yet had such amazing maturity and incredible joy in her heart. To flash me a smile for the mere gift of a bottle of water required only a wonderful heart. I was so humbled.

Even now when I look at the picture of these three, I can't help but think about the lessons they taught me that day. For a moment, there in that ancient city I was the pupil and my teachers were three little girls. I never forgot what they taught me. They thought I had given them a gift but in fact I was the recipient.

Through our interpreter I learned that a mortar or rocket fired by an insurgent had crashed into the kitchen of her home. The Iraqi doctors were able to save her life but there were no burn centers and her wounds were left to harden and pull her chin to her chest. In the States I knew she would have had a different outcome and that our doctors and facilities would have been able to provide her with a productive life but as she was a girl in a land that has little value on females, I knew her life would be hard. I hoped that one day she would be able to make it to America but the likelihood of that was very doubtful.

The little girl did state that she hoped to one day receive a surgery that would allow her to lift her head but she seemed to know it was probably not going to happen. Well, I can tell you that these little girls had me wrapped around their fingers and every night they would come by and every night I had water for them and sometimes I would have special treats as well.

Now, I am no fool. I knew I was in a warzone so I was very careful to watch the distance to see if the girls were trailed by anyone seeking to use them as suicide bombers. I would watch their clothes to be sure they did not look bulky underneath. I trusted the girls and cherished their friendship but I knew this was a warzone and the girls would be powerless against the demands of an insurgent with a gun to the head of their mothers.

Thankfully the little girls were never bothered and our nightly checkpoint visits were something I always cherished and I suspect they did as well. After all it is the "gift of giving" that really matters.

Triple Boom Whoosh!

It was September 2006 and I was a short timer which of course carried maximum weight of superstition. Military men are superstitious about things, about sayings and about the routines they undertake each day. One of the most feared was being a "short timer."

A short timer is someone who has almost completed their tour of duty and will soon be going home to family and friends. The saying was, "Thirty days and a drag bag." Throughout our country's history of battle, warriors have dreaded this time because it seemed that it was an invitation for death to come knocking. In Vietnam it became so bad that some unit commanders would hold their short timers back when they had a week left "in country." What could be more horrifying than surviving months of close combat only to die from an obscure piece of shrapnel intended for no one in particular.

I can tell you that as September grew older my days seemed to grow longer. Is my door locked when I sleep? Is there a scorpion in my boot in the morning? Is my helmet on before I leave my room? Am I presenting an easy target by sitting here in the shade? Am I safer making a run for it or should I just shelter in place? Vigilance. Attention to detail would keep my chances of leaving alive. Overall though the best thing to do is just stay busy so that's what I did. I filled my days with activities and worked so long and hard that I would immediately fall asleep when my head hit the pillow. My new motto was, "Stay busy and stay alive."

In mid-September a large group of the K9 handlers and our dogs made the short trip over to the Grand Festivities Square where Saddam used to hold his grand parades of military might. The grounds are famous for the Swords of Qadisiyah[86] that greet travelers. The crossed swords are probably the most famous landmark in the city. One could often see US military units taking photos under these famous swords held aloft by the molded hands of Saddam Hussein.

Pulling onto the parade ground and passing under the swords each K9 handler then drove his truck and trailer to the nearest shade tree of which there were plenty. Temperatures were high and the dogs required a rest from the relentless and glaring sun. Thankfully the parking area was large and liberally sprinkled with plenty of beautiful shade trees.

The tree I parked under had large leaves that provided a nice canopy to shelter from the heat. These trees were about fifteen to

---

[86] Opened to the public on August 8th, 1989 the monument took three years to complete. It was based on a design concept by Saddam Hussein. Iraqi sculptor Mohammed Ghani Hikmat completed the work. The site selected had the historical significance of being the location of the Muslim Arabs defeat of the Persians in the year 636.

twenty feet in height and they grew out wide at the top. The branches would extend outwards towards the other trees on both sides, as if they were reaching out to one another. The lower branches were about 8 feet above the ground. These branches caused the tree limbs to bend slightly downwards, which gave them the appearance of umbrellas made up of various colors of reds, orange, light greens, yellows, tans, and sandy colors. I noticed these softer shades were due to the fine dust which covers everything in the "Green Zone."

We'd refer to this substance as moon dust. If anyone has seen the news footage of Neil Armstrong and Buzz Aldrin walking on the moon, you'll recall the soil covering the moon's surface was like baking flour. When the intrepid astronauts took their steps the fine soil made an upwards and outwards bursting cloud but left perfect imprints of their foot falls. It was this same scene that came to mind when we walked anywhere in Baghdad. Of course there was a huge difference being that our moon dust was not majestic but rather annoying and drab. The dust covered everything including the leaves diminishing the few colors nature was able to provide in this environment. There was something sad about this.

Ever the optimist, I found myself acknowledging the contrast of beauty and ugliness in this revolting war. All my life, I've always paid attention to small details around me, such as these leaves. For just a few seconds I was removed from the heat, the stench, the dust, and sounds of war off in the distance. I felt a calmness which surprised me; it was a wonderful feeling, knowing I was able to recognize a bit of beauty in the midst of the massive destruction and sorrow which I found in every corner of this place.

I suspect these trees had been neglected for a few years, no doubt because of the war. It was certain they had not been manicured in quite some time. Of course there was really no need for it as there were no more speeches being given by Saddam. The parade fields no longer hosted the Iraqi army marching in review before Hussein, his generals and the people. The stadium and many of the buildings were burnt, showing the devastation meted out by US airstrikes. The main building bore testimony to the destructive power of a single missile. The sad, silent buildings would be ideal for our training purposes.

I looked over at my K9 partner and said, "Let's get the dogs out to stretch their legs and get some water." I knew what was coming next, as soon as we passed the crates the two dogs started barking. Today I had Laky with me and my partner had a dog named Sonnie who was a female fawn colored Belgian Malinois with a black face. She was absolutely gorgeous. She was doing what Mals do, spinning in circles in her crate. Both dogs were yapping at us as if to say, "Come on dudes, get us out of these crates and let's find those odors, so we can play with our Kongs!"

I told my K9 handler to go ahead and water his dog first; I'd follow once he was finished. My partner had a unique collapsible bowl which he brought out. I always wished I had one because they were so cool but I knew the time might come that I would forget it so I trained both Laky and Toris to drink from a water bottle, something that would always be handy.

It was my turn to water Laky so I jumped up into the back of the truck, Laky was barking his head off. I got to his crate, pulled out a bottle of spring water from the side pocket of my cargo pants, and then took my K-bar knife from the sheath on my right hip. With the tip of my knife I poked three to four holes in the top of the water cap and then stuck the top of the bottle cap through the top bars of Laky's crate door. I'd then squeeze the bottle and crystal-clear water would come out nice and easy. The entire time Laky is enjoying the cool bottled water.

Now it's time to get Laky out of the crate, and off the truck to give him a potty break. With working dogs worth thousands of dollars you don't just fling open the crate door and hope for the best. There is a process to opening the door because it is the one time Laky will have to make a bolt for it. These are highly trained dogs but they are dogs, and they will see an open door as an opportunity to get out and stretch their legs.

I put my right knee up against the crate door and I'm commanding him to "Stay," several times.[87] I'm keeping Laky's mind active, thinking about the commands I am giving. It is extremely difficult for a dog to think about two things at once so by giving him these commands I am taking his mind off of rushing past me.

While saying "Stay" I reach down with my left hand to unlatch the crate door. In my other hand I already have my leash which rests across my shoulders and I have the brass clasp at the end of my leather leash ready, in my hand and opened to quickly hook onto the "O-Ring" on his two-inch leather collar. As I'm reaching for the latch a slight wind caresses us bringing with it the odor of fish from the Tigris. Then I also noticed the odor of seal oil which I had used the night before to keep my leash in fine shape. Odd how such things stick in your mind through the years.

I begin to slowly open the crate door while continuously commanding him to stay. Then I reach down with my left hand, slip it between the top of the crate and the crate door, grasp his two-inch leather collar, remove my right knee from the crate door and then allow the door to open just enough to where he could get his head out. Once his head was out, I then snapped the leash clasp onto the big shiny "O-Ring" of his collar. I now had control.

The process isn't over yet though for there are still opportunities for mistakes. I allow the crate door to swing all the way open and as I'm about to head to the tailgate to jump off the back of the truck I scan the area in front of us, to the left side and right side of the truck to make certain no one will be in Laky's pathway when coming off the truck. Then as I'm coming out and off the truck I'm yelling out

_____

[87] We had different words for commands. In this book you see we gave commands like we had a household pet in the States, "Sit", "Stay" and "Lie down" but it was not the case. We used a foreign language when giving commands to our dogs. I do not reveal those words in the book so that readers don't get themselves in trouble. One word could get someone accidentally bit by a dog.

in a loud voice "Dog Coming Out!" Safety is paramount. One bite to a military person, a civilian or any contractor in the war zone is to the advantage of the enemy.

Someone who is bit may not be able to return to their vital work and my war dog will be placed in quarantine for at least ten days. We have two vital assets now off their duties. Such a circumstance only benefits the insurgents so safety and attention to detail was paramount at all times.

With our dogs watered and bowels relieved we placed them both back in their crates in the shade and made our way over to the designated assembly area. As we're walking towards the other handlers I looked back towards our parked truck and as I suspected both Laky and Sonnie were watching us intently. Once Laky noticed I looked back at him he gave me a loud German Shepherd bark, then three more in rapid succession. Sonnie barked once and then began to spin in tight circles in her crate. Hilarious. I'm convinced they were saying something in dog language which I could NOT put in print.

Our K9 trainers prepared a special day of sessions and searches in which our dogs would retest and maintain their proficiency. I say, the dogs "maintain" but it was also just as important for we the handlers.

I always valued proficiency training because it kept me and my dogs sharp. When I became a trainer, I would often tell my students, "There are two things you don't want to happen as a K9 handler: one, to do something right and not know you are doing it right, and two, to do something wrong and not know it." That was the purpose of these exercises with our dogs and I relished them.

At the same time we were conducting training exercises with our bomb dogs, there was a large group of Marines who had gathered on the parade field. They had brought along two M1A1 Abrams tanks made famous by the early stages of combat in Iraq. Strung out between the two tanks they had stretched out a huge American flag.

It was an awesome sight and would make an amazing photograph. I smiled looking at these Marines, proud they were our men.

Meanwhile a contingent of Iraqi police had entered the parade grounds with a flatbed 18-wheeler truck, which was hauling several brand-new Iraq police vehicles. There were several Iraqi policemen assembling and getting into position for a group picture under the famous Swords of Qadisiyah.

As each of our K9 teams was called by a trainer to the building, the trainer would tell each handler where they did not want the K9 team going.

As I was searching Laky turned around a corner wall momentarily out of sight. When getting around the corner, my headlamp illuminated stairs leading to a lower floor. It was very eerie. The stairs led down to a floor smothered in darkness. The building had been knocked out in the opening days of the war and there was still no electricity here so the darkness was almost palpable. Laky started pulling me down the stairs. We had gone about four steps when I noticed the darkness was actually water that reached the ceiling of the lower floor. I was startled by the sight. I could not imagine the force that had created this destruction. I quickly commanded Laky to stay and I must admit that I turned and we left the spectacle rather quickly.

While waiting to be called up to the building to search for hidden explosives, the other handlers could walk their canine, groom their dog, or just sit and relax with their canine. Some handlers chose to put their dog back in their crate. These were good learning opportunities for certain.

There would always be one or two handlers who'd pull away from everyone else, just to be by themselves with their canine. I believe they were trying to deflate and unwind. There was a lot of stress in the war zone and being alone with a dog and just petting him or her helped remove the stress of war. There was also stress during the training exercises, no one wanted their bomb dog to miss a hidden explosive, planted by our K9 trainers, and I'm speaking from personal experience of course.

While wrapping up, we could hear the distinctive sound of helicopters coming in. Two black hawks swept in low and landed right in front of the viewing stands where we were working our dogs. Within a minute or two a caravan of US Army HUMVEEs drove up and soon the two groups were mingling for some photo ops. This was a popular place.

It was time to go though as we had both finished and passed our proficiency training. Laky and Sonnie were loaded up into the back of our truck, one at a time, of course. Once into their crates we double checked to make certain the crate doors were double locked, which was a must because of the horrible conditions of the roads and streets in Baghdad. One thing a K9 handler does not need, is for a crate door to open because of rough potholed roads. It has happened.

My K9 handler jumped into the passenger seat and I got behind the driver's wheel. He turned slightly to his left to glance back through the rear window, checking one last time on his bomb dog. I turned to my right to glance through the rear window to check once more on Laky, all looked good!

We both rolled our windows down and I then put the key into the ignition to start the engine. I pushed the clutch in, shifted into first gear, slowly pressed down on the accelerator, and slowly let out the clutch. Our vehicle began to move forward slowly. I was taking my time being sure not to jostle the crates in the bed of our truck. I looked at the speedometer and noticed we were moving forward at 5 MPH, I then turned to my left to look at the US Marines standing between the two tanks and the American Flag held up in front of them in this group picture. Man they looked sharp.

I then heard three distinct sounds off in the distance which I recognized, they were either three mortars or three rockets which were fired at that very instant. I was certain these enemy projectiles were coming in on us because of the juicy target we presented to them. This was a mistake by all of us. We had grown complacent not remembering what a juicy target we presented. The insurgents have spotters and informants and the word had been passed along about all of this activity on the parade grounds. I was furious at myself. I knew better and as soon as I heard the sounds, I knew we had committed an age-old mistake.

I was still looking out to my left at the Marines and Iraqi Police and realized one of these three booms was coming from my left. The Marines and Iraqi police were targeted, they were all running for cover. I noticed two Marines running towards one another, they were both holding the American flag at each end and while running toward each other they were ensuring the flag didn't touch the ground. Everyone else ran for cover but these two protected the flag. I was so proud. As the two Marines passed each other one took control of the flag and pressed it against his chest and sprinted for cover. I had witnessed the whole thing and can testify that the flag never hit the ground. Salute to these two Marines.

Keep in mind, this is all happening within seconds and though proud of these Marines I knew my life was still in extreme danger. I looked quickly to my front and began to accelerate. At the exact moment I stepped on the accelerator I heard a huge explosion to my right. I could not see where the impact had been but what met my eyes next, reminded me of a scene from a monster movie. Leaves from trees in the distance began to cascade to the ground. More trees began to lose their leaves and we could hear little rattling sounds as twigs, branches and leaves were shredded. The movement of this phenomenon was approaching our direction in milliseconds. I knew the trees were being shredded by shrapnel that was slashing the air in our direction. We could do nothing but duck down and pray. I knew that death was coming down on us in a hurry. It was surreal.

Now the falling green leaves and twigs, were falling ever so close to our right and it was then that I slammed my foot onto the brake pedal. Suddenly we could see a wall of shining hot shards of steel ten feet in front of us above our truck, and as low as the hood of our K9 truck careening through the air.

I could tell this wall of death was about out of strength because the shrapnel was coming down like a plane coming in for a landing. Still very deadly to anyone in its path. Several of these shrapnel pieces were flying within inches of the hood of our K9 Truck. It was over in a matter of a few seconds.

With the truck in park we both jumped out to check on our dogs. Sonnie was fine, happy, looking around with a happy look on her face, panting from the heat of the day. It was a different story with Laky. He was quiet, still and shaking like a leaf in a windstorm. He had been displaying some signs lately of being skittish and I was afraid this latest explosion might have really impacted his psyche. I would get him out of the crate once we were back at the kennel and love him up and see how he was doing.

I could see some of the shrapnel lying on the ground so I quickly ran over and picked up a piece. I knew that if I had been driving faster it would have come through our compartment windows or perhaps pierced the dog crates. It had been a close call. The shrapnel in my hand was still hot so I was passing it from one hand to the other when several of our K9 guys ran up to see if we were all ok. "Yeah, we are fine, thank God" I said and then added, "Here, catch." I tossed the hot shrapnel to a K9 handler who quickly realized it was a hot potato so he passed it to another guy who passed it back to me. We were all laughing.

My next words came fast while I was briskly walking toward my truck, "Listen, those bad guys are still out there. Let's get out of here." Everyone agreed. I jumped into the truck and drove out of there like a bat leaving a Texas cave.

No one killed and no injuries. It was a miracle. The truth was though that there was one injury, my dog Laky. Baghdad was starting to eat away at his nerves, the explosions of rockets and mortars, suicide bombers blowing themselves up, it was all stacking up in Laky's brain. He was showing signs of PTSD and I knew my buddy would never see another war, well, at least I was praying it would be so. He would be retired. It would be impossible to get him working again. My heart wanted to burst. I felt so bad for him. Dogs

263

are a lot like people and just like people they have different mental makeup.

Toris had been through three tours in Iraq and two in Afghanistan yet he was always ready to go to work. Explosions represented the enemy to Toris, something he wanted to take on. Weapons fire was an everyday occurrence that seemed ordinary. Yet to Laky these sounds were unfamiliar, terrifying and to be avoided at all costs.

Laky was born in Russia and trained in South Africa. He had come to Iraq with a South African handler.[88] I did not have the chance to work with him prior to our contract here so I had no history with Laky.

As it turned out, he was too young and should never have been brought to Iraq. I had done my best to give Laky direction and he had proven spectacular in searching for explosives. It had worked out quite well but the last few weeks had been full of devastation all around us evidenced by the shockwaves of VBIEDs and IEDs constantly reverberating through our checkpoint. I would glance at Laky and see him lower his head and drop his ears. I knew in my heart he was done but we had to survive these last few weeks and then maybe I could adopt him. I had a feeling that I would be able to but we would see what the future held.

For now I needed to get his mind off of our environment and back onto fun things, his Kong, doing practice searches, rough housing with me and enjoying his meals. What would the last few weeks hold? I prayed that they would be peaceful so Laky could rest. Nothing to do but take it one day at a time. That night I sat beside Laky in his kennel, just talking to him. Spending time with him. I looked into Laky's eyes as I scratched the top of his head, and with all of my heart and all of my being I implored my buddy, "Come on Laky, hang in there bud. We're almost home."

---

[88] In the chapter "Enter the South Africans and Laky" I talk about this matter

Laky and I during proficiency training.

Laky and I undergo proficiency training in the review stands at the Grand Festivities Square Complex. Note the Sword of Qadisiyah at top right.

The review stands for the parade grounds of the Grand Festivities Square. The same stands from which Iraqis would watch Saddam Hussein famously fire a rifle into the air during military parades. (Handler/Trainer blocked out for security reasons)

Showing the shrapnel that skidded over the engine compartment of my truck in background. The inset photo shows the piece in relation to a US penny.

When Falcons Explode

It was October 10th, 2006 and I was working the 1500 to 2300 shift (3pm to 11pm) and it was a relatively uninteresting day. The sun had been down for about three hours so the city had grown relatively quiet. Government workers were long gone and the construction site was closed for the day. Occasionally a gravel truck would come through with a late load of product but for the most part it was very quiet.

Suddenly, around 1930 hrs. the sky lit up as a giant explosion about a mile away mushroomed into the night. Within a second or two the sound reached us, the all too familiar "whump" but this was the mother of all "whumps." I looked at our guards and we shook our heads. We all had the same thought, "Here it comes. This is it." The explosion was to the south of us and from the Red Zone. Then several more enormous explosions ripped the sky and shattered windows for five miles around. They could not shatter our windows though for ours had already been cracked by previous explosions. Our imaginations ran wild with the possibilities. We checked our weapons and prepared for the worst.

Turns out the insurgents had fired a mortar and made an unusual shot in that it hit a good target for them, an armory at an American Forward Operating Base called Falcon. The original hit was not that devastating but it ignited a fire that defeated all efforts to extinguish it. Then ammunition began cooking off and the firefighting efforts came to a halt. When the stockpile exploded in mass it created a chain reaction of explosions that lit up the sky. The initial explosion and large ones that followed were so huge and devastating that they actually registered on seismology equipment miles away.[89]

---

[89] The explosion was recorded by American servicemen and can be seen on YouTube. Just type in the date, October 10, 2006 and add the words "ammunition dump explosion"

Raining Rockets

I tried to remain positive and upbeat during my last few weeks in Baghdad and even had an idea that perhaps the insurgents would lay off trying to kill us. Why should they? I was definitely hoping they would ease up on their efforts. Being a short timer provides an added level of stress because no one wants to die when so close to getting home.

Standing near our checkpoint, I was waiting for my turn to search a vehicle when off in the distance I could hear a familiar sound approaching. A rocket! It was low and it was coming in fast. It sounded very similar to a jet and was tearing through the sky just as fast. I could tell by the trajectory that I did not need to seek shelter so I stood and watched as the rocket impacted short of our checkpoint into the Tigris River.

The explosion was magnificent to behold as a giant geyser of water erupted several dozen feet skyward. The cascading water sounded as if someone had taken a large fire hose and was spraying the surface of the river. Even though I was a hundred yards from the impact site the sound was incredible. It was so odd how such pleasure could be derived from something so deadly. The scene would be forever seared into my brain.

This would be the only rocket fired on this day for the insurgents had learned that the longer they remained in the open the more likely they were to be discovered and eliminated by a helicopter gunship or roving patrols.

The following day was business as usual. Sweat. Heat. Hydration. Shade. Searches. Gatorades. Vigilance. Dedication. More Hydration.

I was on a break enjoying the shade and guzzling down some water. Nearby two of my guys stood chatting near the entryway of our concrete building that had once been a barber shop. Concrete barriers twelve feet high had been placed around the building making the enclosed space our "go to" place when mortars and rockets were inbound.

When American tanks had first rolled into Baghdad and created the Green Zone the owner of this establishment had been invited to leave. I am sure he was compensated but his choices would have been few. He was leaving.

We liked the building because it was quite sturdy, having been made of concrete. With the construction of the new US Embassy the former barbershop took on new significance as the office for Checkpoint Miami. Looking back, I am not sure how our checkpoint acquired the name Miami but it definitely sounded way cooler than its official title of Checkpoint New Embassy Compound (Checkpoint NEC).

Because our small building was made of concrete it provided good protection from incoming enemy fire but it was also resistant to the radiating effects of the heat. This was a benefit we all enjoyed, men and canines. The inside was always cooler than most buildings and to make it even better we had two window mounted air conditioning units which surprisingly worked quite well.

Toward the rear of the building were two beautifully tiled shower stalls. Forward thinking people had secured iron bars over the entrances to these two stalls, thus creating holding kennels for our dogs in the air conditioning. This area was used sparingly though because we did not want our canines being accustomed to cool air. Having our dogs shut down because they were unaccustomed to heat would be a disaster so it was rare that we used the air conditioners. Most days we just left the windows and door open and allowed the dogs to lay on the cool tiles which the canines adored.

Most handlers at the checkpoint, including myself, chose to leave the dogs outside under the shade of the camouflage netting I had acquired. We also had the option of placing our dogs in the small "cool down" pool I had created. I had worked hard to make our checkpoint more comfortable for the dogs and handlers yet being careful to not decrease their effectiveness and desire to work in the heat.

So, as I'm enjoying the shade and some cold water from our ice chest, I'm listening to two handlers talking about the FIFA World Cup that had taken place in Germany in July. The soccer tournament turned out to be the most watched in the seventy-six-year history of the tournament. In fact, the final game between Italy and France was seen live by over 700 million people across the globe. It was a big deal and the fellas were talking about some of their favorite moments. I forget how the conversation even began but myself not being a fan of soccer had nothing to add so I just listened, enjoying their passion for the subject.

Soon the conversation turned to families back home and that was something I definitely could provide commentary on. We laughed and smiled listening to the misadventures of raising families back in our respective homes. This was a nice moment, a rare moment of peace, just three guys enjoying each other's company and the thoughts of home. It was great.

Coming in fast and low I could hear the familiar screech of death on a trajectory that seemed to be locked on to us. A rocket! The two handlers were directly in front of me and my back was to the search lane, perhaps twenty-five yards from where I was standing with my men. In a fraction of a second, I looked at the guys and could see they had not picked up on the imminent death fast approaching, they looked unconcerned.

Wham! Deadly close! Dirt, debris and dust filled the air and rocks and clods of dirt were pouring down all around us. I could hear the chunks hitting the roof of the tiny building and could feel small bits of rock pepper the ground all around. My ears were slightly ringing and I discovered that I was on the protective side of our "T-walls" lying atop my two K9 handlers. I had no idea how we all got there. The blast?!

One of the men was talking to me. His eyes were huge circles of white with small marble sized iris' in the center. I could see his mouth moving but was having a difficult time discerning what he was saying. I shook my head and slowly stood. I did a quick inspection of my body, no injuries. "Are you guys injured?" I was shouting because of the adrenaline and because my hearing was a little impaired. "No! We are good!" was their reply. "Check again!" I demanded, "Look over every inch of your bodies and be sure!"

Exiting the concrete barrier protection I looked over at our security search teams, the Peruvian and Chilean guards and shouted at their English-speaking supervisor, "Is everyone ok? Do you have any wounded!?!" I could see everyone was checking their limbs and the supervisor was running here and there inspecting his men. He was a great leader. They all checked out ok.

This was all happening in seconds but it felt much longer as I made my way over to the machinegun tower and yelled for the supervisor to check his man up there. He did and proved to be fine. Meanwhile I yelled for the handlers to inspect their dogs for wounds. They were on it. As I am running here and there checking on dogs, handlers and guards the supervisor is doing the same. Everyone, canine and human were fine. It was a miracle.

This rocket hit within thirty yards of our checkpoint, right near the banks of the Tigris River, on our side. I picked up a radio and called in the hit because EOD liked to be informed of such occurrences, to see what the insurgents were using. I also made a call to the Green Zone Fire Department because the grass and bulrushes alongside the river had caught fire and were sending large columns of gray smoke skyward. Soon the firemen were on scene as was EOD who were busy gathering pieces of the rocket.

I took in the scene and then once our nerves were settled, I told everyone I wanted to speak to them. This request was extended to our guards as well and the supervisor agreed and began to gather his men. Our checkpoint was closed during this time so I desired to use the calm to pass on some military knowledge. As we were waiting for the Peruvians and Chileans one of the guys I had been chatting with had a question for me.

"Dennis," he asked, "how did you do that?" I had no idea what he was talking about and admitted as much to him. He continued, "When that rocket came in you picked both of us up, one in each hand and threw us into the protection of the barriers and then you laid on top of us. How did you do that?" I had no recollection of even doing it.

Once the rocket exploded, I felt the blast wave pass through us and that was all I could recall. My next recollection was lying on top of my two guys but I had no idea how I got there. The two guys were looking at me in amazement but I had no recollection of the event. To change the subject and bring some levity I said, "Well, you guys were blocking my way into the entrance so I had no choice other than to throw your butts out of the way." Everyone laughed and the subject was not brought up again.

Within a minute or two all of the men, the handlers and the guards, were gathered around, quiet, serious. Most of the time I was jovial and tried to keep things lighthearted and positive but the message I had for these guys was deadly serious and my demeanor sets the tone, just as the rocket a few minutes before had set the atmosphere.

"Come in close. I want all of you to listen to what I have to say. These insurgents are coming for us, they want us bad. We are probably their very highest priority right now. The property we are standing on is United States soil, the grounds of the US Embassy and these guys know that. What better place to send a message than the ground we now stand on? We are a hot target."

"What's taking place here is simple and if you have a military background you'll understand and see this very clearly and perhaps already figured it out. Yesterday the insurgents fired a rocket at us that landed in the Tigris, perhaps one hundred yards from here. Today they fired a rocket that landed thirty yards from our checkpoint. They are walking the rockets in on us. They either have a spotter out there in one of those buildings across the river or somewhere else close that is helping them make what's called a 'Range Card.'"

Looking around at the men I could see they were all intently listening, "Yesterday when the rocket landed in the river an insurgent was watching and marked on a map where the rocket landed. He then called up his buddies and delivered the impact point. Adjustments were made to their rocket firing platform and today, using the new settings, they landed the rocket thirty yards closer. Right now as we stand here there is an insurgent on a cell phone relaying the news that will bring a rocket down directly onto our position tomorrow."

The news was taking hold. Some nervously licked their lips while others glanced down at the ground. They were processing what I was telling them and it was bringing it all home. Tomorrow we would get hit and it would be on target.

My briefing continued, "I'm telling all of you right now, make sure you're wearing your battle gear tomorrow. Everyone. No exceptions! Guards and handlers wear your helmets and your flak vests because tomorrow we are going to get hit. Tomorrow they are coming for us!"

I had effectively made my point. Having served in the military for twenty-one years I could pull from all of that experience. I was determined to keep my guys, our dogs and myself alive.

The following morning, the big day, the tension was palpable and as I did not report to the checkpoint until 15:00 hrs. I made several checks during the morning and early afternoon to ensure the men were ok and that the expected rocket had not come in. So far it had been quiet.

Soon it was time for me to pick up my two dogs and head to the NEC. I grabbed my flak vest, Kevlar helmet, gloves and dog gear and said a prayer as I left making one last glance at the pictures of my family resting on the table next to my bunk. Game face, time to go.

Laky, Toris and I arrived at the NEC Checkpoint for our 15:00 hrs. to 23:00 hrs. shift. It was a very hot and clear day. My first order of business was to unload my dogs which was of course one at a time, as two alpha dogs side by side is a recipe for disaster. So first I placed my leather leash on Laky's collar and then jumped off the back of the truck bed. Then with Laky down I reached up with my other hand and placed my palm inside the crate and lifted it out. I have Laky in one hand and the crate in the other.

I quickly glanced around in all directions to be sure Laky is not going to intercept paths with a stranger or another canine. All clear, so I yell out, "Dog coming around!" I then walk to the shaded area beside the old barber shop and place the crate on the ground. With the crate door open I have Laky re-enter his crate and as he turns, I unclasp the leash and tell him to stay while I am securing the door in place, double locked. I then return to the truck and retrieve Toris who is barking at me, angry that I had seemingly left him behind.

At the same time I'm unloading my two German Shepherds and my gear, the off going shift is loading their canines and gear into their truck. It's been a long hot day for them. They'd been at it since 07:00 hrs. but they survived another day in the war. Prior to departing they briefed me on anything which had taken place during their shift, information like the most recent info on vehicles and the plate tag numbers and letters of suspected insurgent vehicles. They then briefed us on any new tactics being used by insurgents to gain access through our checkpoints.

We were also briefed on any expected large convoys coming in from Kuwait, delivering building supplies for the new United States Embassy. We'd receive intel on incoming new third world contractors hired to perform work on the US Embassy. These were always men and were just who'd you expect, carpenters, cement workers, plumbers, electricians, etc. Briefings were always time consuming but vital.

On this particular day we were told that there would be at least twenty-five or more new workers arriving. Prior to the arrival of these new men I consulted with the Peruvian and Chilean guards discussing the most efficient way to handle the large influx of human traffic. The K9 teams brought a new aspect to searching a bus load of workers and we laid out the best way to search for each and every one of them.

The bus arrived and our guards boarded with an interpreter and told the men they would all be searched and their bags. They were instructed to hold their belongings and not place them down until instructed where and when. The guards debarked the bus and soon the men started filing out.

The workers were pointed to a large area I had selected. The space allowed me to have three rows of personal items placed on the ground. One by one the men were shown where to lay their gear being certain that it did not touch other items and that there was at least four feet of space between the items of each man so that our K9 teams could maneuver through and around the conglomeration of bags and suitcases.

I was very strict about personal belongings not touching another person's because if there was explosive residue in any of these items, I did not want it cross contaminating other bags. Such an occurrence would have created a log jam in our checkpoint, something we could not allow to happen with so many utility trucks coming through with goods bound for the embassy.

The workers followed our instructions to the letter and while our K9 team searched the bags the guards searched the men and then conducted a visual check of the bus for explosives. Once this was completed, we had one of our K9 teams search the bus for explosives. Everything came back clear so the men were allowed to return to the bus with their gear and the bus drove off delivering the newest batch of workers for the US Embassy construction project.

As the bus drove off, I could see two civilian vehicles had driven up into our search area. I began approaching the vehicles with Laky at my side, checking the wind direction to set up for our downwind approach. Laky was doing good today. He really seemed to snap out of that funk he had been in after the close call endured at the parade grounds with the incoming rockets. I was proud of him and his heart.

We set up downwind and I had Laky go to the "Down" position. I could see tiny hairs on his back were erratically twitching in the soft breeze that came through our area. I was watching for any sign that Laky was picking up explosive odor. He was not so we went forward and followed his search pattern. All went well. We then approached the second car which likewise proved clean. I turned toward the guards to signal them to raise the bar allowing these two cars to enter. As I was lifting my hand up to give him a "thumbs up" sign there was a loud "Boom!" and then darkness.

Veterans of combat often say, "You never hear the one that gets you." I am sure there have been thousands of military men and women who have heard the one that got them but I can tell you I had no idea that anything was inbound from the enemy. Everything in my world was per routine and then suddenly there was a loud "Boom!" like a train being dropped from a tall building and then darkness. Weird how I did not hear this one coming in because I had always heard them in the past.

We had rockets pass over all the time at Checkpoint Two and of course at our current checkpoint, there would be a few seconds to take cover and then boom. This was different. On this day it was everyday noise: the engines of small cars, the distant sound of helicopters, gunfire, the chirping of birds in the trees around our checkpoint and then "Boom!"

So disorienting. I always thought I would have a few seconds to prepare and set my mind for the actions I would need to take but it was not to be. I recall that though everything was complete blackness I could still hear the goings on around me. Though I could open my eyes I couldn't see a darn thing. I was aware that an explosion had happened and that it had been very close. I could hear the sound of scratching, incessant scratching, like nails on a hard surface and I instantly knew it was Laky trying to run away. He was pulling hard and he was incredibly strong, pulling left, then right, back left, then straight and then right and all the while the sound of his nails on the road trying to get traction to run and get to cover.

If I completely lost consciousness the chances were high that I would lose my grip on Laky's leash and then he would be running free. I could imagine him running and running and not stopping until he had ended up outside the Green Zone never to be seen again. I could not bear the thought. I knew Laky, dragging a leash behind him, would be found and that the American flag on his collar would be a death sentence for him if he were caught by an insurgent.

Truly amazing how much a brain can process in just a second of time. All of those thoughts flashed through my mind and stiffened my resolve to wake up. Fortunately I was able to maneuver my grip in such a way that allowed the loop of the leash to move down my hand, and over my right wrist which meant that if I passed out Laky would have to drag me wherever he went.

All of this was done in seconds and in total darkness because my eyes were still not working. All the while I am shaking my head from side to side trying to unscramble what is wrong with my brain. I keep saying to myself, "Don't pass out! Don't pass out!" I could feel the heat of the day on my skin, I could sense the sweat pouring from my body and the disgusting grubby taste of dirt in my mouth.

Suddenly my legs gave out and I knew I was falling to the ground. My immediate thought, "Well, I guess this is it" and then I hit the ground hard with both of my knees but in that moment of pain my eyesight returned. I was back into the world of hell on earth. I could see guards hunched over running for cover. I could see bodies lying in the dirt face down and I thought, "Oh crap, I've lost some men!"

I blinked my eyes to refocus and looked again at the men lying in the dirt and noticed that they had their hands over their heads and that they were quickly looking side to side. They looked to be scared but ok.

Back up on my feet, I looked down at Laky and yelled, "Let's go boy! Let's find some cover!" Laky was right by my side and

277

following my lead. We ran to the concrete building that had once been a barber shop. Once we were inside, I knelt beside Laky to check him for wounds. He looked to be fine. His skin was intact and there was not even a hint of blood anywhere on his body. Frankly, I was surprised. Grateful, but indeed surprised. I did a quick check of myself and was shocked that I seemed to be ok.

It was Laky that I was worried about because he had already been showing signs of stress and I knew that K9 PTSD was a high probability. I had a hard time getting him to stand. He felt safe in the building and had no desire to go outside. His body was trembling and his tail was tucked up way under his body. In that moment I knew he was done as a war dog. He had reached his limit just the same as a guy in Vietnam under constant mortar attack would have reached his limit.

There was difficulty in coaxing Laky to stand but I knew I needed to get him thinking about something else. Standing would be a first step. He finally did but was still showing a little tremor in his body. I had to get him into the back room of the barber shop into one of the shower stalls that had been converted into a kennel for our dogs. I picked him up and rushed him into the stall, laid him down on the cool tiled shower floor, quickly shut and secured the metal door. I told him, "I'll be right back buddy. I have to check on the other dogs and my guys."

Fifteen minutes later I returned to Laky after I had checked on all the men, the guards and our canines. Everybody checked out fine. Well, everyone but Laky and I. My poor boy Laky would never be the same. I struggled to get him back to work but from that moment on every little noise, or crack, or screech of an air brake would cause him to flinch and cower to the ground. Laky was no longer able to function as an Explosives Detection Dog. His working days in Iraq were over.

As for me I had suffered terrible injuries to my ears. I had constant ringing which would go on to last for almost four years. Once back home in San Antonio the doctors at Wilford Hall Medical Center would conduct many tests on my ears but the treatment could only be rest and time. My body would have to recuperate and extinguish the annoying and irritating ringing in my ears. Thankfully they did heal and to date the ringing is gone.[90]

I'll never forget the feeling of that tugging on my wrist as Laky was trying to run away. The sound of his nails on the ground still haunts me. The feeling that I would be yet another foreign warrior to die in this ancient dust was one I will never forget. I was thankful I had survived of course but then I thought, "What if the rockets had been raining down." I shuddered to think about it for I knew I would have been killed. The insurgents had worked the firing problem like professionals and over the course of three days had "walked" it right into the kill zone.

The only reason no one had died or been injured could only be left to God to answer. Perhaps He had things we all needed to do. For me, I knew I was going to take full advantage of the bonus time given to me. Short timer. Gosh. I only had a couple more weeks to go. Would I make it out in one piece and would I make it out with my dogs? Time would tell.

The Land of Oz

We were tired. Laky, Toris and I had been working almost nonstop for weeks at a time. The constant threat of death and the ever-present sound of explosions wears you down both mentally and physically. I was having great difficulty sleeping. I knew I had just about reached my breaking point. Like Laky I was collapsing inside and I knew that if I had to stay any longer than expected there might be an issue.

I was so incredibly sad. I had seen so much death and destruction that it no longer made an impact on me. I was as alert and attentive

---

[90] I do have occasional hearing loss but it seems to correlate with my wife asking me to do a chore around the house.

to detail as ever but I was having to exert more and more internal strength to get through each day. In addition I was seeing my dog Laky deteriorate on a daily basis and this was also breaking my heart. I had to get him out of here. I had to get Toris out of here. Crud! I had to get out of here!

I had been working a swing shift this day, an eight-hour shift that ran from 15:00 hrs. to 23:00 hrs. There was nothing unusual about the day, in fact it was quite ordinary. All of my K9 teams were now on post, everyone had been briefed by myself on the most recent intelligence reports regarding current threats by insurgents. In addition I had given the daily safety briefings which covered weapons, canine and personal safety. I finished up by reminding everyone to keep themselves and their canines hydrated. "Be safe everyone and watch your six."

It was a normal day of searching vehicles for small explosives and car bombs, making certain that all cement trucks which pulled up to the checkpoint had the mixing drum of their truck turning. The sight immediately brought to mind a Defense Department video of a cement truck pulling up to a hotel in downtown Baghdad. In the video it is plainly seen that the bowl is not turning. Seconds later the truck explodes killing several standing around.

With this in mind, not a single cement truck was ever allowed to approach our checkpoints without the drum rolling. If they showed up and the drum was not rolling, they were told to turn the drum on. If they did, we knew then that the truck was not loaded with explosives. If they did not want to turn the drum on, then it would be guns on the driver, get the driver out of the vehicle, search the driver, search the vehicle with our bomb dog. Tense, deadly, straight up, simple!

The shift was about to come to an end and I was on a break. I thought I'd walk with Laky down to the Tigris River which was about fifty yards or so from our checkpoint. We reached a small cement wall which stood about twenty-four inches in height and was about fifty yards long. I had no idea why this small wall was there and for the life of me I could not figure out what purpose it served.

Yet there it was so Laky and I used it as a perch so we could see the Tigris a bit better. It was just a bit after 22:00 hrs. in the evening so I was not worried about being seen by snipers.

I suppose I was there making a memory with Laky because I knew we would be leaving soon and I knew I would never return to this historic and deadly land. With Laky seated at my left side on this ledge we both took in the view.

It was a comfortable night, not real hot and not cold, it was just the perfect temperature with the breeze coming up off the Tigris. I looked down at Laky and was able to see his beautiful German Shepherd face. The rich golden colors of his muzzle and from his nose up to his eyes was jet black fur. Above his eyes the fur continued upwards with the rich golden colors and in the middle of his forehead above the eyes and right in the middle of the rich golden brown fur was a black line about half an inch to an inch wide coursing upwards to the top of his head, then meeting a full crown of black fur between his beautiful full strong standing ears.

I'll never forget how he looked up at me, looking deeply into my face, our eyes locked onto one another. I could see the reflection of the moon in his eyes, I could see his devotion and love for me and I was hoping he could read the same thing in my eyes.

I reached over in the moon lit darkness and scratched the top of his head with my left hand. He pushed against my hand which told me he was enjoying it. Laky displayed his real enjoyment by squinting his eyes as I was scratching his head, he was in heaven at this moment. I then glanced over at the Tigris River. I could see the reflection of just a few lights along its banks. The glow of the moon highlighted the swift swirling currents of this historic river. I was feeling rather peaceful, almost serene. For a moment I was transported to an Iraq with no inkling of war and death and I must say it was quite nice.

Suddenly all of this comfort and peace was ripped from me in a flash. Laky and I were thrown back into the terrors of war as a huge explosion off to our left across the Tigris River illuminated the sky.

I knew immediately it was a VBIED because of the deep double rumble sound it made. A giant rolling ball of fire broiled heavenward several hundred feet into the air. The explosion was enormous with the ball of fire almost as wide as it was high. Buildings surrounding the blast were perfectly illuminated by the blow torch of flames.

I could see dark objects twisting and turning, jettisoned through the air illuminated by the ball of fire. Then came enormous clouds of gray and black smoke that emanated from the fireball and seemed to consume everything in its vicinity. I was only about six or seven football fields away from this latest bit of destruction but I could not take my eyes off of it.

Within seconds after the initial explosion, I could hear automatic weapons fire now mixed in with the screams of women and children and at times I could hear the voices of men yelling along with the others. The wind was blowing in my direction and I could smell the stench of death and smoke but I could also discern the screams carried by the wind. It was the all-too-familiar sounds and smells of death, of Baghdad, of Iraq and I was sick and tired of it. One minute tranquility and peace and the next second fear, death, devastation. I was done.

Then, it was over. Two minutes of sheer terror over. The light retreated and the darkness regained its supremacy. Laky and I both stared into the darkness and I could not help but imagine the scene of terror taking place. At the moment I desired nothing more than to be on an aircraft with wheels up and Baghdad disappearing behind me. My mental faculties were showing cracks and I was so thankful I was leaving to return to the States.

I glanced down at Laky, he was tense, his eyes displaying fear. He was mentally done, checked out and had been for weeks now. In my mind, I was well aware that not far from where Laky and I now stood an insurgent, hell bent on destruction and death, decided to obliterate himself. The insurgent knew that he was going to kill and injure many men, women, and children yet it made no difference to him. Perhaps he had been an unwilling cooperative; cajoled and intimidated into the deed, but in the end, it made no difference for the act was still deplorable. At what point does a man say enough is enough? Did insurgents hold guns to his children and demand he perform the deed? My mind raced with these thoughts and I knew if I kept dwelling on them my mind would crack. Yes, time to get out of this land.

Still my mind raced even though I yelled and pleaded for it to be silent. My traitorous mind flipped back to the scene across the river and allowed me to imagine the insurgent who at that very moment was holding a video camera recording the horrific scenes of death. The video would be used to proclaim their agenda for all the world to see on venues such as the internet and Al Jazeera TV. I hoped for the day when such men would meet their death at the receiving end of a Hellfire missile fired from an Apache gunship or a five-dollar hunk of lead fired from the rifle of a US sniper. My heart was getting darker and my emotions were running high. I pleaded with my mind to retreat from this train of thought yet it kept rolling through my consciousness.

Do something! Snap out of it. I had to remind myself of something from home, something to snap me out of this funk and with the thoughts and longings for home so strong on my heart I knew what I had to do to escape, even if only to jostle myself from this destruction.

I looked down at Laky at my left side, I looked at the strong flowing currents of the Tigris River illuminated by the reflection of city lights. I stood erect, at the position of attention and clicked my heels together three times and said, "There's no place like home, there's no place like home, there's no place like home." That did it. I was back from the abyss and quickly turned on my heels and told Laky, "Come on boy."

Walking away from our perch I could hear an occasional scream and discharge of a firearm but I kept my face forward looking toward our checkpoint. I ignored the scene I could do nothing about. I kept repeating the words in my mind, "There's no place like home, there's no place like home." Over and over and over.

Oh how I wished at that very moment that Toris, Laky and myself were back home in America with my dear loving wife Debbie, my children and my grandkids. I had been in <u>the land of Oz</u> long enough and it was time to go home. Time was running out for me. I knew it and could feel it in my core.

The following day our supervisor was driving through the checkpoint. He must have seen something in my eyes. He knew I was thinking about extending because the roster had some empty slots. They had offered me some monetary benefits that were substantial but when my supervisor saw my face he said, "Dennis, you have to go home. You've done enough. Get out of here while you can." He was right. There were few that I esteemed higher so when I heard these words, I knew I was leaving.

He smiled, we shook hands, "Thank you" was all I could say. It was such a relief to have his permission to leave. My sense of duty had almost convinced me to stay and help them out but this messenger knew what I needed to hear, I needed confirmation that it was okay for me to depart. I felt a huge weight leave my shoulders. I had done my best and kept people and canines alive. I had given my all for my men, my dogs and my country. Time to leave The Land of Oz.

Laky on the ledge that overlooks the Tigris River.

Three Little Kisses

I was so excited to be leaving I could barely contain it. Excited but still vigilant because I had one last shift to do before my departure back to America and I didn't want to be that sad story of the guy who got "whacked" on his last day on post. So, I was exceptionally sensitive to my surroundings and the shift of course dragged on and on. It seemed that the clock was going back one hour for every two it advanced.

A call came out that I had visitors approaching. I looked at my watch and knew immediately who it was. My three little angels. The little girls who had visited me every night for the past couple of months had returned one last time. I had told them that I was leaving to go back home to Texas so they were aware this would be goodbye.

One thing stood out to me immediately, their appearance. For months these little girls had worn haggard dresses that looked to be handed down from other siblings. In this environment I could understand the practice. Their feet were always bare. Tonight though they were all in beautiful clean and ironed dresses and their hair was brushed and it shone like it had just been washed. I could smell the aroma of soap coming from them. I wanted to cry. I was so moved by their desire to send me off in proper fashion.

I bowed slightly, smiled and said how absolutely beautiful they all were. They all looked at the interpreter with expectant looks to see what I thought of their appearance. I could see the translation taking effect as their eyes sparkled and their smiles broadened. As they grinned, I could see their teeth. They giggled and looked up at me shyly. It was then I made their smiles even bigger.

What they did not know was that I had previously asked my wife to send me some toys and goodies from home so that I could load these little cuties up with toys and snacks. You should have seen their eyes when they saw the little coloring books, crayons and "Etch A Sketch" that I had for each of them. In addition I had chips, donuts, soda and candy of all kinds for them. Their arms were bulging with this treasure and their smiles could not have been wider. It made my heart swell to see their excitement. My interpreter was smiling just as big as the kids and what was that? Did I see a tear in the interpreter's eye?

My little friends had to make two trips with all their loot. Once they were back, I walked them over to the ice chest to hand them each some water. As I turned the smallest girl who looked to be about six years old raised her right arm, extended her index finger and motioned for me to bend down. I bent down to her level and she took her hands and placed one on each of my cheeks and then gave me a kiss on the left side of my face. The other two then came up and did likewise, though with some difficulty for my little friend with the fused neck. I stood and now I had a smile as big as my home state.

With the interpreter standing at the ready I poured my heart out to my little friends, "I'll always remember the three of you and will tell others of your sweetness. I'll miss the three of you, be safe, and have a good life as you grow up." They received my words with silence and dignity above their years. I then handed four bottles of ice water to each of the girls. Their eyes were again so full of happiness for it's hard to find cold bottled water for most people in a war zone.

Slowly they turned and began their trek back to their home. As they walked off through the glare of lights from our checkpoint, I could not help but wonder at the life ahead of them. Would they live to be women? Would they be able to dream and then follow those dreams?

When they were just about to step off into the darkness out of the glow of our generated light, they all stopped and turned. They all waved as best they could with their hands so full and the youngest did her best to blow me a kiss. I waved, smiled and blew them a kiss in return. Just like that they were gone from my life but not from my memories or my thoughts and prayers. I prayed for their safety, for their pursuit of their dreams and for surgery that would allow the oldest to hold her head up high. I prayed that they would never forget me and that perhaps when the evil men came indoctrinating, that perhaps they would remember the American who loved spending time with them and counted them as his cherished little friends.

My three little angels on the night they got all dressed up to say goodbye.
The one on left reminds me of my granddaughter Brooke. She motioned
with her finger for me to bend down.

288

Fates Unknown

With my departure looming there was a deep and oppressive heaviness on my heart, the thought of leaving my two war buddies Laky and Toris behind. We had survived so much and our bond forged in war could not be equaled anywhere back home in the States. Leaving them behind was asking me to leave my arm, or my hand. I felt like I was being asked to amputate a limb and it really sucked. I knew there were thousands of war dogs in Iraq and that I was not the only one who wanted to take mine home but the reality was that both dogs were not my property.

I could not bear the thought of boarding a plane, bound for the land of comfort knowing my two war dogs would be left in this place of sand, heat and death. I was sure that no one could take as good care of Toris and Laky as I had. I doubted that another handler would take the time to brush them, play with them and nurture them as I had. I knew they would be fed and cared for but I guess I was being selfish and feeling sorry for myself. I had a pit in my stomach knowing they would have to stay.

My big worry was Laky who had shown signs of severe K9-PTSD and required constant encouragement just to perform basic tasks like walking outdoors. The slightest noise caused him to cower and hug the dirt. I feared that he would be put down after I left. He was so sweet and had such a loving heart. The thought of him left in a kennel day after day with no task to perform and no one to hug him and brush his beautiful coat troubled me deeply. I could imagine him staring at the door of the kennel day after day expecting me to show but to always be let down. I feared he would wonder where I had gone and why I had abandoned him. I had to get him out of Iraq. I had to bring him home, but how?

Toris was not the dog I worried about in the least. He was a tried and true veteran of many campaigns and many enemy attacks. He thrived under pressure and was always ready for a fight. Toris had the heart of a champion and I loved and respected him for it. Sure, I would love to take him home but the reality was that he was too valuable an asset. I knew I would have to say goodbye to him and I knew I would cry when the day came.

I did not want to leave them behind in this filthy environment, the bullets, rockets, mortars, suicide bombers, hordes of flies, and stinking lousy heat. My mind wandered to the K9 handlers of Vietnam. My heart truly breaks for the K9 handlers who had to leave their war dogs behind in Vietnam. It was such a horribly tragic black smear on our government for allowing that to happen.

I was sitting at my laptop stressing over Laky and Toris, staring at the screen but not pushing any keys. After a few minutes I glanced at my emails and saw one which looked very interesting. In the subject line it read, "Toris." Intrigued, I clicked on the message, "Dennis, Toris has served his country well in several countries and several campaigns. It is time he was retired. Would you like to adopt him?" I laughed out loud. I could not believe my eyes. Would I like to adopt Toris? It was a laughable question. They might as well have asked me if I would like to keep my arm. My answer was quick before they changed their mind, "Yes, I'll adopt him."

The only stipulation on keeping my veteran Toris was that I had to pay for his transportation home. Not a problem. Well, the money would not be a problem but the logistics might be another matter. I knew I would make it happen and I was thrilled!

My joy of adopting Toris was quickly overshadowed by my grief of having to leave Laky behind. The following day the head K9 trainer came by to tell me he was going to pick Laky up that evening in his truck and take him to several different checkpoints to see how Laky fared with other handlers.

I was worried about Laky because of his K9-PTSD and I knew that if a "strong handed"[91] handler was given Laky it would be a

---

[91] It is putting too much force, too much "compulsion" on a dog that does not need force or compulsion. A handler who "pops" the leash or scolds their dog in an aggressive manner. Some dogs require this technique. Experienced trainers will know which technique to use with various dogs. Laky was a "soft handed" dog who responded to praise and encouragement.

290

disaster. I knew Laky would shut down and not perform. I also knew that some handlers might get rough with Laky trying to coax him into being more aggressive. Having worked with Laky so intimately I knew that Laky needed a soft hand and that he needed constant praise and encouragement.

That evening the head trainer came by for Laky and as they walked out for a long evening of work a sick feeling welled in my stomach.

Later that night the trainer returned with Laky, "How'd it go with Laky today" I asked. The trainer looked grim as he shook his head, "Not good. Not good at all Dennis. Every noise, even car doors slamming, would freak him out. It was almost impossible for the handlers to keep him searching." I reminded the trainer about the recent rocket attacks that had almost killed both Laky and I. I told how Laky had tried running away and how he had been cowering and jumpy ever since.

I continued, "I can work with him, and keep him working, but ONLY because I trained him and can read his body language very well. I think he is suffering from K9-PTSD."

The lead trainer nodded and added, "Dennis I'm keeping track of eighty-five war dogs in proficiency training, so as you can imagine there's much to remember. I do recall your rocket attack a few days ago but had no idea it had impacted Laky in this way. It seems you're the only one who can read and work him." He stood silently, staring down at the ground and then looked up, "Dennis I'm going to conduct a 'stress test' on Laky, to see how he can handle other stress factors. I'll be running him myself on the leash." I then responded with, "Ok, I'll see you tomorrow then."

The next day, around midmorning, the lead trainer showed as promised. He hid explosive odor up against a huge generator which provided the electricity for our checkpoint. He allowed the odor to sit for thirty minutes, which is a standard set time if you want to allow the odor to build up in that area. He took Laky out of his crate and played a bit with him and a Kong. Of course Laky just loved this. Then it was time for a potty break to keep his mind on searching and not his bowels.

The trainer then began working Laky toward the generator that hummed with a loud mechanical noise. Working toward the explosive odor Laky had his head down sniffing the ground. About this time a truck had pulled up to the checkpoint behind Laky and the driver had exited and slammed his door shut. Laky's ears immediately went down and his body quickly lowered to the ground. I could see Laky's tail had gone between his legs. The trainer was watching Laky intently and had seen this display as well.

To Laky the loud sound must have meant the same thing as a mortar or rocket exploding. I felt so bad for him and could only imagine the fright he was feeling. It was not hard to imagine because I knew the fear firsthand. I could see in his body language that he was terrified and no longer searching. Laky's mind was on survival.

The experienced and awesome trainer did everything he could to help Laky find the explosive. In fact, he did everything but show him the explosive even walking within five inches of the hidden explosive odor. Laky walked right on by, with no indication he was picking up any odor at all.

Okay, a second try, the trainer then hid a stick of C-4, Plastic Explosives under a 4x8 section of beat up and worn looking plywood lying on the ground. After the required thirty minutes the trainer ran Laky on this odor as well. This time there was no one slamming any vehicle doors, and for that matter there were no vehicles in the search lane. The checkpoint was considerably devoid of noise. Laky was worked from the downwind side, and then worked crosswind, starting at about thirty yards away. The trainer walked Laky right on top of the plywood. Nothing from Laky. Not a nod of the head, not a wag of the tail and not the slightest bit of interest shown in any odor whatsoever. Laky's mind was miles away in the far recesses of his consciousness.

The trainer then put Laky up after giving him a water break. He then said, "Ok Dennis, give him about a twenty-minute break and then I will watch you work Laky on these same two hides."

After twenty minutes, I got Laky out of his crate, gave him a pee break, let him drink a small amount of water and ran him on these two hidden explosives. Laky was totally relaxed walking beside me and when on the search quickly found both explosives with his "Final Sit Response." The trainer looked at me and said, "You're the only one who can read him, you know him so well. You see the smallest things in his body language which no other K9 handlers could see, including myself. You know how to keep him motivated when you suspect he's getting uncomfortable with anything."

We stood in silence and I could tell the trainer was in deep thought. I glanced over at Laky in his kennel and he was looking at me, panting. My heart ached for him and his broken mind. The trainer broke the silence, "Dennis, I'm going to recommend to our Director that Laky be retired and if you want him, you can take him home with you. Do you want to take him home?"

I could not believe what I just heard and had to ask him to repeat what he just said. I wanted to make certain I was hearing him correctly, so, he brandished a huge smile and repeated the question I thought I had heard him ask. Tears filled my eyes. My heart seemed to enlarge and my chest swelled with emotion which I kept in check. After a few seconds to compose myself I replied, "Yes, I'll take my boy home with me."

The following day I was told that Laky's retirement had been confirmed and that both Laky and Toris belonged to me and that as my property they both had to be out of Baghdad in two weeks' time. Eureka!

There was a lead on a shipping company inside the Green Zone and once in their office I was told it would cost $14,000 to ship Laky and Toris home. There was no way I could do this because I had just spent almost $6,000.00 that week in having new central air conditioning installed in our home back in Texas.[92] I walked back to my room, praying and asking God to help me, to guide me to someone who could assist me. A favorite verse of mine came to mind when I was walking back to my quarters. It came from the book of Proverbs Chapter Three, verses 5 and 6,

"Trust in The Lord with all thine heart, lean not unto thy own understanding, in all thy ways acknowledge Him, and He shall direct thy paths."

This particular passage of scripture had been a standard I have tried to live by ever since I had accepted Jesus Christ as my Savior back on June 30th of 1982. The verses have helped me many times to trust God and allow Him to take care of whatever I was facing when I desperately needed His help and this was definitely one of those times.

The next day I had stopped by the director's office to see if he had any other suggestions which might help me get my two boys out of this war and home with me. As I was walking through the K9 administration office I heard a phone ring off to my right. I kept walking towards the director's office when I heard a familiar voice of a staff member yell out my name, "Dennis! There's a call for you from an Air Force Colonel."

Perplexed, and not having any idea why an Air Force Full Bird Colonel would be calling me, I took the phone, smiled and said, "Thanks." My friend handed me the phone and looked at me with this look of, "What the heck is going on? We never have any dealings with the upper brass, especially in the Air Force." I just shrugged my shoulders, as if to say, "Your guess is as good as mine."

With the phone in hand, I said, "Hello, this is Dennis Blocker, how can I help you Sir?" The response from the Colonel was simple, and straight to the point, of course! He stated the following, "I understand you have two German Shepherds you're trying to get

---

[92] Central air is a must in Texas. Visit in July if you wonder why.

out of Iraq, and back home with you. I also understand you all have been here 13 months, and that you extended longer because there was a great need. I have come to learn that you and your two war dogs had been working in the 'Red Zone' and being a Team Leader over seven other K9 teams protecting the IIG (Iraqi Interim Government) and the Iraqi Prime Minister. I am aware that you were also the K9 Team Leader in the protection of the world's largest US Embassy, being built here in the "Green Zone" along the Tigris River."

Ok, this was a bit much. Who was this colonel? How did he know so much about me? Why was he calling me? It was then that I started to interrupt the Colonel, but being in "Command and Control", he stopped me cold in my tracks, "Excuse me Blocker, I'm not finished!" Of course, I knew it was time for me to take a back seat and keep my mouth shut. "Sorry sir" was all I got out and then the Colonel stated, "I'll continue now. I also understand you have a German Shepherd named Toris, is that correct Blocker?" Pulling from my twenty-one years in the Air Force I answered, "Yes Sir, that is correct Sir!" "I was told so!" retorted the mysterious Colonel. I had so many questions but I had already been put in place once before and did not desire a second go around so I kept my mouth shut.

There was a quick moment of silence and then, "Here's why I called for you Blocker, because Toris served our country at New York City during 911 protecting the Empire State Building for almost five months I've arranged for a flight for you, Toris, and Laky, leaving out of here on the 2nd of November. You make sure the three of you are on that C-130 aircraft. I don't want you leaving your boys back here in this war. You all need to go home and enjoy your lives together, by the way, tell Toris I said, 'Thank You!'" I was stunned but quickly responded, "I sure will Sir. You're an answered prayer Sir!" The Colonel emphatically stated, "Good! That's all Blocker. Catch your flight and, thank you!" I was about to ask him, how he found out all of this information about me, but, the next thing I heard was "Click." He hung up. Without any reservation, I knew God had used someone else, to talk to the Colonel.[93]

The day arrives, November 2nd, 2006 and I'm so very excited, knowing it truly appears I and my two war dogs, Toris and Laky are getting out of this stinking war, alive! No more bullets, rockets, mortars, suicide bombers and ungodly heat ever again!

I found the US Air Force aircraft and was not surprised to find the loadmaster was waiting for us, fully aware we were coming. As we are loading up onto the C-130, the Load Master and his crew are pushing and pulling the crates holding Toris and Laky into the wide-open rear of the transport aircraft. Toris of course has to feel like he's in charge so he's barking orders at the Air Force crew. Seriously, I mean Toris is growling and barking at this crew with his deep German Shepherd voice. He's all business and setting everyone straight on where he stands as a canine in this environment. I smile. Gosh I love these dogs.

When the load crew approached Toris' crate to ratchet it down with the straps Toris attacked the sides causing the crate to rock back and forth. I could see the smiles on the faces of the crew. Each and every one of them knew this was an exceptional dog and that he was all business. I kept giving Toris commands in a European language to stop this barking but of course I knew it would fall onto deaf ears because he felt these guys were invading his space which he was going to defend. Did I fail to mention that Toris hated all men? The

---

[93] Today's date is 3 June 2019, twelve years and seven months later, I just realized who God used to get that flight arranged for the three of us, it was our K9 Director Mitchell Raleigh. He was a tremendous leader and obviously a very strong Christian. He did not push his beliefs onto you but would always say things like "Praise the Lord" or "Thank God". He always prayed over every meal. He was a very good man which is a compliment all true men envy. He was a man one could learn from if they so desired. I always gave him 150% in everything, no matter the request. He was retired military just as I was and we both had retired with Senior Rank. We both understood mission requirements and working as a team. We understood what the term "Having Your Back" truly meant. I'm convinced, 100% it was Mitchell Raleigh who God used to get Toris, Laky, and myself out of Iraq.

thought made me smile that if these had been a female crew, he would have been trying to give them doggie kisses through his crate door and windows. Toris loved the ladies.

I looked toward the center of the aircraft and spied my luggage along with everyone else's. Then there were other large items which this crew was transporting for other agencies and our own government. This was a huge mound built up with accuracy and sorted by a crew that had distributed the weight evenly. I was proud of the crew and proud to be Air Force myself. This crew was good.

The load crew then secured a huge net over the entire load of goods. I watched as the experienced crew used headsets to talk among themselves and coordinate their efforts. Soon the net was in place and secured to the deck of the aircraft. I was standing off to the side snapping a photo here and there admiring these professionals.

I decided to grab a quick sit down next to Toris and Laky, giving them each a scratch on their noses which they both loved. I turned and asked one of the passengers if he could take a quick picture of me in front of the two crates. A photo was taken and the moment captured in time.

Soon the engines rumbled to life and I began to really believe that I just might make it out alive. One of the crew jumped up and ran over to a seat near a window where a machine gun was mounted. The trigger man pulled the charging handle back seating a live round from a belt of bullets neatly stored in a box of ammunition. The weapon was now ready to deliver death should the need so arise on our departure. The scene reminded me that we were not out of danger yet because there was an obvious need for that gunner to be there. I swallowed hard and rested my head back against the wall of the vibrating aircraft. I must say though once again I was glad to be in the care of an experienced crew.

Looking around the compartment I noted that all of the passengers, including myself were wearing helmets, flak vests and ear plugs. Everyone is battle ready on an airplane. I can't wait to get out of here. What kind of a place requires civilian passengers to wear such gear? Iraq does.

We can feel the aircraft hull and floor start to vibrate as the pilot is running the prop engines harder. The motion and increase in noise even got Toris attention who is now quiet. I guess he came to the conclusion that he was not going to out bark this aircraft so he clammed up, laid flat in his crate and decided to enjoy the ride out of here, NEVER to see, smell, or hear the sounds of war ever again in his lifetime.

This whole time Laky has not made a single sound. He lay sullenly still in his crate staring out the bars seemingly resigned to his fate. I felt sorry for him but instantly thrilled to know the wonderful life that awaited him if we could survive the next few minutes.

The C-130 aircraft now started to move slightly forward and picked up more speed but still only going about 10 mph. I knew we would have to traverse the various lanes and paths of the airport. My attention was drawn to the rear of the aircraft where the large cargo door was beginning to rise up and shut out Iraq from my sight forever. My eyes were fixed on the scene as the far-off buildings and drab trees gave way to the interior of the ramp door. The ramp was now closed and this "Freedom Bird" was now ready to depart.

Within these few seconds the war was gone from my view, no more, never again! The happiness and relief I felt at that moment was exhilarating, "No More War!" I looked over at Toris and Laky and yelled out, "Toris! Laky! That's it boys! You'll never have to hear the sounds of war ever again!" They both slightly turned their heads and looked at me but they wouldn't even lift their chins up from the kennel flooring. They were comfortable and seemed to know what all of this meant. Perhaps their gaze meant they didn't believe it was all over. Perhaps they knew better than me and would only be happy once the aircraft was out of Iraq altogether.

Perhaps they were just plum tired. I know I was, for it had been a wild last twenty-one hours filled with last minute packing, final processing, turning in gear, getting my room cleaned up for the next K9 handler or trainer coming in to take over my room and then cleaning my two kennels out at our K9 facility. I suspect though that the sound of the aircraft was now almost hypnotic, like a car gently rocking a fussy baby to sleep, as Laky and then Toris both closed their eyes and drifted off. There was a steady hum in the aircraft as we slowly moved along the taxiway and the entire time, I had the biggest smile on my face. Yes, Texas sized once again!

We were now making a turn from the taxiway to the active runway and as the pilot was making the turn, he increased the power to the engines which in turn caused our aircraft to move faster. I knew this experienced pilot was not going to sit on the taxiway and present a target, he was going to keep moving and sure enough as we straightened out, he pushed the controls and the aircraft leapt forward.

I had no window to look out, but I've flown enough to know this pilot was not messing around. The engine noise was louder, and louder, and louder and then the aircraft began shaking just a bit and as we were picking up speed, I looked over at Toris and Laky with that huge smile on my face, I yelled out to Toris and Laky one last time, "No More War Boys!" Again, they just turned their heads and looked at me, unconvinced. Suddenly…BOOM! BOOM! BOOM! I could feel the concussion of a blast on one side of the aircraft, then two more concussions coming from the other side of the aircraft. At the very same moment the pilot put the "Pedal to the Medal" and the aircraft jerked forward with so much force it pressed our bodies sideways against the straps and shoulder harness. Now I knew why we were strapped in like race car drivers.

I quickly looked over at Toris and Laky. Toris was doing what he always did when we were being hit with rockets or mortars, he was standing up and barking his deep loud bark, as if saying "Come on, bring it on, I'm ready for you! I'll gladly take you down with a good German Shepherd bite!"

Laky, my poor battle weary Laky was still holding tight to the bottom of his crate with eyes wide open. I could see the white of his eyes and noticed that his ears had dropped against the top of his head. I could see he was shaking and knew it was not only from the vibration of the aircraft but that his nerves were shot. I hoped we would make it out of here so I could show Laky a whole new life filled with nothing but love and tons of fun.

Next our pilot did something that really shot us into the air. The C-130s coming into war zones were retrofitted with rocket pods on each wing. In an emergency these were lit off and the resultant propulsion gave the aircraft such speed and forward momentum that lift offs were completed faster and with crazy angles. Well, when our pilot lit off the rockets, we shot skyward like an amusement ride rollercoaster. The G Forces were amazing and took away my breath for a moment. I would guess that our angle of assent was at least 55 degrees on a math protractor. Not kidding. It was impressive, frightening but effective and that was what we desired.

The wheels left the ground, the plane shot skyward and the dirt and death of Iraq drew further and further below us. It is hard to describe my elation. The higher we climbed the safer I felt and soon I was totally relaxed and I knew it. We had made it out alive!

Looking back I marveled at the sullen look of both Toris and Laky before we lifted off. Did they sense the mortars were coming? Their looks seemed to indicate they doubted we were leaving. Coincidence I am sure but one thing is certain those last three mortars were thankfully off target and Iraq was forever behind us and would soon only inhabit our memories and our dreams, for home was on the far horizon.

Up Up and Away!

Laky was lying flat against the bottom of his crate and shaking. It really bummed me out to see him trembling like that. I knew it was not from the vibrations of the aircraft or because he was cold. No, there was something internal going on. His mannerisms were classic fear impulses; his ears were back, flat against his beautiful head and his eyes were bigger than normal. He was frightened.

Laky just rolled his eyes in my direction, nothing more. He was wasted. Those last three mortars did him in. As they say in boxing, "He was down for the count." I felt so sorry for him but then I also felt extreme joy because I knew that he would never have to hear the sounds of war again. He was bound for a new life full of laughter and love.

After we were up, up and away, and safe from ground fire one of the passengers yelled into my right ear that the pilot had kicked in the "Rocket Thrusters" on each side of the aircraft. It seems the rockets were there for an extra boost to expedite our exit from Baghdad's airspace. I can vouch for the quick lift off and extra boost. It was exhilarating to say the least. Guess I wasn't the only one to be in a hurry to leave this place.

There was no sense in attempting to have a conversation with anyone on the C-130 because there was way too much noise from the engines. I just laid my head back against the bulkhead[94] of the aircraft and tried to rest as the reverberations through the hulk of the plane caused my helmeted brain to vibrate. Though the helmet was uncomfortable I made myself wear it because I knew it would protect me from flying shrapnel should we get hit.

I crossed my arms over my bullet proof vest and turned my head slightly to the left so that I could look at my two boys: Toris and Laky. They were both already peering at me. I smiled at them knowing this was it, "No more wars" for either of them. I said a silent prayer thanking God for His protection during my thirteen months in Iraq, "Now God, if you could manage to look out for myself, Laky and Toris a little longer that would be great. I have a long journey and I sure could use your help. I sure would hate to die on the way home. Amen."

---

[94] Wall of the aircraft.

Part Three

After the Dust Settled

Jordanian Touchdown

The flight from Baghdad, Iraq to Amman, Jordan was a short one; about an hour and a half. Most importantly it was very uneventful. I had passed through Amman several times before but never with two canines directly under my care so I was a bit nervous about what awaited us. Always in the back of my mind was the bounty on the life of these canines. My head would be on a swivel.

Truthfully, I wished I could have taken this American C-130 all the way to Europe. I didn't care about the comfort of a chair, a cool carbonated drink in my hand or a hot towel on my face. I was more concerned with the security of my war dogs and I was fearful that I might lose sight of Toris and Laky at the airports we would have to use. Well, one step at a time. First, Jordan.

The wheels of the C-130 connected with the tarmac and we were soon ambling toward our allotted parking area. This was not a Continental or Lufthansa airline so there would be no giant air-conditioned passenger boarding bridge meeting us at the door of the aircraft. This was a C-130 and we would all deplane down the cargo hold and direct onto the pavement. My goal was to keep an eye on my dogs. I was dreading the long lines that usually are associated with International travel and customs agents. I also knew that most Arabs looked at dogs as filthy and unclean animals so I worried that my boys would not be shown the respect and care that they had earned and deserved. I prayed for no hang-ups.

The cargo door was down and the aircrew were busy as squirrels rushing around the pallets of gear and luggage, unfastening here, pulling there and communicating everything being accomplished and tasked. It was cool to watch their efficiency. Made me proud. Go Air Force!

The floor of the C-130 has hundreds of rollers incorporated into the deck of the aircraft making handling large pallets exponentially easier. So, as the loadmasters pushed the pallets off of the aircraft a forklift lifted them and placed them neatly onto the bed of a waiting truck. Then it was time for the pallet that held Laky and Toris. I was relieved to see the care and concern shown by the forklift operator who hoisted them up like they were a shipment of fine china. In a matter of minutes word was given to the driver that he was loaded up and he pulled away to a terminal area fifty yards in the distance. I kept my eyes on the truck and the two dog crates it carried.

A small bus had pulled up and the passengers all boarded for the very short trip over to the terminal area. My eyes were constantly locked onto the freight truck and my anxiety was relieved by the sight of the truck's brake lights illuminating. It had begun to slow and then stopped. Our small bus pulled up near the luggage and we all stood to the side as the forklift once again professionally handled the pallets.

As the cargo was being unstrapped and cleared, I walked over to my two buddies to let them know I was with them. I knew Laky would be extremely nervous. Toris, nah, wasn't worried about him in the least but I still wanted to see him and I knew he would love to see me as well.

I couldn't help but smile as I approached because Toris was letting everyone know that they had better not screw with him. Once I poked my head around the corner of his crate, he instantly fell silent and pressed close to the crate door. I poked my fingers through the cage bars and he licked them, "Good boy!" I said as he let me know everything was all right. Yeah, Toris was solid. Never worried about him.

Peeking in on Laky I could see he was drooling from both sides of his mouth. His face was pressed against the floor of his crate, his ears were flat against his head and I could see the whites of his eyes; he was stressed out. I stuck my fingers through the crate bars and he slowly rolled his eyes over to look at my fingers. After a short delay he slowly crawled forward and gently licked my fingers. I scratched the top of his head and he then moved in closer so that the side of his face was pushed against the metal bars. Tufts of his soft black, brown and tan fur puffed out between the bars. I reached over, poked my fingers through and scratched the top of his nose. I could see drool was still coming out the sides of his mouth. He was terrified but I reassured him as best I could that he was safe, that I was with him until the end and that he had an amazing life ahead of him.

My heart ached as I peered at the widening pool of drool on the floor of the crate. I looked into his eyes and instantly knew what Laky wanted so I gave it to him. I bent down low and pressed my face up against his. Screw the drool! This was my war buddy who had my back for months on end and there was no way I would not have his now. I needed to reassure him that it was going to be okay. I pressed my face up against the wire mesh of the crate door and he in turn pressed his up against mine. His right eye was looking into my left one and instantly his breathing began to slow. He was relaxing. All the while I was scratching the top of his nose with the fingers of my right hand and whispering how proud I was of him and that I was so sorry he had come home damaged from the stinking war.

I backed my head up and away just a few inches to see what Toris was doing. He was looking down at Laky and I through the side windows of his crate. It was a special moment I'll never forget. Toris was uncharacteristically quiet, still and I'm sure he was in the moment with us; this special moment held by three veterans of war.

Toris shattered the silence when a stranger approached us. Barking, lunging and gnashing his teeth; Toris was doing all he could to warn the intruder that to proceed further was dangerous. I glanced over at Laky who had shrunk back down to the floor.

The stranger was actually the loadmaster of the C-130 whose eyes were locked onto Toris, "Sir, you need to get your backpack and any other luggage from the pallet. The pilot said that we need to roll out." My answer was quick, "Roger that, coming now!"

Up ahead I could see that the other passengers were already pulling out their bags and gear while members of the Air Force load crew respectfully urged the passengers to retrieve their gear and, in some cases, helped pull out their bags. My backpack was easy to spot because it had a big word written on it, "K9."

Every few seconds I would glance over at Toris and Laky to be sure they were still there. I trusted no one. Not after everything I had been through.

With my backpack slung over my right shoulder I turned toward the Air Force crew and thanked them for everything. I signaled the guys in the distance with a "thumbs up" which they returned with smiles and a wave.

Ok, Iraq is behind us, the U. S. Air Force is leaving, I'm in an Arab country with no fellow countrymen around and now I'm alone with two "unclean animals.' Meanwhile, hanging over my head is the bounty on the life of my dogs.

I still had Jordanian customs to clear because my next flight was not until the following day. As I had lots of foreign travel through the years, I knew that the one place where plans go awry is at the customs agent desk. I had no choice. I would have to stay overnight and there was no way I would leave the side of my dogs. How is this going to play out? A deep breath, a silent prayer and my first steps to the next part of this journey.

Assassins or Bodyguards?

I am standing near Laky and Toris waiting for the next part of our journey to begin. I had been through Jordan three times prior and each time there was an American contact who would meet me at the airport. The contact always knew I was coming and had everything arranged: transportation, hotel and itinerary. There were not a lot of people about so it was a bit alarming that no one was there to greet me and my two boys.

Off to my left I can hear the familiar sound of hard rubber wheels clattering across the pavement. The sound reminded me of the flatbed shopping carts at a hardware store back in Texas. I turned and sure enough it was one of those flatbed carts but this one was being maneuvered by two guys who appeared to be making a direct line of approach on me. Oh boy. Who are these guys?

I assumed the men worked for the airport and were doing me a favor by transporting my dogs into the terminal where I hoped my American contact would be waiting for us. I asked if they spoke English and it turned out that only one of the men did. The English speaking guy said, "You are Dennis Blocker, K9 out of Iraq?" My answer was concise, "Yes." The man nodded and continued, "We are here to escort you and your dogs to the hotel. Our boss will greet you just inside and through those glass doors." I nodded my head and we made way toward Laky and Toris.

First Laky's crate was lifted onto the cart and then Toris. While the guys are lifting Toris' portable kennel I was telling him, "Be still. Be quiet. It's ok." I didn't need these guys afraid to move the crates. I wanted to get through this process as quickly as possible.

With Laky and Toris loaded up and secured we began to move toward the building where I assumed the customs agents would be. Up ahead I could see four glass doors which appeared to be the rear entrance to the airport terminal. As our cart rattled toward these doors one of the men assisting with my cart sprinted ahead to open the door for me. As I passed through I noticed that the crate holding Toris and Laky did not pass through the glass doors. In fact, the guy who held the door for me now went to the crate and stood guard over my two boys with another man outside. These guys were professionals.

At this moment I was approached by a well built, squared away looking guy who appeared to be in his mid-thirties. He wore jeans and a pull-over shirt that looked to be one size too large, but I suspected this was to conceal a holstered weapon. I recognized his bearing immediately. He had to be either military or law enforcement. The dude looked "official."

The first words out of his mouth, "Are you Dennis Blocker?" Ok, this guy has my attention and I am wondering, "How does he know my name?" I do a quick pan of his face, his eyes, hands and clothing and answer, "Yes, I am." Then he asked, "Would you please hand me your passport and your documents for the dogs." Ok, the moment of truth. There is no way I am just going to hand over these items he is asking for so I counter, "Before we go any further let me ask, who you are? Who do you represent?"

It's been several years so I can't remember his name but he did introduce himself and stated, "I have been instructed to escort you and your dogs through customs and the airport as quickly as possible. Then we will protect you on the journey from the airport to the hotel. Basically, you will be under our protection until you leave tomorrow on your next flight."

Now I had been through Jordan three times prior but had only ever dealt with an American contact. This guy was Jordanian. Granted, this was my first trip with dogs at my side so it was understandable that there would be an elevation of security. However, there was a hefty bounty on my life and on that of Laky and Toris. I figured bounty hunters would look for a moment away from the airport. I knew it would be when I was most vulnerable.

I then remembered that back in Baghdad our K9 director, Mitch Raleigh, had given me a packet with some letters. One document contained the name of a person who was to meet and escort us to the hotel. I pulled the document from my backpack. While I retrieved it, I asked the man to produce identification for me so that I could verify his story. In short order everything checked out and I placed my life and that of my dogs in the care of this stranger and his team of men.

You know, there was always a little voice in the back of my head that wondered if these guys really were who they claimed to be. However, what other options did I have? I couldn't walk home or hitchhike. I couldn't swim home so I had to risk it. There was no turning back now.

For those readers who have been in war you truly understand my mindset at this time. My father-in-law had fought the Japanese in WWII at the islands of Saipan, Guam, Tinian and Iwo Jima. To the day he died he never trusted the Japanese. We would rationalize with him and tell him that not all of the Japanese were evil but he would never relent. His brain would tell him that obviously it was true that not all of the Japanese were bad but when he would see one, he would only see the bodies of his buddies laid out with their brains and abdomens blown out on the deck of his gunboat, the LCI (G) 449. It was the same with me. I KNEW that not all Arabs were insurgents or terrorists but when around them I couldn't help but remember all of the explosions, the friendly fire incidents and death. I was always on edge and if my father-in-law is used as evidence, I guess I always will be. Time will be the author of truth to this, in time, we will all know the truth, but not until then.

I handed over my passport, and documents, for Laky and Toris and hoped for the best. "Wait here, this will not take long," and he was off, running toward a man standing at a booth. I closely watched as my papers were handed over and the customs agent looked in my direction. In a matter of seconds my bodyguard was running back toward me and as he did, he glanced to the side, began waving his arms about and yelled out something in what I assumed to be Arabic. The words took immediate effect on a group of men standing off to the side in a long hallway.

I hadn't even noticed these other men. I had been intent on keeping vigil over Laky and Toris who were on the other side of those large glass doors. Well, this is it, moment of truth. I have a large group of Arab men moving toward me. Are they here for the bounty or to take me to the hotel? I had already made up my mind before coming to the Middle East that I would never be taken alive. There was no way I was ending up on television having my head sawed off. I was going to take as many with me as possible and make them kill me on the spot.

As the Jordanian runs up, he blurts out, "You're cleared to leave now. I've taken care of everything." He then hands me my passport and papers and continues, "My men will now bring your dogs through the airport and rush them into the van backing up to the doors on the other side of the hallway there." He points to another area opposite where my two boys are sitting in their crates. "Let's move now!" With this command he extends his right arm in the air and with a motion sparks all the men around him to action.

Move they did! Laky and Toris in their crates were hefted to a long metal table that rolled smoothly atop stout rubber wheels. Several men had gathered around the table and they were moving them quickly, briskly. They were actually running down the hallway, pushing and guiding the cart with them. Of course this meant that I was also running, following their route just a few feet behind my two war dogs. I was sensing a theme here. Everything this team did was meant to get us out of this facility pronto. We were a target and we needed to change locations NOW!

As we ran down the long hallway we turned and two men bolted ahead to open a set of glass doors. I could see a large white van backing up to the doors. This was the transport for the dog crates and me. Passing through the doors I looked around and could see that my security detail had blocked off all the roads to our area. Drivers sat patiently waiting, looking in our direction.

A few more yells and both Laky and Toris were loaded up into the white van. I glanced behind and could see that two men in our escort refused to allow passengers to approach the hallway. This team had sealed off the area around us and no one was getting in. I smiled to myself and felt sort of special. I had no idea I would be afforded this level of security. This was all new to me. There was only one person who could have made this happen, Mitchell Raleigh, my boss. What a great man. He saw to it that we were safe and secure. I will never forget this show of concern on our behalf.

I was instructed to run around to the side of the van and jump in. Once I did the door was slammed shut and locked. Then my escort jumped into the front passenger seat and we were peeling out of the airport parking area.

As we are speeding away from the parking lot, I noticed that my escort consisted of several other vehicles that were blocking roads and entry points into the area.

This was like a scene from a movie with James Bond or Ethan Hunt from Mission Impossible. We flew down the highway at incredible speeds. Zip. Zip. Zip. The street signs flashed by so quickly that I could not focus on the lettering. Looking out the side window I would notice cars creep up, keep pace and then back off. The driver and passenger were both Arab and were all clean shaven. They were extremely well groomed and dressed casual but clean and obviously expensive. Jeans and pull-over shirts seemed to be the theme of these guys. They each wore sunglasses and looked like hitmen for the Devil himself. I was a little concerned until my Escort Team Leader noticed my expression and informed me, "Not to worry. Those are my men. They will allow no one to pass us or move in close behind." I smiled. These guys were awesome.

I spoke up, "I saw those guys pacing us and wondered if they were going to open fire on us. I was thinking that I had survived thirteen months in Baghdad only to get killed on a highway in Jordan." I laughed but my escort did not. He flatly stated, "I'm aware of all things during an escort. Those are my men providing protection for you during the journey to the hotel." He wasn't rude. He was a professional and good at what he did. I had to say something, "I want to thank you for your awesome team." My guardian looked over his shoulder at me and said, "Mr. Dennis, don't thank me until we get to the hotel. We are not safe yet. Once we get there, I will gladly accept your thanks." He smiled and then faced forward and spoke into his radio. I liked him and it seemed the feeling was mutual. Two men who shared a similar warrior code[95] and now the same vehicle.

---

[95] "The Warrior Code" varies between military branches and various countries but the values are essentially the same. I think the US Army "Soldier Creed" says it quite well, "I will always place the mission first. I will never accept defeat. I will never quit. I will never leave a fallen comrade. I am disciplined, physically and mentally tough, trained and proficient in my warrior tasks and drills. I am an expert and I am a professional. I stand ready to deploy, engage and destroy the enemies of the United States of America in close combat. I am a guardian of freedom."

The trip took no time at all, especially at the speeds we were doing. Of course the fact that our escort shut down all roads intersecting our path helped quite considerably.

Suddenly we began to slow and I heard the head honcho say, "We've arrived."

Hotel Jordan

Up ahead I could see the hotel and it was absolutely beautiful! I had never slept in a five-star hotel before but if I had to guess this probably was one. The buildings were clean and well-tended. The beautiful lawns featured trees of at least a dozen varieties and the grass was a crisp, startling green. I hadn't seen such colors in a long, long time.

Once again, our vehicle escorts were blocking all traffic so we arrived without a hitch. We arrived at the entrance like an arrow; in a hurry. The driver remains behind the steering wheel watching his mirrors and glancing forward. It is obvious he is looking for threats. Meanwhile, the security chief has sprung out of his door and is delivering instructions and reminders to his guys who set off in different directions on various tasks. I wait until instructed to leave so that the security team can take up their overwatch positions and make sure no one attempts to break the perimeter they are setting up.

The driver places his hand to his ear listening to a microphone and then turns toward me, "Ok Mr. Dennis, it is ok to go to your dogs." The door is opened and I proceed immediately to the rear of the vehicle. Off to the side I can see a member of the security detail had previously collected a cart and is patiently waiting for the word to approach. The hand signal is given and then both of my boys were hefted out of the van and placed on an opulent cart made of polished brass. Laky is of course silent as they carry him out but Toris has to let everyone know his opinion on the new surroundings, and the strangers gathered round him.

Toris' barking was drawing attention so I commanded him to stop. He did. I praised him and then reached through the metal bars to scratch his nose. I needed him to settle down a bit. I glanced in and he flashed me that amazing German Shepherd smile. I then noticed that people in the lobby were looking out toward us. It's almost impossible to escape attention when you arrive in the fashion we just did. I looked in on Laky who was glued to the bottom of his crate. I reached through the bars but he wouldn't budge. I was so thrilled to get these two home with me.

My escort walked me over to the counter so that I could check in. The clerk behind the desk was not a happy dude. His body language was telling me volumes. I knew that in their culture dogs were considered unclean so his discomfort was understandable. However, he was in the hospitality business so he needed to pull himself together.

The first thing out of the clerk's mouth was, "I'm sorry but your dogs will NOT be able to stay with you in your room. The dogs will be housed on the fourth floor and you will be on the fifth."

Ok, here we go. There is always some joker who wants to put in his two cents and puff out his chest. I had to set him straight quick, "Well, that's NOT going to work. I go where my dogs go. There is NO WAY I'm losing sight of my two dogs. If they have to stay on the fourth floor, then that's where I'll stay." The clerk looked in my eyes and could see he screwed up. You know, I'm not sure what he saw in my eyes. Maybe it was weariness. Perhaps it was death, not his of course, but just the shadow of the ominous specter that had hung over us for thirteen months.

Whatever he saw caused his voice and his bearing to change, "Sir, you don't understand, it's not as clean as the fifth floor where you have a room reserved for you. You will be more comfortable on the fifth floor." I was rock solid, "Well then you'll have to unreserve it and put me in a 'dog room' on the fourth floor, with my two dogs. If that is not possible then we will stay in the lobby and sleep. As you can see, I'm NOT budging on this!" The clerk gulped hard, looked down at his desk and said, "I'll have to talk with the hotel manager and see what he wants to do."

I looked over at my lead guard and his face was unchanged. Still hard. Ever determined. I took this to mean that I would get a nice room on the 5th floor one way or another.

After a few minutes the shuffling and stammering clerk returned and sheepishly stated, "The hotel manager states he will make an exception this one time for you!" Obviously, this guy did not like telling me the news. I warmly smiled and pleasantly replied, "Thank you, and please convey to the hotel manager my deepest thanks!"

Toris, Laky and I were escorted up to our room on the fifth floor. The team leader stated his men would search the room first but I said, "Why let these perfectly good, tried and true explosive detection dogs sit idle. How about I take Toris and search the room?" The Security Team leader loved the idea so we conducted a complete search of the entire room. No explosives. The room was clean. As I placed Toris back in his crate the team leader said, "I should get one of those dogs for my team." I smiled and said, "Yes you should."

I must say though that I was struck by the beauty of the room and the attention to comfort of guests. Everything from the furniture to the pictures on the walls were pristine and extremely clean. I also noticed that there was not even the hint of a layer of fine dust on the tables, counter tops or the television. Believe me, I looked. The place was spotless. Yeah, we were not in Baghdad anymore.

"Mr. Dennis if you need anything you can call room service. There will be a guard standing in the hall outside your door so if you require something you can always ask him. You will have protection all through the night so sleep well. I want to introduce you to him." We stepped out into the hall and I shook hands with the man who had my life in his hands that night. I then thanked the security team leader and said, "Right now I need to take my dogs outside so they can go pee and poop." The team lead spoke into his radio and then turned back to me, "There will be a guard to accompany you when you go outside."

I looked over at my boys and they were both quietly looking up at me through their crate doors. They instinctively knew it was time to get them out. Laky was the one I most worried about so I would take him first.

When I opened the door of my room leading to the hallway I called out, "Dog coming out." Stepping into the hall I was approached by my squared away muscular bodyguard who said, "I will show you the way."

As we walked toward the elevator my guard walked ahead of us, checking corners and making certain he was the first person to look in the elevator when it opened. I assumed that the head of security most likely had a team of guys bunked down on the same floor as I and that they were probably sleeping in shifts so that they could relieve each other and be fresh during the night shift. I felt important until I realized that I had come through Jordan three times before and had never been shown this much attention. I laughed to myself. This security was for Laky and Toris! I just happened to be the handler benefiting from their security detail.

Once we were outside the guard showed us to an area behind the hotel where there was grass and some bushes. The escort kept looking down at Laky. His face showed not the slightest bit of disgust but rather curiosity and almost a sort of reverence. I was mystified until the guard spoke up, "Is your German Shepherd friendly or aggressive?" I said, "He's very friendly." I was floored by his next question, "Can I hold his leash and can you take a picture of me with him? I've never been near a real war dog in my life." I couldn't believe I was saying it but before I knew it the words, "Sure, not a problem" were spewing from my mouth. I suppose I was thinking, "It's the least I can do since you are protecting us."

This guy was all smiles. I mean it beamed from ear to ear. I could tell that this man held Laky in the highest regard. Perhaps it was a part of the warrior code again. Warriors recognizing and respecting other warriors who have seen and endured combat. I took the picture and he profusely thanked me for the opportunity.

As we walked back to the hotel room, I noticed that Laky was relaxing and that he had that famous jaunt of his down, that cool swagger when he walked. This was a good sign.

As Laky and I entered the room it was dead quiet and Toris was sitting, staring at us. I placed Laky back in his crate and when I released Toris he shot out like a current of pent up water released at a dam. He jumped up on the bed, did two quick spins and then jumped to the floor and ran around the room a couple times, trying to expend that pent up energy from the long day of travel. He then swooped up to my feet jumped up, placed his front paws on my shoulders and licked my face several times.

I always felt safer with Toris. I loved them both of course but Toris had the heart of a warrior and was always ready for a fight. Toris had my back and I his. If an enemy approached in these halls, I knew Toris would take him down.

Once outside my friendly guard asked if he could have a picture with Toris. I smiled and said, "That would be a very bad idea. This dog is aggressive and does not like men. If you were to get bit then it might delay our trip back home. I can't afford to take that kind of a chance." The guard understood and Toris went about reading the "Doggy news."

It was time to return to our room and as we prepared to enter, I thanked our guard and asked, "Will you be guarding us tonight?" He smiled and said, "No, I will be relieved in a short while. There will be another guard during the night. I'll introduce you to him before you go to sleep Mr. Dennis. This way you'll know who your assigned guard during the night is." I thanked him for protecting us and wished him well.

I was famished so I picked up the phone and ordered something to eat from room service. I fed Toris and Laky, made sure they had plenty of water for the evening and within thirty minutes my food was delivered. I could hear conversation in the hallway so I looked through the peephole in the door and watched as my guard conversed with the porter. I had previously told the guard not to touch anything on the cart. If there were explosives, I didn't want him getting blown up. I informed the guard that he was not to allow the cart into my room and that after the porter left, I would bring Toris out and have him sniff for explosives. The guard smiled and said, "It's a great idea."

After the porter left, I poked my head out into the hall and smiled at my bodyguard who smiled back; our plan was a go. I brought Toris out of his crate, opened the door of my room and told the security guard to step away down the hall a few feet so I could bring Toris out to search the cart with my food. I gave Toris the command to search the cart, which he did with no indication of any explosive odor. I praised Toris for a good job, put him back into his crate, secured the crate door, then pushed the food cart into my room.

It was wonderful to eat a meal on proper dishes. I relished the taste of this professionally cooked meal and took my time. When I was done, I placed the tray outside on the floor, looked to the left, saw my guard standing there and gave him the "thumbs-up" sign. He smiled and returned it. With the door now closed and secured I immediately let Laky out of his crate for a good hour and a half. I did the same later with Toris because I knew that beginning on the morrow, they'd both be in their crates for many long hours.

In preparation for this I massaged their legs, groomed them and played tug of war with them. All with the intent of exercising their muscles and minds and getting them prepared for the long day of travel on the morrow.

Next Stop, Paris

Laky, Toris and I were escorted down to the hotel lobby where we met up with the rest of the security team. Things were already clicking along like a well-oiled machine. I looked out the entrance

317

to the hotel and could see that all of the escort vehicles were in place. Convoy style. In no time flat the crates containing Toris and Laky were once again loaded into our van. The catch was flipped, the spring shot forward and our caravan was off at lightning speed.

Arriving at the airport, I could see the other vehicles separate and block off roads intersecting with our intended route. As Laky and Toris are brought out several of the guards fan out and close down hallways and entryways that might allow someone to approach us.

Several of the guards surround Laky and Toris and push their cart along while keeping a vigil on civilians passing nearby. Once again, they are jogging. Even though we are on time, everything is completed in a hurry for the detail knows this is the most vulnerable time. I am right behind them as we all jog in stride. The contents of my shoulder slung backpack clanked and chinked as we moved as a unit. I have to admire these guys. Professionals.

Every door we proceeded toward was immediately opened, each counter bypassed and not surprisingly the official at the customs counter looked bored as he dutifully stamped my passport and documents. It was almost a given that he was going to stamp them. I thought to myself, "I wonder if these airport and customs employees have all been paid off." I was fine with it. This was the reason Mitchell had hired these guys, to keep me, Laky and Toris alive and to expedite us through customs. I felt like royalty but then I remembered that it was my dogs who were royalty, I was just along for the ride.

At one point we approached a line with at least three dozen people. We were at the back. No, no we're not, we are now at a trot moving around all of these travelers and passing right through a door being held open by an airport employee. My head escort, the leader, would just yell out some words in Arabic and everyone ahead of us would just part, like Moses when he parted the Red Sea.

In no time flat we were at a private area where no one would disturb us or ask questions. It was just Laky, Toris, me and our security team. We had two hours before we had to board the plane.

318

At this point I knew my dogs would have to go into the cargo hold of the aircraft but I didn't know when they would need to board. Everything was taken care of and I was assured I would be informed when things needed to happen. I took the opportunity to thank my Security Escort team leader and asked him to please convey my thanks to his team. He stated they would stay with us until we were on our aircraft and wheels up.

Soon we were heading to the aircraft to board. I went one way and my boys Laky and Toris went another. Airport employees came over and wheeled Laky and Toris toward the aircraft. Right beside them were two men from our security detail who would remain with them until they were safely tucked away in the cargo hold. Did I mention how impressed I was with the security we had been provided? These men were true professionals, seeing a job to completion right up to the aircraft doors. I of course watched to make certain I could see Toris and Laky being loaded onto the aircraft. There was no way I was getting aboard until I witnessed them enter the cargo hold. Once I saw their crates disappear inside the aircraft I exhaled and took the final steps toward the cabin door. Once at the door I turned, waved at my amazing security detail, smiled, flashed them the "thumbs up" sign and entered. The Security Team Leader saluted and I'm certain that he and his men didn't leave their posts until the wheels of our aircraft were up. Just like he had said the day before.

The flight from Jordan to Paris was sweet because Toris, Laky and I were getting further and further from the sounds, smells, and terrors of war. My seat was tilted back as far as it could go and the air smelled fresh. I had a smile on my face and let out a sigh. Time to relax.

No, that wasn't going to happen. All during the five-hour flight hordes of screaming and crying children would run up and down the aisles chasing each other. I just listened to music, kept my eyes closed and prayed for God to grant me serenity.

As I looked around the cabin, I could not help but feel uneasy. This was five years after the attacks of September 11th and people were still leery of folks dressed in traditional Arab attire. One of those folks was me but not only because of 9/11. I had come from a war zone where Arab looking people stole Police uniforms and Iraqi military uniforms and then opened fire on unsuspecting Americans.

As I lay back in the seat my mind wandered and I recalled a scary incident at Checkpoint Two. There was an Iraqi Police Lieutenant assigned to work at the Iraqi section of CP2 and every once in a while, he'd drift his way up to our K9 checkpoint to sell us cell phone cards which were much cheaper than what we were paying in the Green Zone. One day I walked into our small little break area building at our old CP2 area and found this guy rifling through my jacket pockets. I immediately grabbed him, spun him around and pushed him out the door. I wanted witnesses. I shoved him up against the wall and pulled my 9mm from its holster and shoved it into his back so he could feel the muzzle. At the same time I "Jacked Him Up" in spread eagle fashion, kicking his legs out to put him at a disadvantage. As I knew he spoke English I am yelling commands at him, "Spread your legs! Spread your arms!" At this point he tried moving off the wall but I shoved him back and yelled, "DO NOT MOVE AGAIN!"

For me, at this moment, I considered him a possible insurgent and I'm not taking any chances. This is war. This is real. This is the Red Zone and the stakes couldn't be higher. I then started my search of his body to see if he had taken anything from the pockets of my jacket. Sifting through his pockets I found they were full of photographs of my wife, my son, my daughters and grandkids. Yeah, this guy was working for someone and as he had not taken anything but photographs, I assumed he was not after monetary items. This of course meant he was an insurgent or at the very least working for the insurgents. It was also glaring to me that we must have made an impact at the checkpoint because they were after items about my family. My carnal desire was to shoot the guy on the spot in the back of the head but I didn't want to spend the rest of my life in prison. I also knew that this scumbag parasite could possibly provide some good information on bad guy networks.

I called this in and everyone showed up: the Iraqi Police, Iraqi Army, the US Military, and a civilian guy who looked like a Special Forces type. I suspected he may have been CIA. Anyway, they all showed up and everyone wanted a piece of this guy. I passed on what had taken place and that was the last time I ever saw the chameleon Iraqi police officer.

I briefed my guys to watch all Iraqi Police and Iraqi Military and that no nationals were allowed near or in our break area.

So, was it any wonder why I did not trust anyone? The thought was a bit ironic because I trusted this group of Jordanian security men with my life and would do so again in a heartbeat. Never-the-less, the feeling is imbedded in there and is something I will struggle with, to the day I die I'm sure.

The screaming and rowdy children jerked me back to the reality of my situation. I was safe and aboard an aircraft bound for France and then America. My two war buddies were with me and we would all be home to a new life soon enough, but gosh almighty those kids were annoying. Finally it happened, some weary war-torn warrior stood up and yelled at the top of his lungs, "Would someone please SHUT these kids up and make them sit in their seats!" The entire plane heard this, all of the kids ran to their seats, parents turned and gave evil looks at this tired American. I think it was obvious that he could care less what these parents thought, or anyone else for that matter. I wanted to shout out my approval but refrained. He sat down, leaned back, pulled the bill of his baseball cap down over his eyes, crossed his big arms and that was it, finished.

Not a sound for the next hour from these brats, then of course, once it was still, they started creeping out into the aisles one by one. This time though they were quiet. It was obvious the parents had told them a story that in my mind made me smile and went something like this, "If you get loud, scream, and cry that big American will throw you out the door of the plane and the sharks will eat you once you land in the ocean!" For me I wanted to high-five the tired American warrior for shutting down the madness.

Within an hour during the blissful silence we began our descent into Paris and I could see the Eiffel Tower. The sight brought back many fond memories of when my dear sweet wife and I were very young, seventeen and nineteen. I had been stationed in Germany with the military and on my days off we would travel all over Europe visiting the various countries and of course Paris.

Exiting the aircraft in Paris I made way to claim Laky and Toris. To be sure they made the connecting flight to Chicago. It's funny the things that stand out to you when you leave a war-torn country. As I walked the short distance to baggage claim I inspected the countertops and picture frames for that familiar fine layer of dust but it was not there. The lack of dust delighted me because it meant I was getting yet further away from the war.

I'd not had this slight taste in my mouth of dirt, or clay. I'd not be spitting every few minutes to the ground to remove mud from my mouth. I would not have to clean my cameras daily to remove this fine dust. I'd not have to spend time cleaning my laptop daily. It may seem crazy to some of you reading this, but this small insignificant little thing called dust had been a big problem in Iraq. I was leaving all of that crap behind and I was thrilled.

I'm now at the counter to claim my two boys. I could hear Toris barking on the other side of the door. I smiled. Instinctively I knew what the problem was but said nothing. The clerk at the counter was pleasant and spoke very good English with the most wonderful touch of a French accent.

The clerk smiled and then glanced at my tickets. He quickly looked up and said, "Oh, you're the American who is bringing along with you two German Shepherds from the war in Iraq." I smiled and answered, "Yes Sir, that's me!" The intrigued clerk continued, "I looked at your dogs, they are so big and beautiful, but the one keeps barking at one of our workers. No one else but him. Do you know why?" I grinned and asked, "This one worker, is he from an Arab nation?" My new friend was enthralled, "Yes he is." I explained, "That's why. You see, in Iraq our dogs were taunted and hissed at by the Arab looking men. They would tease these dogs and thus our

322

dogs developed a hatred for these guys." The astonished clerk gulped but said nothing.

I could hear the barking coming closer and closer so I guessed they were on the move. Sure enough here comes Toris and Laky on a big cart being pushed by a young Frenchman. There was a guy keeping his distance, walking alongside and he looked to be Arab. I knew it. Toris hated those guys.

I showed them my ticket stubs, they released my boys to me and then it was time to find my next gate where I'd board my flight to Chicago, USA!

Fortunately my gate was not too far away and I had enough time to push my boys around and look at some of the shops; shops with no fine dust anywhere! The entire time I was pushing them around looking at the shops at the Paris International Airport, Toris didn't bark one time at anyone. Laky? No way. He was chilling out, as was Toris. Both were taking in the sights and people watching.

It was time for me to check in for my flight to Chicago. I wheeled my cart up to the counter but the pleasant clerk informed me that I had to check my dogs in at another station, which thankfully was quite close.

I thanked the clerk and wheeled Toris and Laky to the next station to check them in. It all went very smooth. To expedite things they wanted to take them directly back behind closed doors. I said this would be fine as long as it was possible for me to stay with them prior to our boarding time. They cordially said it would be fine. During this time I made certain Toris and Laky had plenty of water and just a bit of food in their bowls attached to their crate doors. I'd open up their crate doors and give them each head and body scratches and massage their legs and thighs, knowing they had to be stiff from the flight from Jordan. I couldn't take them out for a potty break so I figured I would have poop and pee to contend with when we arrived in America.

The clerk at the counter motioned to me and as I approached, he said in his French accent, "Sir, it's time to allow us to take your dogs to the aircraft now." I nodded, turned and had a few comforting words with my two boys. They pressed their furry faces up against the crate door for me to scratch and give them each a kiss. Then Toris flipped his body around so that his stubby tail and rear end were pressed up against the crate door. This was his way of telling me to scratch just above his tail, so I did with a smile on my face. I looked at him, his head was turned towards the crate door and his eyes were squinting.

The clerk took charge of Toris and Laky and pushed their cart through two big double doors which swung on rolling hinges. In a matter of seconds my boys were out of sight.

I walked briskly over to my check-in counter and discovered that people were already checking in and proceeding to the aircraft ramp to board. This whole time I am watching the cargo hold of the aircraft and have not seen Toris or Laky loaded. I waited a few more minutes allowing that it might take them as long to drive the dogs over to the aircraft from where we were. Minute after minute ticked by but no dogs in sight. I thought that perhaps they had reached the plane before me and were already loaded. But there was no way they had already been loaded.

I looked around and discovered that everyone had already boarded the aircraft. I was the last one. The clerk asked if I was ready but I said, "I am waiting to see if my two German Shepherds that were with me in Iraq made it to the plane but I have not seen them arrive yet. The clerk mentioned that two dogs had been loaded earlier. I replied, "Maybe, but they weren't mine. There is no way they could have made it from the place I left them in such a short amount of time. It's impossible."

There were a few seconds of silence and then I asked, "Would you please ask the pilot or crew to check and make sure the dogs were loaded. These dogs survived war and there is no way I am leaving without them." The clerk smiled and said she would.

324

The clerk said something into a radio, waited a few seconds and then received a reply that I could not hear. She turned to me and said, "Sir, they are checking inside the aircraft cargo area for you." I smiled and said, "Thank You!" A few minutes later I heard her radio receive a transmission. She looked at me with a surprised look on her face, "Sir, you were right, your dogs had not yet been loaded onto the aircraft. I'm so sorry to have given you bad information. The pilot himself asked me to express his deepest apologies to you." She then pointed out the window and said, "LOOK! There they are on the truck now being taken to the aircraft!" I quickly turned my head in the direction the clerk was pointing. It was dark outside but the huge airport lights furnished enough light so I could clearly see both Toris and Laky's crates being taken directly to our aircraft.

I thanked the clerk for assisting me and she smiled, shook my hand and walked me to the boarding gate. As I walked down the long ramp, I thought of the error that had just been avoided. I looked up and there standing at the open hatch to the aircraft was the Captain of the plane. As I drew near, he smiled, stuck out his hand and with very defined English and a soft touch of French accent apologized for the mistake. I shook his hand and stated, "Sir, I accept your apology. No worries. It has all turned out well. My two dogs are on board the aircraft and we are heading home after a long thirteen months in the war in Iraq. Sir, please take us home to America!" We released our handshakes with smiles! The Captain then said, "Sir, it will be my pleasure to take you back to America. We will make your flight as enjoyable as possible. My stewardess will escort you to your seat."

Soon we were racing down the runway at a high rate of speed and up we went into the air ever so swift and smooth. I could hear the wheels being locked up in position. I peered out my window seat and reveled in the view of Paris at night with her thousands upon thousands of lights. It was a magical moment I shall not soon forget. There, off in the distance, as the pilot made a slight turn the Eiffel Tower came into view. The cherry on top. I could not help but reflect on the time my dear wife Debbie and I had scratched out a heart with our initials etched into the center. I wondered if it was still there on the second story level.

The Eiffel Tower was now no longer in sight and the lights of Paris were slowly disappearing as we entered a cloud. Then a sudden break in the cloud and with it a quick and final glimpse of Paris, then clouds and the sights were gone. I smiled, exhaled and relaxed. I was preparing for a nice nap when I noticed one of the stewardesses walking the aisle. She was looking at me and brandishing a huge smile. As she approached, she handed me a bottle of cold Champagne and said, "A gift from the Captain who wishes to express his regret for the mistake with your dogs." I smiled, accepted the gift and asked her to deliver my appreciation to the captain.

I didn't have the heart to tell her I didn't drink alcoholic beverages. It was a nice gesture and I didn't want to hurt the good captain's feelings. I tucked the bottle into my carry-on bag, leaned back in my seat, closed my eyes and my last thought was, "Chicago! America! Here we come!"

Windy City

The flight to Chicago over the Atlantic Ocean was very comfortable, peaceful. In other words there were no kids running up and down the aisles and screaming. Total peace. Of course, the knowledge that I was bound for America, my home had much to do with my state of mind.

Looking back on that time I can say that I enjoyed everything about that flight. The meals served on the plane were awesome, the passengers quiet and the ride absolutely smooth. Everything was perfect. I had a book with me but as soon as I started reading, I must have passed out from being just so comfortable, so at peace. The hum of the aircraft and the fresh, cool air blowing in my face lulled me to sleep. I was safe. My two boys in the cargo hold were safe. We were heading home.

In a matter of what seemed like minutes a voice came over the intercom announcing our imminent arrival to Chicago. I couldn't believe I had slept the whole journey but I sure was thankful that I had. I was giddy, excited and kept peeking out the window to see the night lights of the famous "Windy City." Nothing but darkness. We were over Lake Michigan, thus the absence of any lights. I couldn't help but smile. I was like a little kid on Christmas morning. Then down below I noticed a faint light shining off the waters. Suddenly I could discern white capped waves and then brighter and brighter lights. Then bam! The city blossomed below in all of its thousands of elegant lights; buildings, vehicles, streets all lit up to welcome me home. It was beautiful!

After touching down on American soil I was in a hurry to find my two boys. After retrieving my carry-on bag I made way for customs which I hoped would not take too long as I'm a citizen of this amazing country.

The line for Americans was moving quickly so I was happy about that. Well, happy until I noticed that there was an agent swabbing bags and testing for what I knew to be explosives. Crap! I had lived with and around explosives for thirteen months. While in Baghdad I had actually carried explosives in my backpack, the very same pack now over my right shoulder. Oh boy, this should be interesting.

Readers must recall that this was November 2006 so the attacks of 9/11 had only been five years before. The impact was still strongly felt and on everyone's minds. I had no doubt my entry would all eventually be worked out but I just did not want to miss my flight and possibly have Toris and Laky continue to Texas without me because of my potential hold-up in Chicago while my story was checked out. Ok, here we go. It's my turn in line.

I was hoping they would just wave me through and for a second, I thought they might because the dude looked absolutely bored. As I approached, he spoke to me, "Sir, place your backpack and laptop on the counter please." Oh man, here we go. I did as instructed and watched as the agent began to swab my bags. Ok, time to start talking, "Sir, I must tell you now that you're going to discover that my backpack and laptop have the odor of every explosive known to man on them." Bored, he asked, "And why is that?" Ok, here goes what cops call an alibi, "I was a K9 bomb dog handler and trainer for the past thirteen months in Iraq and I had to carry explosives with me every day as "Training Aids/Drop Aids" for my two bomb dogs. By the way they are waiting for me to pick them up in cargo."

After a short pause he looked at me and said, "Well, let's see what we can find." He placed the swabs into a computer system and within seconds it started to spew out a long white paper that resembled a receipt. In fact, as I watched, the paper kept coming out and then truly did look like a grocery receipt. My thoughts at the sight were simple, "Oh crap!"

The agent reached down and tore the paper from the spool and held it up. Studying the readout he stated, "You're right. It lists almost every explosive we concern ourselves with. Now I've got to ask you for documentation, paperwork, orders, something which confirms what you've told me."

Producing documentation was easy. After checking my papers, he then handed them back and said, "We get a lot of you K9 guys coming through here with explosive odor on your bags. Good thing you had all the right papers otherwise this would have turned into a different situation for you and caused a huge delay in all of your plans." I retrieved my papers and said, "Thank You Sir!" He smiled and responded with, "No, thank you and your two bomb dogs for your service for our country." He hesitated and then remembered something, "Oh, Sir, allow me to be the first to welcome you back to the United States of America!" I smiled and said, "Thank you for your kind words. Man, it sure sounds good to hear that." He grinned and said, "Welcome home."

Now it's time to find my two boys, Toris and Laky!

I followed the signs to where I was to pick up Toris and Laky. As I was getting closer and closer to where I was to sign for them, you guessed it, I could hear Toris barking his head off. I get to the counter, show the necessary papers and the clerk says to me, "Mr. Blocker, those are two very awesome looking German Shepherds you have. The one whose name is Toris, he's very selective in who

328

he likes and doesn't like." My response to him, "Yes, you could say that. He does not like men, especially if they look Middle Eastern." I took a few minutes to tell him how Toris would be teased. The guy loved the stories about Toris and Laky. I could see he truly admired them both.

Suddenly the door opened to the cargo area where Toris and Laky were being held and a man emerged and approached the counter. He had a few words with the clerk I was chatting with and then the man turned to me brandishing a huge smile and an outstretched hand. We shook hands and then the young man said, "Sir, I don't know why your dog Toris doesn't like me. All dogs like me. In fact, he's the first that seems like he wants to get out and kill me. Why is that sir?" I asked this kind and hard-working man which country he was born in. He said, "India Sir!" I then explained the history of Toris and Iraqi men. The young guy said, "Oh, now it makes sense. I understand."

I asked for permission to visit with Toris and Laky. I knew it was most likely against regulations but I had a feeling these two K9 admirers would allow it. "I'm not supposed to but Toris would be happy to see you I'm sure." He then quickly added, "By the way, what's your other dogs name," I said, "Laky's his name and as you've noticed, he's not vocal at all. Unfortunately he's been traumatized by the effects of war and has developed K9 PTSD in Iraq due to the explosions and red tracers flying over our heads. They were just too much for him. As you can see right now, he's very concerned about what's going on in his young life."

I was escorted back to where my boys were held and Toris spied me from a distance and started to emphatically bark at me. He was both happy and scolding at the same time. Those readers who have a German Shepherd understand this type of bark and I'm certain as you're reading this you have a smile on your face as I do. You're probably shaking your head up and down acknowledging what I've just said. It's a great bark of communication for certain!

Meanwhile Laky stood and was peering through the metal grate windows on the side of his crate. He just stood there, sullenly watching me. He had been in this funk ever since the three mortars had almost killed us less than forty-eight hours before. The best I can do for him now is love on him and this I did right away. I asked the man escorting me if we could cut the zip ties from his crate door so I could lean into his crate and give him several hugs, scratches on his head, and plant a few good kisses on top of his head between his ears.

The escort was terrified but had a dilemma on his hands, "Man, I'm not supposed to even let you in here, but I have a soft spot for these war dogs we see come through here." As he's saying this, he is looking around to see if the coast is clear. He continues, "I appreciate so much what they are doing for our country. I can't say no to you. So, yes, I'll cut the zip ties. I have plenty of those things here to secure the crate door once again."

The zip ties were removed and I unlocked Laky's latch on his crate. He walked towards me and immediately I could see fear resonating in his eyes. I reached in with both of my hands and grasped him up around his shoulder blades and pulled him towards me. Laky moved into my left front chest with his head turned sideways and rested his head right there, pressing gently but firmly, as if to get ever so much closer into me. I was patting his sides with both of my hands and turned my head slightly downwards and placed a kiss on the very top of his head. I then heard his tail striking the inside crate walls. This was a golden moment. His body language told me that he was enjoying our special moment. I gave him one last kiss on the top of his head and said, "Ok buddy, time to go, this is the last leg of our trip home."

He immediately lifted his head up off my chest and backpedaled into his crate. His eyes looked happy again and his German Shepherd smile was back. My escort quickly zip tied Laky's crate door. While he was doing that, I leaned over to Toris crate door because he wanted some loving as well. I told the escort, "Don't worry, Toris doesn't need a hug and kiss from me. He's just fine with a head scratch and a few good words. Toris is a seasoned war dog, very tough, and has no K9 PTSD issues like Laky." My escort looked relieved because he was very intimidated by Toris. Respectfully intimidated I would say.

As I had previously done in the other airports, I quickly made way to my boarding area so I could make certain Toris and Laky were both loaded onto this final flight into San Antonio. HOME!

To make better time I stopped one of those airport electric golf carts which move people up and down the halls of airports. I'm glad I did because just as soon as I arrived at my boarding area and approached the large window, I could see Toris and Laky's dog crates moving towards the aircraft. I let out a sigh of relief and boarded my final flight.

I found my seat which turned out to be the accursed aisle seat but, on this trip, I was just happy to be on the aircraft. I would have sat my rump on the floor if need be. Shoot, for that matter, I would have curled up in one of the dog crates. To my right sat a very nice older lady and next to her a man I assumed to be her husband. We all said hello and prepared for the three-hour flight to San Antonio.

Next stop, HOME!

G.T.T.

In the United States in 1819 there was a huge collapse of American banks causing many families to lose their homes and land. This particularly impacted farmers who, unable to pay their debts, found themselves in a hopeless situation. During this time the Mexican government opened its doors to Americans seeking a new life. The door to Texas was thrown wide open and thousands of desperate Americans made the journey. Many of these destitute families left a sort of "forwarding address" in the form of a board nailed to the door of their old farmhouse with the phrase "Gone to Texas" painted on it. Some found they had not enough room or patience for the entire phrase so it was shortened to, "G.T.T." Everyone knew what it meant. The family had packed up and moved to Texas. This story was now mine as I had figuratively nailed the sign on my lodgings in Baghdad and now approached the borders of the greatest state in the union, Texas![96]

I tried to sleep so the time would pass more quickly but it was impossible. I was too excited. Every time I closed my eyes, I visualized my family getting ready to meet me at the airport. I imagined the hours my wife Debbie had put in making sure everything at the house looked perfect. She has always made our home so comfortable.

About an hour and a half out from the San Antonio airport I heard a sound come from the plane that had not been there before. It was a sound coming from the bowels of the aircraft. Barking! It was Toris. The barking lasted for about ten minutes and then stopped. A few minutes later it began again but this time Laky joined in. It was clearly audible. I looked around the cabin and could see people were whispering, looking around and smiling. I looked at my watch and did the math.

Toris, during the entire trip had not barked once in the cargo hold of the multiple aircraft, we had flown in. Now, he is barking. Why? Well, at first, I thought it was because he was tired of the journey but then it dawned on me. Toris had been trained in Texas. Looking at my watch and knowing when we had crossed into Texas, I knew he was most likely picking up the scent of his home State. He could literally smell home. It reminded me of the times we would take trips with our family dogs and they would start barking when we got close to home. Toris knew we were getting close. Laky must have picked up on the excitement of Toris because having never lived in Texas he must have thought, "If it makes Toris happy well then what's coming must be awesome." So he started barking as well. Of course I was guessing but the thought made me smile.

---

[96] Notice I did not say biggest. Yeah, we know you are bigger Alaska but we don't talk about that.

About an hour out from landing one of the stewardesses kneeled down next to my seat and asked, "Sir, do the two dogs barking belong to you?" I smiled and said, "Yes, they do" She then asked, "Can you tell me anything about them?" I thought this was very strange, so I asked her, "Why?" Her answer, "I suspected you were coming back from the war in Iraq or Afghanistan. You look like you're military and you have a very dark tan. I suspected you came from Iraq or Afghanistan. Am I right?" I chuckled and responded, "You're right on target. You're good. You ought to be a cop!" She smiled, laughed and said, "Several of my friends have told me the same thing over the years."

I took a few minutes and expounded on the impeccable service record of Toris and Laky. I told of their service in Iraq and how Toris had served multiple tours in both Iraq and Afghanistan. She listened intently, holding on to every word. Then she smiled, shook my hand, thanked me for my service and for that of my dogs. Real nice lady.

About fifteen minutes from San Antonio I heard the intercom overhead crackle and then the voice of the captain. He spoke clear and sure, "Ladies and gentlemen, for the past hour and a half you have been listening to two dogs barking in our cargo hold. Well folks, allow me to tell you who they are. They're two German Shepherds. One is Laky and the other is Toris. They're both returning to America after serving in Iraq for the past thirteen months. Their handler is aboard escorting them back home to become his pets now. A new and peaceful life for them both." At that moment, the entire plane broke out in loud applause which lasted for a good minute. I of course broke down and started crying. I was just so darn happy and thankful that my two boys were being recognized for their service to our country.

As I'm wiping my eyes and cheeks, drying my tears, the kind lady sitting next to me squeezed my right arm and said, "Thank you. Welcome home!" Well of course this really turned on the tears for me. Every day not knowing if it was my last. The explosions, the pillars of smoke, the stench of death, mortars and rockets, the screams of terror all came back to me with the realization that I would experience it no more. That Toris, Laky and I were safe, that

I was home and that I was surrounded by people who appreciated the sacrifices made by dogs and men. It was a powerful moment I will never forget.

Soon the aircraft internal lights were dimmed and everyone was quiet again. I peered out the windows looking for the lights of my hometown. Looking for familiar landmarks: The Tower of America, the Quarry, the cowboy boots of North Star Mall and the streetlights of Loop 1604 and the traffic congestion of Loop 410. Yep, there it is in all its magnificent glory.

In a matter of seconds we touch down on Texas soil. I'm home. Home at last.

Homecoming

The foot race is on once again but this time I am bound for the arms of my family. As I debark the aircraft and make my way toward baggage claim I'm taking in all of the sights. The hustle and bustle of passengers. The fresh smell of the air and the absence of dust on all of the surfaces. I'm surrounded by hundreds of people who have no idea how fortunate they are to live in this amazing country we call home. I can't help but reflect on the previous months that I had somehow survived.

My heart rate increases the closer I get to Baggage Claim because it's where my family will be. I know there's a goofy grin on my face but I just can't help it. Debbie will be there as will my son Dennis and my daughters Marnie and Sarah with their husbands and children. One more turn in the hall, down the stairs and they will be there.

A few more seconds now, a final step, I look up and…nothing. They are not there. I looked all over and there is not a familiar face in view. What in the world! I have traveled all this way with the whole anticipation of this moment and they are not here. To say I was bummed out would be putting it mildly. I won't even pretend otherwise. Everywhere I look there are families hugging and kissing, smiling, slapping each other on the back and here I stand, leaning against a pillar trying to figure out what in the world happened.

Then I see her, my bride and I can tell by the look on her face that she was upset that she was not there to greet me. Turns out the airport had listed the wrong terminal I would arrive in. They were there on time, waiting, but at the wrong terminal. My wife hates being late for anything, especially something so significant as my return from a war zone. I knew she would be heartbroken but now it's time to celebrate. She hasn't seen me yet so I started walking toward her. Our eyes meet and the fireworks are lit off!

We hold each other and just enjoy the moment. There are tears of joy and relief. It's as if a giant weight suddenly dropped from my shoulders and I could finally exhale. I never thought I would survive. I never thought this was my future. I felt guilty being here when so many others had died or were still stuck in that grueling sandbox. I was here and I knew that others would wish me to enjoy it so I chase the guilty thoughts from my mind and enjoy the arms of my wife. Soon I'm surrounded by my children and grandchildren all waiting for their turn for a hug and kiss.

What a reunion it was! My grandchildren were holding signs featuring pictures of Laky and Toris and a picture of myself, "Welcome Home! Our Hero!" I didn't feel like a hero. True heroes come home in caskets draped with their countries flag. I was simply a guy who had done his best, every day. I had given my all and I was proud to say that my checkpoints had lost not a single man or canine. To me the heroes were still there in Iraq, covered in dirt and sweat, swatting flies and bracing for the inevitable IED or VBIED. I knew I would never forget them. How could I? For now though, enjoy the moment, the hugs and kisses.

The family were all so excited as you can imagine, waving their American flags in the air and at the same time rocking their homemade signs back and forth. Everyone was talking at once and it was so much fun trying to decide who to answer. The one question that kept coming up was, "When can we get Laky and Toris?" I would have to remind them, "We will have to give these war dogs a couple days to get used to this new life. They are not like our dogs at home. These dogs have lived through some terrible times. Soon you will be able to love and hug Laky all you want. He is very gentle and loves hugs but Toris is different. He's a true war dog who has known the sounds of war his whole life so you'll not be able to hug him. Most likely never."

The grandkids eyes were glued on me as they took in every word. Of course this made them want to see Toris and Laky even more so we set off to retrieve them.

With my left arm around Deb the grandkids clamored to hold my free hand. My son Dennis took charge of my backpack and my daughters Marnie and Sarah walked alongside with huge smiles on their faces. I can assure you though, no one's face was smiling any brighter than mine. I'm HOME!

Approaching the area where I'm to claim Toris and Laky, I was shocked to see their crates were already near the counter and resting up against the wall, away from prying eyes and indiscreet fingers. Someone behind the counter held these animals in high regard and I appreciated the gesture.

I got the feeling that my two boys knew we were home because they were both very chill, lying in their kennels idly watching the folks passing by. Suddenly Toris locked eyes with me and he was up and spinning in his crate, barking, fussing at me. Then Laky was up, doing a sort of dance in his crate and brandishing the biggest smile this side of the Rio Grande. Yeah, they knew...no more war.

Trying to leave the airport was interesting as we were stopped by multiple travelers asking about the dog crates we were wheeling out. Working dogs are special but dogs who put their lives on the line are another tier all together. My boys were celebrities leaving the airport as folks asked to have their pictures taken with them. I was pummeled with questions: "Where are they coming from?" "Are these war dogs?" "What are their names?" "What kind of war dogs are these?" You've have to love a military town. I was thankful my boys were being recognized but I was also in a huge hurry to get home and introduce Laky and Toris to their new "forever home" and spoil them rotten. Let's face it, I also desperately needed to take a hot shower.

When we emerge from the terminal and are outside a white truck pulls up and out jumps a K9 friend of mine who greets me with a smile and handshake. I was a bit surprised to see him and had a bad feeling his presence had some terrible meaning which he in fact confirmed, "Hey Dennis, I was tasked with taking Laky from you and evaluating him this week to determine just how bad his K9 PTSD is." I couldn't believe it. All this way and on my dime and now he's being taken away. I was respectful but also tired as I replied, "I was told he and Toris were both mine when I arrived home. I have the paperwork" My friend said, "I don't know anything about that Dennis. I'm just following orders." I shrugged my shoulders and quipped, "Ok, I'll be out soon to talk this up and see what direction this is going."

As you can imagine I was extremely irritated. I knew what was going on, but it still didn't change my mood. Of course my big concern was that Laky would be thrust back into the system. I realized that a great deal of money had been spent in training Laky and maintaining him but I knew he was done. He was mentally checked out. Trainers in Baghdad knew that as well so I knew it would only be a day or two before they realized the same here in Texas.

I helped load Laky's crate onto the truck, opened the door and gave him a huge hug and kiss. I scratched him all over and said, "It's ok buddy. I'll see you soon. Get a good night's sleep." I gave him another kiss between his eyes, closed up his kennel door and shut the tailgate on the truck with a light slam. I knew I loved this amazing dog and seeing him drive off like that broke my heart. It was such a damper on what was supposed to be a jubilant occasion. As the truck drove off, I slowly turned to my family and with as big a smile as I could muster, I said, "Let's go home."

The ride home was a shock to my system. For one thing the cars were moving at such incredible speeds. Driving around Baghdad in the Green Zone was always a slow go. Speed limits there were necessarily slow. So racing along Loop 410 at sixty-five miles an hour felt like a roller coaster ride. I kept looking into the mirrors to be sure a vehicle coming up fast was not setting up to detonate a VBIED against us. My nerves were shot. I was on high alert and every vehicle seemed to be targeting our truck. Swooping in and out of lanes the other cars seemed destined for death. I couldn't wait to get home and out of this environment. I turned my attention to my family, ignored the mirrors and lost myself in conversation.

Soon a feeling of complete joy overtook me as we passed North Star Mall and the famous cowboy boots that tower above. Off in the distance on the skyline I could see the Tower of America and the familiar landmark brought a smile to my face. The familiar sights were beckoning me from my hidden recesses. This was real. I had made it. The giant Indian chief with handheld high above the car dealership seemed to welcome me home. I smiled and chuckled. Yeah, I'm back.

Pulling into our neighborhood I could not help but revel in the beautiful colors of the homes and the stark green of the grass. I smiled as I witnessed carefree people mill about their yards and chat with neighbors. Not a care in the world. No fear of insurgents. No bombs. No machine gun fire. No pillars of smoke billowing into the sky. Peace and quiet.

We made the turn onto my street and there's my home. What an awesome sight and beautiful moment. The American flag is flying in front and I thought of how many exceptional people I had met who had served and died for that very fabric. I will never forget that moment. Stretched in front of the house is a large banner all the kids and grandkids had made, "Welcome Home from The War!!!" My eyes filled with tears but I laughed at the excitement of the grandkids running around and pointing to their contributions on the banner. I yelled out with a huge smile on my face, "I LOVE IT!"

I was not the only one home. Toris, my battle buddy, was home too and everyone stood back as I took him out of his crate for a much-needed stretch of the legs and potty break. This time I had to press against him as I opened the crate because he was raring to go. Understandable. It had been a long day of international travel. Toris had a blast running around the backyard sniffing everything and marking his new territory. I just sat and watched as he frolicked around as a dog with no job, no searches, no obligations other than to enjoy life. I watched and thought, "Enjoy this Buddy. You've earned it!" Three tours in Iraq. Two tours in Afghanistan. One tour in New York City at the Empire State Building following 9/11. I felt humbled to know him, to have him, to love him and I just wished that America could have known of this warrior who steadfastly stood at the front lines for so long.

Well, now YOU do.

Home in Texas with soft green grass and an absence of explosions. Toris, the grizzled veteran enjoys his new life of peace.

Finally in the arms of my wife Debbie

My daughter Sarah with grandson Caiden in her arms. My wife Debbie and my grandchildren (L to R) Seth, Alexis and Austin at the airport.

Laky

It had been about four days since I had seen Laky and I was anxious to see him and get a report on his status. I had not received any news or updates and I must admit I was irritated that they were dragging their feet. I knew they were busy and that Laky would be a secondary priority so I hoped my sudden appearance would create a stir.

One of the trainers told how Laky had been put through several trials and searches but had failed. The final test was one I was actually asked to be involved in. A trainer stood seventy-five yards from Laky and I. In the trainer's hand was a .357 handgun. Walking straight toward us the trainer would fire the .357 off to the side. Bam! Take a few more steps and Bam! Few more steps and Bam! Laky's whole body was shaking and he tried to turn and run away. The trainer immediately stopped in his tracks, looked up at me and we both knew that Laky was mine. Laky's wartime service was over. His problem was not his nose, his intelligence or his drive. It was finally and certifiably determined that Laky was suffering from severe K9 PTSD and was unfit for further duty. He was retired (again) and officially handed over to me (again).

I was beaming from ear to ear and could not wait to get him home! No more cement slab for this boy. From now on he would have air conditioning in the summer and heat in the winter. His would be a life of comfort and love resting on a Kuranda bed.

Many of my acquaintances wanted to chat about my experiences but I was in a hurry to get Laky home with me before someone changed their mind. I politely excused myself.

As we approached the car Laky did something he had never done in his life, he entered a vehicle without being in a crate. Stepping up into the driver's side of the car he scooted over to the passenger seat. This was a new experience for him and he was jerking his head left and right taking in the sights and the new perspective. When I sat down behind the wheel Laky leaned over and gave me a huge doggy kiss across the face. This was a rare thing for him and I loved it. I smiled and said, "Next stop is home!"

I'll never forget the scene as we drove home. The sun was setting and the orange hue of light was splashing against our faces as we drove off into the Western sunset. Laky edged over to the half-opened window to smell the air. His eyes squinted and his lips began to part as the wind cascaded against his face. Laky glanced over at me and our eyes locked. In his eyes I saw contentment for the first time. I was so happy for my boy!

When we arrived home, my sweet wife Debbie greeted us in the driveway and of course she greeted Laky with high toned sweet words and soft scratches on his head and neck. She bent down to his level and gave him a quick soft kiss on the side of his face and sweetly whispered in his ear, "This is your new home Laky. Welcome home!"

The Late-Night Insurgent

We never saw it coming. I had been home for quite a while and seemingly safe from any attacks. I had been having nightmares but refused to get help assuming I could manage it on my own. The dreams were always centered around explosions and insurgents trying to kill me, my men and our dogs. My wife would wake me and console me but truthfully, I was a bit hardheaded about getting help. I knew that my wife's dad had suffered from terrible nightmares of his time at Saipan and Iwo Jima during WWII. I knew he never went for help so why should I. I would be a tuff guy and handle it on my own.

Bad idea.

My sleep was fitful and I never seemed to feel rested. This constant state of stress became unbearable and I knew that I would have to get help or perhaps my mind would explode.

There were issues with the counselors but this was mostly because I didn't want to talk to anyone unless they had seen combat and been under fire. It seemed that all they wanted to do was push medications onto me and for a while I tried them but I felt slow and goofy. I hated that feeling of being in a cloud, almost muffled. I stopped taking the meds and tried to focus on the issues that were haunting me. Slowly over time I began to sleep again and that made things a lot better. Rest does wonders for your mind and health.

My big issue was regret at not being able to do more and the feelings of being helpless while under fire. I learned techniques to deal with these issues and I got to tell you that it really worked. The big problem was my pride but once I swallowed that down and got to the issues, I really began to see progress. I am sure that I will always have recurrent nightmares but I am so much better off now than I have been in a long time.

With the nightmares at bay and less frequent I assumed I was finally done with my nighttime visits by insurgents. As it turned out there was another visit to be had.

One night, around 3:30 in the morning, I woke with the sudden urge to use the restroom. On my way I heard our wolf/dog Rosealee howling. This was odd because she never, ever howled. In fact, Rosealee never made a sound. She was very unique and quite beautiful with a white and gray coat. Stunning.

So, to hear her howling was significant. I made my way to the middle bedroom, peeked through the window curtains and was surprised to see an adult man in our backyard peering through a chain link gate attached to our cattle fencing. This intruder was speaking to one of our German Shepherd police dogs named Dallas.

This young man did not realize it but he had chosen the worst yard to jump in. The county had previously excavated the ditch behind our house making it wider and deeper. The excess dirt had been pushed up against our fence so this guy only had to make a hop of about five feet to get into our yard. What he didn't know was that I had installed eight-foot-high fencing so what appeared to him as five feet translated into an eight-foot fall on the inside of our backyard. He plopped to the ground with a thud and twisted his ankle. He didn't know it but his problems had just begun.

I had several large German Shepherds and a few were males. One, named Dallas, was a retired Police drug dog. He had been a family pet for years. Because of the dogs, I had cordoned off sections of the back yard with cattle fencing and then because German Shepherds are intelligent, I had placed a metal clasp over the latch so the dogs couldn't flip the latch and open the gate.

Well, when this guy jumped into the backyard, he landed in the section with Toris. Ha! Ha! Yes, Toris. My six-campaign war dog. My dog who had single handedly tore into insurgents with his jaws when they tried to sneak onto an American base by jumping a fence. Well this idiot has no idea how much danger he's in right now. Lucky for this guy Toris was in his kennel with the doggy door cover in place. Earlier that day my son Dennis had cut the grass in the back yard and had forgotten to take the cover off the doggy door when he was finished. As it turned out this was a fortunate error for this guy.

Meanwhile, this guy is standing at the gate trying to get into the second dog run that contains Dallas, my retired police dog. Well Dallas is awake and standing only a few feet from this character. The dude sees Dallas and is whistling at him, gauging if the dog is aggressive. This was the noise I heard in the kitchen, the whistling.

This guy is having an impossible time with the latch because he doesn't realize I had placed a clasp over it. So as he struggles with the latch, he whistles at Dallas to gauge his aggression. Giving up on getting through the fence our hapless intruder decides to jump out of the yard but now he sees that it's actually eight feet that he must ascend. It's then that he makes another startling discovery.

I had strung electric fencing on the inside of the yard against the lower boards of the fences to discourage our dogs from digging or trying to jump out. This intruder gets zapped by the electric fence and decides maybe it's better to face the German Shepherds so he tries the gate again. Dallas is watching the whole scene in silence for he is quite passive.

Hiding in the shadows is another German Shepherd and she is quiet as well. Kiesie was quite unique.[97] She reminded me of the raptors from the movie Jurassic Park. Perhaps you recall the scene when the big game hunter speaks of the raptors and says, "When they look at you, you can tell they are figuring things out." This was Kiesie. She was our personal raptor. She hid in the shadows and remained silent because she didn't want this night stalker to know she was there. Kiesie was hoping he would come through the gate so she could take him down. She was very protective of our family to say the least. She relished the thought of tearing into this guy.

Well, the last thing I wanted was for some stranger to get mauled on my property. I knew this man was in extreme danger and that he was oblivious to the fact. I went to grab my shotgun but for some reason it was not in its usual spot so I grabbed the next best thing, a BB gun. Yeah, that's right. I was hoping the dark would conceal the identity of my weapon.

By this time my wife is up and, on the phone, calling the Police. I also sent her to wake our son Dennis who only fifteen minutes before had returned home, having completed a night shift in the Trauma Center. She threw open the door to his room and yelled out, "Dennis, get to the backyard. Dad has someone at gunpoint!" Talk about a rude awakening. Zero to sixty in nothing flat for my son.

Dennis walked by mom in the kitchen to hear her tell the dispatcher, "Don't worry. He isn't going anywhere. We have him at gunpoint." My son was thinking, "What in the world is going on?" He was still a bit foggy because he had just fallen asleep but when he stepped outside, he saw I had the intruder up against the side of the house, "spread eagle." Dennis looked at me, looked at the guy and then looked back at me. Surprisingly, my son turned and without uttering a word went back into the house. I was stunned.

---

[97] She was the mother of Dallas

Less than a minute later Dennis returned and this time he had a shotgun in his hand. He walked up to me and smiling said, "Its loaded." I smiled and said, "Thanks." My son had seen I was holding a BB gun and went to get me something more substantial.

This guy was saying, "You called a plumber, right?" I couldn't believe the gall of this dude. "No, we didn't call a plumber at 4:30 in the morning and I don't know a plumber that shows up by jumping a back fence in dress clothes." I had to tell him several times to stay against the wall because he kept pushing himself off. I had to reiterate his dire position, "If you make any sudden moves, I will shoot you. Do not get froggy on me." I looked over to Dennis and said, "Go get Toris. This guy is getting froggy on me."

Dennis went pale. He knew Toris' history and that he was not a dog you just hung out with. In fact Dennis had very little interaction with Toris because of his schedule and commitments. "Go get him! Make certain Toris sees the leash in your hand when you open the door." Dennis slowly turned and later confessed to me, "I was thinking, 'Oh crap! Toris is going to eat me alive.'"

As my son approached Toris' kennel I could hear him say in a nervous voice, "Here Toris, Good boy Toris. Don't eat me please." Dennis reached down and opened the door sheepishly saying, "Here Toris." Seeing the leash in my son's hand Toris immediately licked his hand. Dennis knew he would survive the night.

Toris is panting and excited to go for a walk with my son. Well, that is until he sees the insurgent up against the house in the body search position I had taught for years. Toris went nuts, lunging, barking, foaming at the mouth trying to tear into this guy. I took control of Toris and handed the shotgun to my son. Now I felt safe. With a gun there were many variables but with Toris it was a done deal. The dude was going to behave.

I yelled to the guy, "This is my war dog Toris! He served three tours in Iraq, two in Afghanistan and he's taken down three insurgents with his teeth. If you keep pushing yourself off the wall I will feel threatened and I will release my dog. He will attack you. If you turn one more time to face me I will send my dog in on you. Do you understand?!"

The guy yelled out, "Sir! Please don't send the dog. I don't want to get bit!" Meanwhile Toris is doing his job to the letter; barking, lunging forward and loving every moment of it. He's a true warrior. This dude was locked into the side of my house like a spider. He wasn't moving any longer.

Within a few minutes the police arrived and quickly made way to the backyard where the intruder gladly presented his wrists to the officers if they would only remove him from this insane backyard. I had never seen a criminal so happy to see the police before.

Later, talking with the officers I discovered the guy had been attending a neighborhood party and was too drunk to walk the long-distance home using sidewalks. He thought jumping fences through the neighborhood would be a great solution. His drunken stupor almost cost him his life. I asked the officer if I could tell the young man something.

We walked out to the squad car and the officer opened the door. I said, "Young man, I'm a retired cop and spent twenty-one years in the military. You are fortunate you jumped into my backyard because I wasn't nervous. If you had jumped into another family's yard they would have been scared and they would have shot you. Please, next time arrange a ride." The young guy looks down at his shoes and then up at me, "Sir, would you have shot me?" My response, "Yes, I had no idea what your intentions were. I didn't want to shoot you. Only a sick person would want such a thing. However, I was absolutely willing to do it should you have shown any aggression toward me or my family?" The young man shook his head and stared at his feet. "Yes sir," was the reply. I doubted he would remember the conversation.

The officers loved hearing about Toris and they laughed about how happy the guy was to see them. "I've been doing this for a long time and never had a bad guy so happy to see me before," said the officer who'd been first on the scene. We all laughed.

I've said it so many times but I was so lucky to have Toris in my life. He made us all feel so safe. I loved that amazing dog and was thrilled that he added another "bad guy" to his record. I learned something else this night; I was getting better. I had handled a very tense situation with professionalism and had not lashed out in anger. I had been calm and collected. I'm sure the tense situation with Toris at my side was in a way sort of a healing moment for me. It eased me back into my world and I look back on it as a milestone in my recovery.

Toris and the Bridge

Toris and Laky were never placed together to play. Toris was the Alpha. He did not tolerate other dogs at all. I once tried to see if he would at least get along with females so I introduced him to Scarlet, our huge all black and gray German Shepherd.

Running up to Scarlett he placed his big paws on her back shoved her to the ground and was about to take a bite out of her hide when I yelled at him, "Toris! Phooey that! Here!" He obediently came to my side just like the old days but kept an eye on Scarlet. In that moment I knew Toris would never have a companion.

Laky and Toris had shared kennels side by side for month after month in Iraq. They were used to each other's company but there was no love there. No comradery. It was all business with these two big males. When I finally had them both home in Texas, I let them loose in their own individual private fenced in area. They walked up to each other separated by the cattle fencing, Toris immediately turned and urinated in Laky's general area. Yeah, that was a statement and Laky got the message. Toris turned and walked away like a gangster.

No love there. Not even respect from Toris for other dogs. However, he did love and respect me and I in turn loved him. I sort of felt bad for him because I knew he was missing out on a lot of fun

348

things that the majority of dogs enjoy. Family, friends and company. Toris never enjoyed the laughter and pats of my children or grandchildren but you know what, he was ok with that.

Toris was the grizzled veteran who sits at the end of the bar, night after night, enjoying his two drinks in silence. Never causing trouble and never initiating conversation. He has his routine and that is what he loves about his life. It's his, just the way he liked it! That was Toris.

Now Toris did have air conditioning, his Kuranda bed and a comfortable kennel he could go in and out of when he pleased. He had amazing meals and plenty of dog treats. He was doted on, medicated when necessary, vaccinated when required and pampered beyond anything he had known before.

My goal for him has always been that he would finally get to relax. To enjoy his later years without the sound of war.[98] In this we successfully created an environment that he could enjoy. I assumed we would have many years to spoil him. I was wrong.

The day everything changed began just as every other day had begun, with routine. I went out to the kennels to let the dogs out for the day. I guess it was close to around 6:30 in the morning. I always let Toris out first because he had the larger portion of the property to himself.

When I opened the door to his kennel, I was shocked to see Toris standing there with his front legs spread wide and his head hung low, panting heavily. My first thought was the recurrence of bloat that we had successfully fought in Baghdad three years before. His mannerisms and symptoms looked very similar. I knew he needed a Veterinarian immediately.

---

[98] There is a military base close to where we live and on clear nights, we can hear weapons fire. Toris would hear this and stand erect, facing the danger. He was a true warrior to the last.

I pull my cell phone out and make the call to my Veterinarian who I am certain will not be there. I look at the time on my phone and see it's close to 0700hrs., and in that instant know she will not answer because her office does not open until 9. On the second ring she answers. I couldn't believe it. I explained what was going on and before I could explain further, she said, "Bring Toris in right now." I didn't hesitate, "We're on the way."

I picked my battle buddy up in my arms and I'm running with him to my car, talking to him, "It's going to be alright boy, I'm going to take good care of you. Your doc is waiting for you to arrive, and she's going to help you feel better." As I'm running, he's grunting from the jostling up and down which is causing intense pain. I'm holding back my tears with every bit of energy I can muster. I didn't want him seeing me cry.

I'm convinced I was breaking all of the speed limits but I didn't care. This was early morning traffic time and my biggest fear was congestion on the roads. Well, to my surprise it was not bumper to bumper and traffic was moving along nicely. It also seemed like I caught nothing but green lights. This was a huge blessing.

Meanwhile, Toris is breathing harder and harder. I have the rearview mirror situated in a way that will allow me to keep a close eye on him. I swing into the parking lot and screech to a halt. I can see the Doc is waiting outside with a couple of her medical staff. Toris knew all of these people very well and the fact they were all women worked in their favor. First thing Doc said was, "There's no need for a muzzle. He loves all of us and we love him. He knows we're here to help him." I said, "Ok Doc, it's your call!" She then said, "He will not be awake much longer, we will do a quick X-Ray and see what we've got going on with our boy. Once we get the images, we'll know which direction we're going with this."

Within a few minutes the x-rays were finished. The Doc came out and said, "Dennis, no bloat, but I'd like to open him up and see just what's going on with him. He's very stressed, his stomach is large and distended. He has a lot of gas in there. I need your permission to open him up." My answer was quick, "Go for it, I don't want him suffering."

She asked, "Would you like to stay in the surgical suite?" I answered that I would like to. The Doc then wondered if I would be able to handle the sights. I filled her in, "This is the second time I'll have seen him opened up like this. I can handle it. I want to be with my battle buddy." She nodded and said, "Ok, scrub up and put on a gown and mask."

Sure enough, this is a repeat performance of what I witnessed in Baghdad with Lt. Col. Thompson when he and his team were saving Toris' life from the monster known as "Bloat." I wondered what she would find once she opened him up.

After removing his organs and carefully inspecting them she declared, "It's for certain this is not bloat. His stomach has been sewn to the inner lining of his skin preventing it from flipping. I'm determined to find out what this is."

The Doc drew several syringes full of fluids from his stomach and his intestines. The doctor then began injecting medications into his stomach and intestines stating, "This will help settle his stomach down." The Doc reported that they extracted a few berries from his stomach. I told her they were most likely from our China Berry Tree. "You know those are poisonous," she paused for a second and then continued, "but there were so few in his stomach that it would not have made him this sick."

The Doc continued looking at the organs and then looked up at me, "Dennis, the lab results came back, he has been poisoned for sure! The good news is that I believe he will be fine. I think you got him here in time." I was overjoyed to hear that he would be fine but angered that someone had poisoned him. Who would do such a thing?

After closing Toris up he was placed on layers of quilts that rested atop a heating mat. The Vet Techs were like a flock of angels hovering around him and tending to his every need. At one point the lead Vet Tech came in and pulled out her stethoscope. For some reason I figured this was a bad sign. She saw my concern and after listening to his heart smiled and said, "Dennis, his heart is perfect. It's pumping strong with perfect rhythm so there's nothing to worry about. He's beat this. You got him here just in time."

Whew! A sigh of total relief. She stood to walk away but just prior to turning she bent down and gave Toris a little scratch on the top of his head. As she turned to leave, she looked at me and said, "Dennis, if you need anything for Toris or yourself please let us know."

Then a huge smile formed on her face as she looked beyond me pointed to Toris and said, "You have company. Your boy Toris is waking up." Sure enough, there were those big beautiful almond colored eyes looking straight up at me. I of course broke out with a huge smile.

I took both of my hands and placed one on each side of his face and gave him a big long kiss between his beautiful almond colored eyes. When I kissed him, he squinted his eyes; he was being so sweet. I know it made him feel good to see me right there by his side.

I laid my body up close to his and placed my face right up next to his head. All the while I am stroking under his chin and giving him small little kisses on his beautiful golden and black muzzle. I was whispering to him, "You're going to be just fine. It won't be long and we will be going home." He was getting sleepy again so I let him nap. He needed the rest.

One of the Vet Techs came by to hang a new bag of IV fluids. She glanced down at me with Toris and said, "Everything looks good Dennis." I said, "Yes it sure does. I'm so grateful for everything you all have done to save my boy Toris' life!" She smiled and said, "Dennis, you know we all love our boy Toris!"

As he lay there napping, I thought back on the times we had run for cover from incoming rockets and mortars. How could I ever forget the showdown we had with the Iraqi soldiers who were pointing their weapons at us. I smiled when I thought about the giant turkey he had between his teeth, saliva pouring out the sides of his mouth. This is my partner, my war buddy.

He stirred and opened his eyes again. He placed his right paw on my left hand and boosted himself up a bit and licked my face twice. He then slumped back down to rest. I continued running my hands through his fur, reflecting on the many adventures we had shared and survived.

Lori came back to hook up another bag of fluids and make sure his IV lines and drips were ok. I looked up at Lori from where I was lying next to Toris and said, "Lori, I pray I'm wrong, but I believe we have a problem. This is the third or maybe fourth bag of fluids and he's not passed any urine." Lori had a troubled look on her face, she said, "I know Dennis, no one had the heart to tell you, but it appears his kidneys stopped working because of the poison. It was just too much for them."

My heart was in my throat, at that very moment I became very frightened. I felt like a little boy who wanted to pick his dog up in his arms and run away with him. The reality was staggering. I had experienced in two seconds the extremes of both happiness and sheer sorrow. I knew what these words meant but I just could not, did not want to believe them.

The Vet Tech said, "Dennis I'm going to insert a catheter and see if I can get him to pass urine. The Doc wants to see if anything will come out. I'll be right back." I couldn't speak, I just moved my head up and down. As Lori walked away my boy opened his eyes and locked in with mine. I gave him a big smile and spoke in a high-pitched tone "Hey boy! Man you sure are sleepy today, but that's ok, you're going to be just fine my boy." I leaned over and gave him several big kisses between his eyes and a few on the side of his face. Toris returned the gesture many times over. I can tell you that at this moment it was taking all of my will power and energy to keep from crying!

About this time I can hear footsteps approaching from the hallway and I could discern what sounded like a plastic bag being opened. This was the moment of truth. For me it was like a Twilight Zone episode. I hoped I would wake up from this nightmare that was all too surreal. Just last night everything was fine and now today it's all coming to an end. How could this happen? What kind of an end is this for a dog who gave his whole life to protecting Americans? This wasn't fair. In the cosmic order of things how could this be right? This was supposed to be the safest place in the world for my buddy and now here he is lying on a hospital quilt dying. Dying at the hands of an American insurgent. Insurgent! An American did this to one of our heroes. To a dog that protected this idiot's own life. How is this even possible?

I didn't like the look on the Docs face when she entered the room. She seemed a bit too somber. I would have preferred a better poker face but I knew it was hard for her because she loved Toris. This was personal for her and all the staff.

The lead Vet Tech got down on her knees next to Toris. Toris loved and trusted her so he was not concerned with what she was doing. We both slid his body around so she had a better vantage point to insert the catheter. Toris turned his head to see what she had in her hands. Ever the professional she said, "It's ok my sweet boy, go ahead and smell it." She stretched out her hand towards his face so he could smell the bag but not the catheter since it had to be sterile. She then wiped Toris with a cleansing swab, squirted Surgilube onto the catheter and then began to insert it. Inch after inch disappeared down his urethra and nothing was coming out.

NOTHING! NO URINE!

My heart was shattered into a thousand pieces. The Tech looked at me with utter despair written all over her face. In a cracking low toned whisper she said, "I'm so sorry Dennis, but it appears his kidneys have shut down. I'm so sorry." As she's saying these words, I could see tears welling up in her eyes. Seeing her despair broke the dam on my emotions. My shoulders began to heave and shake and I could not hold back the tears any longer. Suddenly I felt pressure on my hand and I looked down to see that Toris had placed his paw on my hand.

Toris boosted himself up and was licking the tears from my face. I cried harder and harder. This was too much. How could this be? I thrust my arms around Toris body and drew him close to me. I could feel his warmth against me. My heart was breaking in half.

I kept hugging Toris so hard against my body and I could hear the Doc crying softly behind me as she watched these heartbreaking moments between Toris and I. I then said in a muffled voice through Toris' fur in his neck, "Could you give me a few minutes alone with Toris, but when you come back, bring with you the items you'll need to send my boy off into eternal rest. I do have a special request, however, please give him the first shot which will put him to sleep as if he were going in for surgery. I want him to be comfortable. After this you can slowly inject the pink fluid which will end his life. Can you please do that for us?" Our Doc quietly and respectfully whispered, "Of course Dennis, anything for Toris. I'll give you both the time you need."

The words I said to my battle buddy are too hard to write. The times we shared under fire had melded us into one. I owed my life to him and he was leaving me way before his time was due.

After a short while the Doc returned with the medications and as I held my boy, I kept telling him how sorry I was and how thankful I was for his love. I thanked him on behalf of the entire country for the years of faithful service he had provided.

The medications were injected as I held my boy tighter and tighter, trying desperately to take advantage of the few seconds I still had to feebly convey my love and thanks. It was an impossible task and I could only try, try my hardest to tell him all the things that passed through my mind. In the last seconds it all came down to one final phrase, "I Love You."

The very last thing my boy saw of me, just before he closed his eyes for eternity, was me coming forward to place a kiss between his two big almond colored eyes. I then quickly kissed him on the lips and at this moment his eyelids began flickering.

And with that my boy Toris, my war buddy, my friend, companion and protector slowly closed his eyes, drifted off to sleep and took that final walk to the bridge, the most beautiful you've ever seen, a bridge whose light comes from a rainbow.

Lying there, hugging the lifeless form of my war dog I wiped the tears from my eyes, stood at attention and made a straight and proud military salute. Holding the salute with my right hand up to my right eye I uttered the following words while maintaining military bearing and staring straight ahead, "This Salute is for an American War Dog Hero. An unsung Hero. Your country does not know of your service but I do and on behalf of the United States let me say thank you. I love you my boy. My war hero!"

With that I dropped my salute, looked down at him for one last time and then asked if I could have some scissors because I wanted to cut fur from his neck. I needed a piece of him that I could always hold and touch. The Doc was standing there with the techs and office workers who were wiping their eyes. Someone ran to a desk and retrieved some scissors and I took some samples of his fur..

It was about eight days later I was told I could pick up Toris in his beautiful wooden box. I did and it truly was a solemn time driving home. I kept my hand on his box the entire drive. I said to him, "Well Buddy, I'm taking you home!"

In my last will there are special instructions that specify that when I am buried at Ft. Sam Houston National Cemetery, San Antonio, Texas, the remains of Toris are to be placed inside the casket with me. For generations to come my heirs will know that with me is my battle buddy, my best friend. A German Shepherd with a stubby tail, named Toris.[99]

---

[99] As I typed this story Toris ashes were never more than ten inches from my left wrist. Also within reach was a container holding his beautiful and soft hair. He'd been right beside me the whole time

Salute to an American War Hero

Toris Blocker

A War Dog whose life and exploits will live on forever, in the pages of this book.

Veterans Day Parade

I was shocked by the request I received, "Would you be willing to have Laky in this year's Veteran's Day Parade?" Of course it only took a millisecond for me to agree to Laky receiving credit for his service. I just wished Toris was alive to participate.

The first Veterans Day parade was actually called "Armistice Day Parade" as it commemorated the official end of World War I. The day of remembrance was held in San Antonio on November 11th, 1919.[100] The celebrations were fantastic and continued throughout the day. A large crowd had gathered on the Alamo grounds where a beautiful wreath had been placed to honor those who fought and died in WWI. News accounts described the spectacular scene as biplanes from Kelly Field appeared overhead circling lower and lower until they dropped flowers onto the Alamo crowd. It was a beautiful tribute to those who had lost their lives.

My first order of business was to make certain my boy looked his best so it was off to the doggy salon. Laky's eyes squinted with joy as he was given a deep shampoo, massage and conditioner. He was in doggy heaven. After a blow dry and nail trim he was ready to go. Absolutely breath-taking! So handsome! Funny, but I think he actually knew what a stud he was. There was a bit of a prance in his step, definitely showing off. He had come a long way from the moon dust days of Baghdad with muddy snot dribbling from his nose.

The folks at the salon were aware he was going to be in the parade and they knew of his service so they had thrown in all sorts of extras at no additional charge, "It's our honor" they said. I thanked them and we left for home where I knew he would be lauded for his beauty.

---

[100] World War I ended on November 11, 1918. The United States suffered 116,516 deaths during WW I and 320,000 wounded and sick. The identification of the day of remembrance was changed on June 1, 1954 by Congress from "Armistice Day" to "Veterans Day."

Back at the Blocker casa, the family was hugging and kissing Laky, raving about how handsome he was. Of course he took it all in, soaking it up like a sponge. He tried to look regal but he wasn't fooling anyone. He was a ham.

I opened the back door so he could take a potty break. About thirty seconds later I thought, "Oh crap, Laky loves the pond!" I bolted to the door, threw it open and yelled, "Laky! Come!" There he stood with paw raised, just about to step into the pond. I had caught him just in time. Whew!

I asked my daughter Sarah, and my two grandsons Austin and Caiden (Sarah's sons), if they would walk Laky in the parade for me. I was physically unable to undertake the long trek because of serious injuries I suffered in Afghanistan.[101] I knew I would never be able to walk the distance of the parade. My physical therapy was excruciating enough and the mere thought of a long hike on asphalt was mind numbing. I knew it would be too much to ask of my body at that time.

Anyway, my daughter was happy to do this for me. Of course Austin and Caiden were excited to learn that they would be carrying large signs that displayed, "LAKY WAR DOG BAGHDAD 2005-2006"

It was time for the parade[102] and there were thousands of people along the entire route which wound through downtown San Antonio. Sarah had Laky on a leash of course and on the left side of Laky marched Caiden while Austin moved along the right. Each of the boys held the sign telling of Laky's service. I was in the front seat of a follow along car with a video camera in my hands.

---

[101] Details of this life altering injury will be revealed in the second book of this series which will be titled, *The Dogs I Have Known in 2 Wars: Afghanistan.* Set for publication December 2020.

[102] For a video of the parade as it unfolded visit the website dogsof2wars.com

As Laky walked the route on Avenue E, I could see we were approaching East Houston Street. There, plainly visible was the north wall of the Alamo grounds. Off to the right stood the Alamo Cenotaph Monument honoring all of the fallen from the great siege of so long ago. I could not help but reflect that I had also lived in a walled-in redoubt surrounded by thousands of bad guys. It was not a good feeling.

What caught me by surprise were the hundreds and hundreds of people up ahead lining the way along the intersection at East Houston Street. I smiled as a teenage girl, who looked to be probably thirteen or fourteen years old, turned to smile at Laky. The pickup truck she rode in was part of the parade and directly in front of us. She could see people pointing behind her so she turned left and then spun right to see what was so interesting. She saw Laky, smiled and waved the American flag in her right hand.

After making a right I could see solemn people standing with their arms at their side suddenly perk up, lift their arms and snap a photo of Laky. Smiles all around. Waving. Clapping. Yelling. It was amazing. Laky was making his presence known.

As we turn left from East Houston Street onto South Alamo my breath is taken away as I can now see thousands of people up ahead, lining both sides of the street. U. S. flags snap in the wind, POW/MIA flags wave and flags from the different branches of the military sway in the breeze. It's an amazing moment. Suddenly, off to the left and above the din I clearly hear a woman's voice, "Thank you Laky!" Tears fill my eyes and with a cracking, emotion filled voice say to my wife and grandson Tyler, "I love that."

To the immediate left people are leaning forward in their chairs, smiling and waving at Laky. He's the star of the show. A little girl, probably eight years old, holds a video camera aloft and is looking through the viewfinder. She swings to the right and is startled to see Laky. Her eyes widen and her mouth opens in astonishment. I love the look of adoration on her face. She was not expecting to see a war dog and she's loving every second of this moment.

A young elementary school aged girl wearing a blue shirt holds an American flag in her left hand. It ripples in the wind as she looks at the white pick-up truck ahead of us. Looking in our direction she sees Laky for the first time. Her gaze is fixed on him and slowly her flag drops down to her lap. Her head tilts to the side and in that moment, there is only Laky and her on the street. She is mesmerized by him and I will always hold dear that moment she had with him.

As we continue down the road, I spy a grizzled Vietnam veteran with the logo of the 101st Screaming Eagles on his shirt. Stoically he sits in his wheelchair surrounded by his cheering family. There is not the least hint of emotion on his face as he stares at Laky, following my boy's path with his eyes. Quiet. Grim. Respectful. I recognize the look. This man has seen friends die. He views Laky and honors his service with dignified silence.

The adulation and cheers of the crowd for Laky now crescendos and reverberates off the walls of the Menger Hotel where Colonel Theodore "Teddy" Roosevelt interviewed candidates for his famous "Rough Riders." The place is steeped in history and the fact that Laky is now making it has not been lost on me.

Soon we pass another veteran of the 101st Division who watches Laky pass. The man reads the sign of my boy's service and quietly nods his head up and down. Solemn. Respectful.

A tiny brown dog on a leash, sees Laky, barks and lunges forward from the crowd. People nearby laugh because Laky pays the little squirt not the least bit of attention. Moving forward, one paw in front of the other, Laky is all business.

Now I see a man with a toddler in his arms squat down next to a person who looks to be his wife. She is sitting on the curb quietly watching the parade pass by. They huddle together and the man allows the boy to stand. As a family they watch Laky trudge past. The husband and wife smile. The little boy is expressionless, hypnotized by Laky. The mom sees her boy's fixation and waves with a huge grin on her face. It's too precious.

Further down the street, near where the old Joske's building stands, I notice three active duty US Navy servicemen clomp by on the sidewalk. They maneuver through the crowd with an important destination on their minds. Suddenly the Seamen see Laky, their expressions change, they slow and watch in silence as Laky passes. The sailors know a veteran when they see one and the respect they show is beautiful to behold.

A woman with a "PRESS" badge is walking across the intersection of South Alamo and Commerce. She is aloof and seemingly a thousand miles away in her thoughts. Suddenly she spies Laky, stops in her tracks, grins and bends down to snap several photos of Laky and the signs being carried by my grandsons.

Now we turn right onto Commerce street and there are more people waving and cheering even as busy policemen wave traffic around. A woman with a rainbow-colored hair wig smiles and waves at Laky with delight. We all smile and laugh.

As I watch from the passenger seat of the vehicle following Laky, I cannot help but reflect back on the amazing journey that has led Laky here. I recall the first time I saw Laky as he drug and pulled the inexperienced handler across the dusty field in Iraq. I recall Laky's amazing nose and how he had saved the lives of the two hapless American contractors who were hammering away at a metal box containing sixteen explosives. Those paws that now softly pad down Commerce Street had once kicked up clouds of dust in the war-torn land of Iraq and I can't help but feel proud of my boy. He made it. He's safe and now receiving the adulation and thanks of an adoring city.

Crowds on both sides of the street wave American Flags, cheer, clap, point to Laky and smile. I laugh as Laky moves his head from left to right looking to both sides of the street. He's taking in the sights, soaking it all up. His mouth is open, his ears straight up and I can tell he's relaxed. He actually looks happy. I can see joy in his eyes. My boy.

As always happens in parades the inch-worm effect of the procession eventually causes us to pause in place as we wait for those up ahead to move on. While panning the camera around, my peripheral vision picks up a lady running out from the sidewalk toward my daughter Sarah. The lady hands Sarah something white, a handkerchief perhaps. They exchange words and I see my daughter bends down to look at Laky's back legs. She quickly stands, turns and waves for me to come forward. Oh crap, something's wrong.

As I approach, my daughter says, "Dad, that kind lady over there noticed what appears to be blood on Laky's back paw." I bent down, inspected the two back paws and was troubled to see that the right rear paw had blood streaks over the sides and top. Looking up at Sarah I said, "As much as it pains me to say this, we have to pull him from the parade, right now." Laky was my highest priority, so I picked him up and carried him to the nearest sidewalk.

My first suspicion was that the pet parlor had cut his nails too short but then I noticed that his other paws were fine. It was just the right rear paw that was bleeding. The thought struck me hard, "He's having an issue with his hips." Having worked with German Shepherds for so many years I knew to always inspect for hip issues.[103] In fact, I had checked Laky every month since we had returned from Iraq so I was a bit perplexed because he had always checked out fine.

When a dog, especially a German Shepherd, starts to develop hip issues often the first sign will be the sound of them dragging their hind paw(s) on the ground. You'll actually hear those paw nails

---

[103] To check for hip issues I place the flat of my right or left hand directly over and on top of the dog's back and hip area. I then have them walk. I'm attempting to discern any bumping or grinding on the palm of my hand. I'd regularly conduct the test with both Laky and Toris but never felt any abnormalities.

scraping against the pavement. I had not noticed this with Laky before so the new development was concerning.

I turned to my daughter and said, "Sarah, I'll go for the suburban and be right back to pick you all up. Hang tight sweetheart." I could see she was worried and that she felt bad for Laky. "Sarah, it's not your fault. We didn't know Laky had this issue until now and besides Laky was having a great time. I'll be right back." Sarah smiled and said, "Ok daddy."

Once I got Laky home, I thoroughly cleaned his wound and he fell right to sleep on his Kuranda bed. It had been a fun filled day for this war dog. Looking down at him I marveled that he had not indicated he was hurting or uncomfortable.

The following day I took Laky to our Veterinarian's office where X-Rays were performed. After inspecting the films the Doc reported, "Dennis, you were right, his hips are perfect! He's getting up in age, and I suspect searching thousands of vehicles in Iraq for thirteen months may have run its toll on his joints. I think arthritis may very well be stepping in because he's starting to feel some discomfort."

I was grateful that the doctor confirmed that Laky's hips checked out ok but I was still disturbed that he was hurting. The thought of arthritis causing Laky pain really bothered me so I was sure to faithfully give him the prescribed medications that would alleviate these issues.

A few days later in the solitude of my office, I watched the video of Laky on the parade route and smiled. It was a roller coaster for me. I laughed out loud as Laky ate up the attention and I cried as cheers of "Laky! Thank you!" burst from the spectators. I was thrilled that Laky had made history in San Antonio as the first war dog in the Veteran's Day Parade. Thousands had stood in honor as Laky passed. I recalled with pride the swelling of applause and cheers that would reverberate off the walls of the historic buildings as Laky passed by. Davy Crocket, William Travis, Jim Bowie and now Laky had made history in that very spot. Not bad for a German

Shepherd that had been born in Russia, trained in South Africa, sniffed for explosives in Iraq and then finally settled down in San Antonio, Texas.

Laky, the "Lone Star" of the parade.

Laky with my daughter Sarah and her sons Caiden and Austin who each hold signs regarding Laky and his service. This was Alamo Street by the Alamo.

Laky Gets His Wheels

It's an unfortunate fact of life that as we age, things in our body start to breakdown, ache, or just stop working. Almost every human on the planet knows that this process of aging and well, deterioration in canines is more accelerated than in humans.

Laky no longer enjoyed running or walking around our backyard, an activity that he of course previously loved. He always enjoyed jumping in our pond and splashing around but it seemed that the simple act of walking now caused him excruciating pain. Of course I gave him supplements so that his body would be encouraged to regenerate and heal but deep down I knew this was only prolonging the inevitable.

This was a frustrating time for me because his mind and heart were still so young, so strong, but the fact was his arthritis made the simple act of walking unbearable. All he wanted to do was lay around. I'd attempt to lift him and encourage him to walk but he refused. My wife Debbie would help me place him in a standing position but he would just teeter and then plop down.

So, this war dog was now confined to a life of laying around. I'd rotate him several times a day so he'd not get sore spots or bed sores. When it was time to go poop or pee Debbie and I would have to lift him up in the grass, hold him erect on his paws. Thankfully he would relieve his bowels when we did this.

Laky was never cooped up in his kennel. No way. I made sure he was out by the pond under the shade tree, lying atop his Kuranda bed basking on layers of soft quilts. His comfort was my chief concern. He was not in pain lying around, it was only when we made him stand that he winced.

One day I got the idea that perhaps the buoyancy of water would help his problems with mobility. I knew he loved frolicking in the cool waters of the pond so perhaps the water would hold his hind legs for him.

So, on a nice summer day I tried it out. I picked him up in my arms and slowly walked out into the water. Bending down he was gently lowered into the water. First to touch the cool liquid was his front legs which went down, strong and sure. Then his immobilized back legs were lowered down and much to my delight they gently floated. Laky knew exactly what to do. His face lit up and I could see that old spark as he frolicked around the pond. Laky turned, looked over at me and barked several times letting me know he highly approved of the arrangement. I loved seeing that happy German Shepherd smile on his face again.

Of course I had to toss him some sticks and floating toys that squeaked when he chomped down on them. Sometimes though I was a bit slow on the toss and he never failed to rebuke me for the error. My boy was lapping up water, splashing around, enjoying being a dog again and it did my heart good.

We did this for a good forty-five minutes but soon he had enough. Laky just stood there in the water, his hind legs caressed and held aloft by the cool water. He was enjoying everything about the moment; the warmth of the midafternoon Texas sun and the comfort of the soft breeze against his water-logged coat. The only sounds were the reverberations of the cicadas in the trees and the droplets of water falling from Laky onto the surface of the now muddy pond. There he proudly stood, the veteran, with a scarred mind and aging body, still holding his red Kong in his mouth. Was there a twinkle in his eyes? You bet!

One day I was flipping through a K9 magazine when I noticed something which immediately grabbed my attention. It was a picture of a German Shepherd standing upright in what is called a K9 Wheel Cart. The German Shepherd in the cart had no use of his back legs any longer, so his family bought the cart for him. There were special straps which gently held his back legs up off the ground and the frame of the cart was built around the dog so there were straps connecting to the entire body. The cart was essentially an extension of the dog. I was intrigued.

The article was a review of the product and the praise was exceptional. I had to get one for my boy.

A week later the cart arrived and boy was I excited. I knew Laky's front legs were strong so this would be a cinch for him. I just hoped he would tolerate the new contraption. This could be a game changer.

The first time we tried it out was at our home. There was a lot riding on this moment. Debbie and I lifted Laky Boy up and placed him in between the support railings, strapped him in at all points as described in the instructions. As we snapped, fastened, pulled and clasped the chair around him, Laky patiently stood on his front legs, allowing us to do whatever we felt was necessary. Occasionally he would turn to see what we were up to. He was a bit concerned but this was understandable and a natural reaction. I knew he would be fine because he had survived much worse.

Ok, he's in and standing tall. I walked over, gave him a big hug around his neck and told him, "Buddy, your life is about to get a lot better in the next few seconds." We were in our front yard so I stood in the street made sure traffic was not coming down the cul-de-sac and prepared to toss his favorite red Kong down the street. I wondered if he would stand there frozen in confusion and fear or if he would bolt after his favorite chew toy.

I held the Kong aloft for him to see. Wow! His eyes lit up, his body stiffened, he started breathing hard and his mouth was open displaying a happy face. BOOM! I threw the Kong down the street, and BOOM! Laky took off like a rocket. He was flying down the road as fast as he could go, and believe me, he was going fast. Those big rubber wheels kicked up small pebbles as he moved like a jet down the street. I was impressed at how stable the contraption was. Truly an engineering delight.

Laky ran up behind the Kong as it was still bouncing around and BAM! he scooped it up with his mouth, chomped on it a few times and then turned that cart "on a dime" (as they used to say back in the day). Now here he comes full force towards Debbie and I. We're both yelling his name and I'll never forget his eyes that emanated such intense happiness. The sight brought tears to my eyes; he was beyond happy! He wheeled up to Deb and I and we both threw our arms around him and smothered him with hugs and kisses and as we did, I could hear him chomping away on his red Kong.

Sometimes I would take Laky to Lackland Air Force Base which is a short drive from our home. I'd take him there so he could run free on the parade field, the same field I had marched on when graduating as a freshly minted airman back in 1969. Laky would have all the room he could wish for and the setting was awesome as we were surrounded by generations of aircraft that had served the Air Force well through the years.

By this time Laky was very familiar with the wheel cart and even knew how many straps there were. Every time I snapped the last clasp he would shoot off like a rocket. He did this every time. He was so intelligent. As soon as that last strap was fastened those tires were already turning, kicking up clouds of dirt and grass. Boom! The Kong was launched in the air and Laky was jetting after it. Sometimes I would throw the ball only a few feet over his head and as it passed, he could hear the gentle sound it made. Oh man this fired him up! He was on it!

Sometimes Laky would see a family with children walking by the track that surrounds the field. The folks were almost always from out of town and were inspecting the amazing display of various aircraft. They would hear a noise coming toward them and turn to see a happy German Shepherd with a red Kong in his mouth rushing toward them, ON WHEELS! They would invariably smile and hoot and holler and love petting him. Laky had always been a gentle dog, eager for human companionship and he loved to be loved.

Of course the questions about Laky would fly and I was always so proud to answer that he had in fact served overseas to protect our country. Well, here come the cameras and the smiles and the poses of families around this amazing dog. I always loved for Laky to receive recognition and adoration from the people he protected. It did his heart good and I must admit that it did mine as well. Yes, Laky was enjoying his new life on wheels.

America the Beautiful & Laky Boy

Well, it's been a good year and a half since Laky was introduced to his wheel cart and now his front legs are developing issues. His muzzle is almost pure white and he's having trouble holding his urine and stool. Unfortunately his debilitations mean that he can no longer use the wheel cart that brought so much joy to his life. I'm happy though that he was given the extra time to be a dog, to run and play.

Laky is eating well and drinking fluids fine but his whole existence is now just lying around. I loved my boy so it was no bother to clean him up when he urinated on himself or to constantly alter his positions so he did not develop bed sores. I knew his time was now limited. Once again this was frustrating because his mind, his organs were fine. His skeleton had failed him, not his heart or mind.

I'm now treating him just like a baby. I have doggie diapers on him which I regularly change and then wipe him clean with baby wipes. I even have a small fan positioned in the area of his groin area thus keeping him as dry as possible. After a fresh diaper is placed, I turn him to the opposite side. I change out his layers of quilts for fresh ones to make sure he is comfortable.

You know, I always loved our family pets and I hated when they passed but there was a special connection between Laky and I. We had both served together in one of the most dangerous places on the planet. Laky and I both had suffered terrible mental damage from the experience but we had overcome, together. I was always there for him and he was there for me. I knew he was in his last months of life but I wanted to prolong the inevitable for as long as I could. I was not willing for him to suffer or become emaciated. I knew that I could take wonderful care of him just as I would a bed ridden family member. So, my thoughts were that as long as he stays healthy, I don't mind all of this extra work. It was the least I could do for this war dog who had saved so many lives.

Well, I'd accepted the fact that he was getting closer and closer to no longer being with me. I knew the time was approaching that his body would begin to shut down, presently though, he was still healthy.

I'd been kicking around an idea for several months and was now convinced I'd make it happen. My idea was to take Laky on a road trip from South Texas all the way to the Northwoods of Wisconsin where my folks lived in a comfortable town called Rhinelander. I really wanted Laky to see and enjoy the vast country he had defended.

So we did it!

I made a perch for Laky that would have his Kuranda bed positioned so that as he lay atop layers of quilts, he could look in three directions and enjoy an unobstructed view of the scenery from both sides and the rear window of the suburban. Those along for the journey were of course my wife Debbie, my son Dennis and my granddaughter Lauren. The route took us through North Texas, Oklahoma, Kansas, Missouri, Iowa, Minnesota and then of course Wisconsin.

As we stopped at various travel stations, I would check on Laky's diaper and be sure to clean him up and change his blankets. These travel stations were usually packed with people who would see the celebrity status of Laky in the back of the SUV and inquire. Of course I loved telling these folks of the many exploits we had shared in Iraq and the journey we were now on. Once again, the cameras came out and photos with Laky were taken. This sort of interaction took place all the way to Wisconsin and back.

I knew Laky would love my home state of Wisconsin because the northern part was absolutely covered in tall beautiful trees. My Mom and Dad's property had been purchased over fifty years prior and it came with a small lake. The place is remote and serene. My son states that it is one of his top three places on the planet.

Once at my folks place it was so much fun to introduce Laky to everyone. Of course all of my sisters had heard the stories about Laky and were eager to spend time with him. One day I prepped one of the row boats so Laky could enjoy a peaceful cruise on the Lake. My son Dennis and my brother-in-law Daryl carried Laky from the house out to the lake. It was such a cute sight because Laky was lying atop his Kuranda bed which as it turned out was a great way to move him to the boat. The bed fit perfectly between the bench seats of the boat.

Pushing out into the water cameras captured the moment but soon it was only Laky and I surrounded by tall trees. It was so quiet, peaceful and memorable. Laky lifted his nose and took in the abundance of new odors: pine trees, White Birch trees, Tamaracks, raccoons, chipmunks, minks, fish, deer, black bears and the aroma emanating from the marsh lands. Laky was loving it.

On the far side of the lake I lay next to my buddy who turned and licked the side of my face. I said, "I love you buddy and I want to thank you for having my back in Iraq. Thank you for serving our country. I'm so proud of you." Laky lifted his nose and was taking in all of the smells carried on the breeze. We drifted for fifteen minutes and were soon approaching the far shore. Laky was trying to prop himself up so he could look. I reached over and pulled him up so he could see down into the water and see the many beautiful lily pads.

A tree branch was just over us and within reach and getting closer. Laky saw it and tried to prop himself up so he could smell it. I grabbed the branch, pulled it closer and was surprised to see that Laky had successfully maneuvered himself so that he could rise up a bit and sniff the branch under his own power. He sniffed it up and down for a few seconds and then his strength gave out and he plopped back onto the layers of quilts and pillows. He absolutely loved the pine trees, their scent enchanted him which of course delighted my heart to no end.

Suddenly a dragonfly landed on the handle of the oar. Laky quickly zeroed in on this beautiful little creature. His ears were erect and his attention solely focused on this visitor. The sun was hitting the insect just perfectly igniting a rainbow of colors in its cellophane-like wings. Laky scooted, shimmied and worked himself closer so he could get a good look and perhaps a sniff or two.

I was amazed that the dragonfly didn't budge. Laky was within two inches of touching it with his nose but it remained still, almost as if it had been sent by God for just this purpose. I could distinctly see Laky working his nose, attempting to get a scent from this little creature. There in that moment on a secluded lake in the north woods of Wisconsin a war dog and a dragonfly stared at each other. Neither budging. Both studying.

I couldn't help but reflect on the dragonfly in Baghdad that had visited me along the Tigris River. On that day in Iraq the tiny insect reminded me that there was beauty everywhere in the world if we would only look. Now, the dragonfly reminded me that small moments in life matter and that if we would just be still for a moment in our busy lives, we might just witness something amazing.

As we drifted across my parents spring fed lake I'd reach into the water and scoop up water into a cupped hand and let Laky drink the ice cold water. He loved it!

I was so glad I had brought Laky here to such a peaceful place. I was thankful that so many members of my family could spend time with him. I knew his time was short and tough days were ahead but for now, in the moment, Laky was happy and enjoying the attention. My goal had been accomplished for Laky had seen America the beautiful and in turn America had seen him and treated him like the hero he was.

Laky during the road trip from Texas to Wisconsin.

Until We Meet Again

The trip to Wisconsin is behind us and we have been home for several weeks now. I smiled as I looked over at Laky resting under the shade tree. I thought back to how far he had come. I recalled the day in Iraq I had first seen him. I also was reminded of how fearful he was of people.

In my mind I snapped back to a problem I had with Laky in Baghdad years before. His fear of people was becoming an issue but I had an idea that might do the trick. I messaged my wife back in Texas that I needed her to send me a couple tubes of tennis balls. When the shipment arrived, I took the tubes to our checkpoint and emptied them into a bucket. As folks walked through the checkpoint, I asked them to reach into the bucket, pull out a ball and throw it toward Laky. Well as you can imagine this was a huge hit with the pedestrians but also more so with Laky who in a matter of three days was over his fear of humans.

The memory had come to mind as I recalled the many wonderful people that had met Laky over the previous months. I was thankful for the attention for my boy. I truly felt that Laky understood their appreciation and most importantly their attention which he now relished.

One day I told my family that I suspected Laky would have to be put down within the next few months. I guessed that he would be fine up to Christmas but after that I was determined that if there was a medical emergency, well, I would let him go. I was having to do everything for him and though he had no skin breakdown I knew this couldn't go on forever.

I had friends ask, "Why don't you just have him put to sleep?" My answer always circled around the fact that he was still very sharp in his mind and heart but the reality was that I could not even fathom the day when I would see my war buddy take his last breath. I mean, how do you do that? How do you extinguish the life of that being you love with all your heart? Rationally I knew that I would be showing Laky respect by allowing him to die. My intellect told me that in the wild Laky would have died years ago as his legs would not work. I had given him so many more years of love and life but I wanted to give him more. I wanted there to be a magical procedure that would restore my battle buddies' body. I thought I would have more time.

It was December 26th, 2014 and I was giving him a nice warm bath full of soap suds. I let him soak for a long time and then I massaged his body to bring comfort to his sides and legs from lying all the time. Laky absolutely loved this.

I rinsed him off three times with the sprayer and then let him drip and drain most of the water before I started to rub him down with two big beach towels. Once satisfied I had removed most of the water, I then lifted him from the tub and placed him on several dry towels I had strategically placed on the bathroom floor. I had also placed a "potty mat" because he would almost always urinate when I removed him from the bath.

I was drying him off further and saying, "I know you loved this bath time again" when he began to pee. This time though it wasn't just pee, in fact it appeared to be more blood than urine. When I saw it, my heart seemed to leap into my throat. I knew what this meant.

I continued to dry him off and clean up the blood before it stained his fur. I then bent down and planted a huge kiss between his almond colored eyes. Laky lifted his head and gave me some quick kisses alongside my face. I laughed and said, "Thank you buddy." The reality was that my heart was breaking because I knew this was the medical emergency I had dreaded. I knew our days together were now numbered.

I placed Laky in the living room on a fresh bed I had made for him. He loved watching the television, especially when there were animals on the screen. I then walked over to the phone and called one of my veterinarian friends. I explained what had just happened. The Doc knew all about Laky's service and medical issues and he agreed that it was time. I asked if he could come by the following day.

I looked down at Laky and could see he was tired. His eyes seemed weak and the spark, though not extinguished, was definitely dimmed. The rest of that night was spent solely in the company of my war buddy. I was sure to tell him how loved he was and how appreciative I was for his service. It seemed like every few minutes I was rubbing his head, kissing him, hugging him and trying as desperately as I could to find a way to be sure Laky knew how wonderful he was.

The 27th of December 2014 was one of the most dreaded days of my life. I awoke from a fitful sleep feeling sluggish, awful, numb. I couldn't believe this was real. Of course I had known for years this day was approaching but I had managed to always find a way to put it off and insure a productive and fulfilling life for Laky. On this day it was different for I was out of options. There was nothing I could do. Helpless. Dreadful.[104]

It was early morning and my wife Debbie went out early to buy a thick steak to cook for Laky. A splendid last meal he would thoroughly enjoy. In addition Debbie cooked up a dozen eggs and a piece of toast. Laky had never been allowed food like this before so I knew he would relish the meal.

Debbie brought the hearty meal to Laky on a large plate. As she laid the plate in front of him she said, "This is all for you, our Laky boy, enjoy!" Laky's nose was working overtime taking in the amazing smell of the specially prepared meal. His eyes revealed pure delight knowing this meal was all his own. People food!

---

[104] As I'm typing this presently, 14 September 2019, I'm still hurt and upset at having to end his life after he protected mine for those thirteen months in the war. Yes, I'm well aware that the decision was made out of love for him. I certainly didn't want him to suffer and after talking with my good veterinarian friend he agreed that it was time to usher Laky into eternal rest. I knew he was right, he's Laky's doctor and our friend and it gave me comfort in knowing this was best for my boy. It still really sucked though. Even to this day.

Laky devoured the entire breakfast and then set about licking the plate clean. Debbie bent down, picked up the plate and kissed Laky on the top of his head.

After his meal I took him out to the boardwalk beside our pond and allowed him to enjoy the cool December breeze and the company of his son Laky Jr. who was now just over a year old.

I had paid to have Laky's sperm harvested and used to make a litter of puppies. The mom who was impregnated with Laky's sperm was a beautiful German Shepherd named Heidi. Her own story was really quite remarkable as she was living under a trailer home. She was covered in sand fleas that had removed most of the hair from her ears. Heidi had never known the feel of a collar on her neck. Once we were able to place a collar and leash on her she yelped like she was being murdered. It was such a pitiful sound.

After taking her to the veterinarian for a checkup and vaccinations we were able to get Heidi bathed, cleaned and after a few months she was revealed to be a quite spectacular German Shepherd. She had such a sweet disposition and when she eventually carried Laky's puppies she turned out to be an amazing mother to thirteen puppies.[105] One of these was Laky Jr. who was now spending time with his ailing father. It was wonderful to see the two spend time together and it was comforting to know I would have a living piece of Laky with me.

I laughed as I watched Laky Jr. try to steal the Kong from his father. Jr. would hunker down and slowly creep closer to the Kong resting near Laky. As the son crept closer, I could see Laky Sr. was baring his teeth and growling. Soon there would be barking but Laky Jr would not move an inch. He remained still, so close he could almost touch the Kong. Soon the Sr. would relax and Jr. would pounce on the Kong and run like heck as dad barked his disapproval. The scene made me laugh and temporarily forget the awful deed ahead of us.

---

[105] Heidi now lives in Arizona where she enjoys a good life with a wonderful family

Then suddenly a beautiful scene opened as Laky Jr came by his dad one last time. He laid down in front of his dad, almost face to face and gently let go of his dad's favorite red Kong. Daddy went forward and quickly picked it up, not sure if his son were thinking about teasing him again. Laky Jr then stood, walked forward just a couple of steps, bent down and smelled the top of his dad's right ear. He then turned and trotted off to the pond which he entered to cool off.

It was now almost lunch time so I picked Laky up and moved him back into the house because Debbie had boiled a chicken for Laky and was even now deboning it for him. On the floor in the living room we had placed half a dozen Kongs and a new toy which looked like a chicken and made a horrendous squeak when chewed. Well, as you can imagine Laky absolutely loved this new toy. Debbie and I laughed but the laughter did not show in our eyes, only in our throats for a glimpse at the clock revealed our veterinarian friend would be coming in only a couple hours.

Debbie now brought Laky a full chicken that had been specially prepared for him. He was so happy getting this opportunity to eat more people food. The food disappeared in seconds and we both laughed at his exuberance. However, I also knew this was his last meal and the thought hit me hard.

My heart was about to burst, how could this be happening! I wanted to go back in time and relive these last few years all over again. I wanted to spend more time with my war buddy and try to thwart these ailments that were taking him from me. All to no avail. There was no avoiding this day. It had been plodding closer and closer for years. I had to relent.

As the time drew closer, I felt such a HUGE tremendous amount of guilt pressing upon my mind and heart, "He took care of me in war, and I'm doing this to him!" Again, stupid thoughts! Irrational thoughts but they were fervently felt. Sure, I knew this was what was best for him, right now, at this present time and to wait any longer would only cause him further discomfort and pain. It was time. The doorbell rang!!!

To tell you the truth dear reader I had the hardest time writing what transpired over the next several minutes. If you've had to put down your family pet then you know what I mean. On top of that, imagine if you will, that it is also a beloved friend that you had survived hell with. Imagine that the precious animal had saved your life on multiple occasions and that now you must watch one of the most treasured beings on the planet take his last breath.

There was the insertion of the IV, the hugging and desperate last second kisses and the words whispered into his ears that came direct from my soul. How do I write about such things?

I walked into my office and retrieved an American flag that had flown over the US embassy in Baghdad for a full day. I walked over to my boy, unfurled the flag and draped it over him like a blanket. He looked up at me with those big beautiful almond colored eyes and looked so regal. I then whispered in his ear so he would be sure to hear me, "I love you with all of my heart my Laky boy! I'm so very proud of you for your service to our country and our allies as well. Thank you so very much for protecting me and having my back when we were in the war together. Thank you for loving me. Thank you for the many times you gave me doggie kisses and allowed me to hug and kiss on you while we were there. It helped me so much in those long hot stressful days and nights. Mommy and the kids and grandkids all love you my boy! Thank you so VERY much for your son Laky Jr. who will be with me for many years watching my back. I'll always have a part of you with me." Laky had his red Kong in his mouth and never chomped on it. He just stared deep into my eyes and took in every word I was saying.

I looked over at my Veterinarian friend and asked, "Do you remember my request? I want Laky to first get a shot that will put him into a deep comfortable sleep, sort of as if he was going to have surgery. Then when he is resting you can give him the pink fluid that will end his life." The Doc answered, "Dennis, it's just as you requested. He'll be quite comfortable and sleeping soundly when I give him the injection that will send him off into eternity."

As the doctor prepared the medications and insured the IV line was patent, I was sure to show Laky the big red Kong he loved so much. Laky lunged forward a bit and grabbed the Kong from my right hand, nipping a finger. I laughed. He still had that amazing ball drive. He was happy that he had taken the Kong from me. I could see that familiar twinkle in his eyes. I started to tug on the Kong; I pulled, he pulled, I pulled, he pulled and I let him win and take it. He was so happy he had beaten me yet again.

During this time the veterinarian had injected the fluid that would put Laky into a deep sleep. I watched the plunger of the syringe sink deeper and deeper and watched the liquid disappear into the arm of this war dog I loved so much. I shrugged it off, I only have seconds now, I grabbed the Kong one more time and tried to pull it, Laky pulled back, I pulled, Laky pulled, I pulled, Laky pulled and I let him win. On this last pull though I noticed it was significantly weaker. He was leaving me. I could still see joy in his eyes but he was getting sleepy.

I then saw his eyes do something I had never seen before, they sort of flickered, as if a light was going out. I only have moments now. I grab the Kong, which is still in his mouth and pull, he weakly pulls back, but he's still in the fight, still in the game so I pull again and this time his pull is almost nonexistent. I bend down placing my face right up to his eyes and I yelled, "Pull Buddy! Pull Laky! You can beat Daddy!" Oh God I want him to win one last time, so I yell, "Come on Buddy you can beat daddy! Pull! Pull! Pull!" and then I could see just a bit of a spark for the last time in his eyes, and he pulled ever so slightly, I released his favorite red Kong, looked deep down into his eyes and yelled, "You beat daddy again!" His eyes blinked and I knew this was the last time he'd see me so I leaned forward and kissed him between his big beautiful almond colored eyes. Just then he slowly began closing his eyes, drifting off to sleep so I gave one last desperate effort, "LAKY!" He opened them just for a second, "I LOVE YOU MY BOY!" He then slowly closed his eyes. I kissed him on his front lips, stood to the position of attention

381

and gave him the very best salute to my "American K9 War Hero, Laky Boy!"

My wife and I held him, hugged him, kissed him and told Laky how much we loved him over and over again. He was absolutely covered with our love, appreciation and the beautiful colors of the flag he had served so well.

All during this time Laky still has his favorite red Kong in his mouth. I wanted to make certain that when he passed away, he would feel and taste the rubber of the Kong in his mouth. I had my head down next to his and I discovered that I could hear his breathing through the holes in the Kong. Laky was very relaxed inhaling and exhaling deeply. The sedation had done its work perfectly. I listened to the beautiful sound of his breathing knowing my boy was still alive, just sleeping. Then I watched as the pink fluid was injected into his vein and I knew it would only be seconds now so I remained silent and listened to the comforting sounds of his breathing through the Kong. Then a deep breath, a long exhale and then nothing. I waited and strained to hear another breath but there were no more. My war buddy was gone.

I remember thinking, "One unsung American canine war hero has just crossed over the Rainbow Bridge." I couldn't help but wonder if Toris was at the end, waiting. I'd like to believe he was, but healed, playful, perfect again and that we would be "Best Buds" for eternity.

As soon as the Doc left, I walked straight to the American flag in our yard and lowered it to half-staff, walked back a few paces, stood at attention and delivered a crisp salute. America had lost one of its best on this day.

Laky, until we meet again. Salute! <u>I</u> <u>Love</u> <u>You</u>!

Salute to an American War Hero

Laky Blocker

A War Dog whose life and exploits will live on forever, in the pages of this book.

(Photograph of Laky by Renee Spade Photography)

Laky enjoying the pond and the water that held his failing bones secure.

Laky and his unresponsive hind legs resting beside the pond in our backyard.

Legacy

It's been a hot summer here in Texas this year. In fact, the year 2019 is making it hard for old timers to remember when it's been hotter. Day after day topping 100 degrees with a humidity level that would make the amazon cringe. In the midst of this heat and crazy electric bills there is a breath of fresh air though. The manuscript for this book is finally nearing completion meaning the story and legacy of Toris and Laky will be ensured to endure for years and hopefully millennia to come.

This has been a labor of love and one that quite honestly, I wasn't sure would ever happen. The one driving factor though was my desire to honor Toris, Laky, Beauty and the other dogs who worked our checkpoints in Baghdad. Their legacy is now a thing of preserved history and this sole fact inspires, delights and encourages me in ways few will be able to contemplate.

A couple years ago my wife Debbie surprised me with a beautiful gift. Two brick pavers. Both were placed at the site of the National Military Working Dog Teams National Monument located at Lackland Air Force Base, San Antonio, Texas. There is a paver for Laky and one for Toris. This was a wonderful gesture for there were times I would play with Laky on the very site. Laky would chase his Kong while attached to the wheel cart that held his useless hind legs aloft. I now have a place to honor my two war buddies. Who knows, perhaps you the reader will one day find their pavers there and reminiscent about everything you learned of them through the pages of this book.

As I sit in my "Think Tank" working on this book, with my son at my side typing away on the manuscript, I am thankful for the time we have shared together. The hours spent rehashing these scenes and making sure the details were absolutely correct to the best of our abilities will be cherished by us both for as long as we live. The valuable input provided by my wife was such a blessing. It was awesome to sit at a table with my wife and son and cover details about the story and realize everyone was plugged in and up to speed. Each of us invested precious moments of valuable time in each story. Realizing we were dealing with "legacy" kept us on course and at times created more work for us, but in the end, it was the force that energized our efforts. This book is the result of that teamwork.

You should know that Laky was cremated a few days after his death and now at the moment of this writing rests not more than a few inches from my left side, my "Heel side." One day both he and Toris will rest with me in my casket at Ft. Sam Houston National Cemetery. So it is decreed in my Last Will and Testament.

Looking into the backyard I love watching Laky Jr. run around the pond as he is now chased and teased by his son Poldark. Yes, that's right, Laky Sr has a grandson. The legacy of Laky lives on through his son and grandson who we get to see every day and believe me, I'm so thankful for that opportunity. Legacy. It's a small word with some hard driving impact that I hope has led you to enjoy this story of service and commitment by some of the most amazing canines I have ever known.

Here's to you my boys and your legacy of service to this great country.

Here's to you Laky and Toris, no longer "unsung" heroes.

But most important of all – Thank you Lord!

Proverbs 3: 5, 6

Glossary of Terms

Air Scenting

- When a dog lifts his/her nose into the air and is smelling different scents that carry on the wind. Especially the scent he/she has been trained on.

Alpha Dog

- The leader, usually a male. A dog that all other canines know is the "Top Dog." The one that all other dogs fear and respect. This type of dog should not have a "Soft Handed" trainer or handler. This type of dog may challenge a trainer or handler by refusing to perform the task it's being trained to do. It is critical to make certain you have the right dog paired up with the right trainer and future handler. It makes a huge difference in the "Working Life" of this Canine. This dog needs to be shown and taught by the trainer/handler that it is not the "Alpha" in the trainer/handler and dog relationship.

AIF

- Anti Iraq Forces

CF

- "Coalition Forces" -Those nations whose troops supported the efforts of the United States and the New Iraqi Government

COB

- "Change of Behavior" - Behavior that you recognize in your dog when he/she has come into the odor that he/she has been trained to detect. It could be something as simple as a twitch of an ear, lifting of the nose, a jerk of the body, the tail might come up and start wagging. Each dog will have its own particular way of indicating it's on odor and will work toward the source/location of the odor. BUT, in order to see this, you have to work with your dog many hours in training to be able to view these "Changes of Behavior." This IS so Critical!

Crosswind
- A wind blowing in a direction not parallel to a course you are taking or facing.

Distractors
- Anything that might pull the canines off of their search. Things like human odor, food, animal scents, noises, cleaning supplies and a myriad of other items or substances.

Downwind
- In the direction the wind is blowing. Allowing the wind to work for you by carrying odor toward your resolute K9. The wind is your friend.

"Duck and Cover" Bunker
- A reinforced rebar and concrete shelter designed to act as a place of protection from incoming rockets and mortars. Key feature is ease of access.

False Sit
- When a dog will sit where the odor is not. He/she is trying to fool you into throwing their reward toy to them. This is often a smart dog trying to fool you into thinking the odor is "here" when you know it is not. **Special Note** - This is always discovered and dealt with in training because in a "real world" environment the handler will not know where the explosive is located. If a dog continues to "false sit" in training they will need remedial instruction. Too dangerous.

FOB
- "Forward Operating Base" - A military base that is used to support tactical operations located away from the "Main Base."

"Going Down the Leash"
- Your emotions travel down the leash to your dog. If you are angry and distracted your dog will pick up on it and mirror you. Shake off your negative emotions before you touch the leash.

Hard/Heavy Handed
- A trainer or handler who puts too much pressure on a dog who is sensitive. These types of handlers/trainers would rather use muscle than brains to work out a problem with a dog.

IED
- "Improvised Explosive Device" - A homemade bomb, constructed from military or nonmilitary components, that is frequently employed by guerillas, insurgents and other non-state actors as a crude but effective weapon against a conventional military force.

Incoming
- A word we would typically shout when we knew mortars or rockets were headed in our direction. This word simply meant, "Get to cover now" and if you cannot get to cover then lay flat on the ground, cover your head. This makes you a smaller target for the shrapnel flying through the air.

Insurgent(s)
- A rebel or revolutionary. In Iraq these were typically religious zealots and mercenaries whose goal was to topple US and Iraqi policies and efforts.

JND
- "Just Noticeable Difference" - An indication from your dog that it is onto odor. This is different from a "Change of Behavior" in that the "JND" is something that only the handler would notice in their canine. This close relationship is only established between a dog and handler who have spent countless hours working together in proficiency training.

Mortar
- A simple muzzle loaded weapon, consisting of a smooth-bore metal tube fixed to a base plate with a bipod mount and sight. These launch explosive shells in high arcing trajectories.

Open Area Search
- Typically a search conducted in a field. You would position yourself downwind and work your dog crosswind.

Reading Your Canine
- You know what your dog is thinking and feeling. It's like reading a book with full understanding.

Residue
- A small amount of odor that remains after the explosive agent or device was removed from an area it had been in.

RPG
- "Rocket Propelled Grenade" - This is a shoulder fired anti-tank weapon that fires rockets equipped with an explosive warhead. There was an abundance of these in Baghdad and were a daily threat.

Soft Handed Dog
- A handler or trainer should not be too "Hard Handed" or tough on this type of dog with corrections. This type of dog requires a trainer and handler who will be "Soft Handed." A "Hard Handed" handler or trainer will shut this type of dog down. Such a dog will NOT want to work for this person or sadly, perhaps anyone in the future.

Upwind
- In the opposite direction to that in which the wind is blowing.

VBIED
- A "Vehicle Borne Improvised Explosive Device." This is a vehicle which has been loaded down with various types of explosives. Often made up of whatever the insurgent(s) could lay their hands on. Explosives could be landmines, rockets, mortars, basically any explosive which could be placed in a vehicle to detonate. It is delivered to the target by a driver and either detonated in place by the driver or by remote.

The Authors with Completed Manuscript!

Father and Son – Mission Accomplished!